Pelican Books

Decline and Fall of the Freudian Empire

Professor H. J. Eysenck, who was born in 1916, obtained his Ph.D. degree in psychology at London University after school and university experience in Germany, France and England. Having worked as psychologist at the war-time Mill Hill Emergency Hospital, he was appointed Professor of Psychology at the University of London, and Director of the Psychological Department at the Institute of Psychiatry (Maudsley and Bethlem Royal Hospitals). He has since retired from the University of London and is now Professor Emeritus. He has lectured in many countries, and been Visiting Professor at the Universities of Pennsylvania and of California. Known mainly through his experimental researches in the field of personality, he has written some seven hundred articles in technical journals, as well as some three dozen books, including *Dimensions of Personality*, *The Scientific Study of Personality*, *The Structure of Human Personality*, *The Psychology of Politics*, *The Biological Basis of Personality*, *The Uses and Abuses of Psychology*, *Sense and Nonsense in Psychology*, *Fact and Fiction in Psychology*, *Know Your Own IQ* and *Check Your Own IQ*. His more recent books include *The Causes and Effects of Smoking*, *Mindwatching* (with M. Eysenck), *A Model for Intelligence* and *A Model for Personality*, and *Astrology: Science or Superstition?* (with D. K. B. Nias). He founded the journal *Behaviour Research and Therapy* and was its editor-in-chief, and is editor-in-chief of the journal *Peronality and Individual Differences*. He advocates the highest degree of scientific rigour in the design of psychological experiments and is very critical of much loose thinking current under the guise of 'psychology'.

H. J. EYSENCK

Decline and Fall of the Freudian Empire

PENGUIN BOOKS

Penguin Books Ltd, Harmondsworth, Middlesex, England
Viking Penguin Inc., 40 West 23rd Street, New York, New York 10010, U.S.A.
Penguin Books Australia Ltd, Ringwood, Victoria, Australia
Penguin Books Canada Limited, 2801 John Street, Markham, Ontario, Canada L3R 1B4
Penguin Books (N.Z.) Ltd, 182–190 Wairau Road, Auckland 10, New Zealand

First published by Viking 1985
Published in Pelican Books 1986

Copyright © H. J. Eysenck, 1985

All rights reserved
Made and printed in Great Britain by
Hazell Watson & Viney Limited,
Member of the BPCC Group,
Aylesbury, Bucks
Typeset in Palatino

Contents

This is a book about Sigmund Freud and psychoanalysis. There are many such books, and the reader might rightly demand to know why he or she should be asked to pay good money to buy a new one, and spend precious time reading it. The answer is very simple. Most books on this topic are written by psychoanalysts, or at least by camp-followers of the Freudian movement; they are therefore uncritical, unaware of alternative theories, and written more as weapons in a war of propaganda than objective assessments of the present status of psychoanalysis. There are, of course, exceptions to this rule, and some of the most important of these are mentioned in the bibliography at the end of this book. Important new books, such as those by Sulloway, Ellenberger, Thornton, Rillaer, Roazen, Fromkin, Timpanaro, Gruenbaum, Kline, and others are long and highly technical; they are invaluable to the professional student, but cannot be recommended to non-professional readers trying to find out what modern scholarship has discovered about the truth or falsity of Freudian doctrines. But for the sake of readers who wish to check for themselves, I have referred in the text to the major historical writers who have carefully looked at the evidence and given detailed accounts of what actually happened, with special reference to factual events, publications and other evidence available to all.

This book, then, is inevitably based on the scholarship of the people mentioned above, and many others whose works have been consulted. It is, nevertheless, special in bringing together material covering a wide range of topics within the general field of psychoanalysis – the interpretation of dreams, the psychopathology of everyday life, the effects of psychoanalytic psychotherapy, Freudian psycho-history and anthropology, the experimental study of Freudian concepts, and many more. I have tried to do this in a non-technical manner, to make the book accessible to readers who have only a passing knowledge of Freudian psychoanalysis, and no professional background in psychology or anthropology. It would have been easier to write a book five times as long and full of technical jargon, but I have found it a salutary experience to try to reduce this wealth of material to the confines of a short, non-technical book. The effort of doing so cleared my mind of many preconceptions, and I am grateful to the many experts whose works I consulted, for clarifying puzzles and paradoxes that created numerous difficulties before.

I have given many lectures on the various topics discussed in this book, and these were inevitably introduced as being 'controversial'. Similarly, I have no doubt that reviewers will call this book 'controversial', but with such an assessment I cannot agree. I have tried to deal with ascertained facts, and to add as little comment and interpretation as possible. The conclusions may be 'controversial' because they disagree with previous assessments arrived at without the benefit of recent scholarship, but that does not make them contentious. It simply means that our knowledge has progressed, that our understanding has advanced, and that facts have been discovered recently which throw a new light on Freud and psychoanalysis.

Much of this new evidence is highly critical of claims made by Freud and his followers, and, as the title of this book suggests, the inevitable result has been a decline in the influence of Freudian theory, and in the esteem in which psychoanalysis is held. That there has been such a decline can hardly be doubted by anyone acquainted with the present climate of opinion among psychiatrists (qualified doctors with specialist training in the medical study of mental disorder) and psychologists (graduates in the scientific study of human behaviour), as well as philosophers, anthropologists and historians, in the United States and the United Kingdom. This disillusionment has not yet advanced as far in South America, France, and a few other countries which still cling stubbornly to outmoded concepts and theories. However, even there doubts are beginning to appear, and gradually they will follow the U.S. and the U.K.

In dealing with Freud's work, I have looked at it exclusively from the scientific point of view. To many people this may appear too strict. They may maintain that Freud's contribution has been to hermeneutics – the interpretation and meaning of mental events – rather than to the scientific study of human behaviour. Others may insist on the social and literary importance of the Freudian opus, or look upon him as a prophet and innovator, a man who changed our sexual and social mores and, like Moses, led us into a new world.

Freud may be said to fit into all these different roles, but I am not qualified to deal with them. To judge the importance of prophets, innovators, or literary figures requires a profound knowledge of history, sociology, or literature and literary criticism. To this I cannot lay claim, and consequently I shall not be concerned with these aspects of Freud's contributions.

I do, however, have something to say about the claim that Freud should be regarded not as a scientist of the ordinary kind but rather as the originator and chief represenative of the hermeneutic movement. Such an argument would have been rejected out of hand by Freud himself, who had this to say:

> From the point of view of science we must necessarily make use of our critical powers in that direction, and not be afraid to reject and deny. It is inadmissible to declare that science is one field of human intellectual activity, and that religion and philosophy are others at least as valuable, and that science has no business to interfere with the other two, and that they all have an equal claim to truth, and that everyone is free to choose whence he shall draw his convictions and in what he shall place his belief. Such an attitude is considered particularly respectable, tolerant, broad-minded, and free from narrow prejudices. Unfortunately, it is not tenable: it shares all the pernicious qualities of an entirely unscientific *Weltanschauung* and in practice comes to much the same thing. The bare fact is that truth cannot be tolerant and cannot admit compromise or limitations, that scientific research looks on the whole field of human activity as its own, and must adopt an uncompromisingly critical attitude towards any other power that seeks to usurp any part of its province.

With these sentiments I cannot but agree. They show, as do many other passages written by Freud, that he aimed to be a scientist in the traditional sense; those of his followers who now wish to denigrate the importance of science and claim for him a place somewhere between philosophy and religion, do him a disservice. Freud, like Marx, often complained about the lack of understanding shown by his followers and, again like Marx, who claimed he was 'no Marxist', stated that he was 'no Freudian'. Freud would have regarded these attempts to deny him the status of scientist, and to shunt him into the hermeneutic cul-de-sac, as a betrayal. I have preferred to judge Freud by his own avowed criteria, and deal with his work as a contribution to science.

In doing so I want to make one point clear. In attempting to judge Freud as a scientist, and psychoanalysis as a contribution to science, I have no wish to denigrate art, religion and other forms of human experience. I have always regarded art as being of the utmost importance, and I cannot imagine a life without poetry, music, drama or painting. Similarly, I recognize that for many people religion is paramount, and much more relevant to their lives than science or art. But to acknowledge this is not to say that science is the same as art and religion; all three have their functions in life, and nothing is gained by pretending that there are no differences between them.

The truth the poet writes is not the truth the scientist recognizes, and the poetic identification of truth with beauty is essentially meaningless. There may be some connection between this poetic truth and hermeneutics, but for the scientist, truth is the statement of testable generalizations of universal validity, subject to proof and experiment. This is far removed from poetic truth, or the truth of music, painting and drama. It is with the former that Freud was concerned, and it is by its criteria that he must be judged.

Let me illustrate the difference between poetic truth and scientific truth. When Keats writes about the Nightingale, Tennyson about the Eagle, or Poe about the Raven, they are not trying to duplicate the work of the zoologist. In each case the poet is concerned with 'emotion recollected in tranquillity'; that is, with a personal, emotional reaction to certain experiences. Introspectively, no doubt, these experiences are recorded truthfully, but this is an individual, not a universal, truth, a poetic, not a scientific, one.

This distinction is relevant to a belief shared by many people, that writers know more about human nature than psychologists do, and that Shakespeare, Goethe or Proust were better psychologists than Wundt, Watson or Skinner. Here again we face the division between individual and universal truth. When Elizabeth Barrett Browning tells us that 'hopeless grief is passionless', does that accord with the psychiatrist's experience of depressed patients? When Shakespeare says that drink 'provokes, and unprovokes' lechery – 'it provokes the desire but it takes away the performance' – is this in fact true? The psychologist would put awkward questions, asking, 'Is this the function of the quantity of alcohol consumed, or the type of alcohol, or its concentration, or is it due to the mixing of drinks?' and so on. Or he would try experiments to show that a placebo (non-alcoholic) drink, consumed under conditions where the subject believes that he has drunk alcohol, has much the same effect as alcohol itself. Alternatively, he might demonstrate that the effects of alcohol depend very much on social circumstances: is it consumed at a party, or by a solitary drinker? He might demonstrate that extraverts and introverts react quite differently to drink. Shakespeare's words contain a truth, but it is a partial one.

In what sense can we say that Othello is the universal protagonist of the jealous person, Falstaff of the conman, or Romeo of the lover? They are all individuals containing their individual truth, but it is a truth which does not generalize. Having read this book, ask yourself to whom you would go for advice if you had to deal with a head-banging child, or an enuretic one, or with an obsessive-compulsive hand-washer – Shakespeare, Goethe, Proust, or the hard-nosed behaviourist who could practically guarantee to cure the disorder in a few months? To ask the question is to answer it. Practical problems of this kind are not the business of the poet, just as the poetic recollection of emotion, or the delineation of the single notable character, cannot be the business of the psychologist. Believers in hermeneutics try in vain to bridge the gap, but the gap remains.

To the scientist, two approaches to truth are particularly important. The first of these is informed and constructive criticism. Nothing is more valuable to the practising scientist than to hear his theories and views debated and criticized by his peers. If the criticism is ill-founded, he knows that his theories will survive. If it is well-founded, then he knows that he will have to change, or even abandon, the theories. Criticism is the life-blood of science, but psychoanalysts, and particularly Freud himself, have always disliked and discouraged any form of criticism. The usual reaction has been to accuse the critic of psychodynamic 'resistances', resulting from unresolved Oedipus complexes and other similar causes; but this is not a good rejoinder. Whatever the motivation of the critic, the points he makes must be judged in terms of their factual relevance and logical consistency. The use of the *argumentum ad hominem* as a reply to critics is the last resort to those who cannot answer criticisms factually, and is not taken seriously in scientific discourse.

Conversely, the same weapon has been used to criticize Freud himself. Thus several critics have suggested that psychoanalysis is an essentially *Jewish* kind of theory and that in forming it Freud drew upon his Jewish upbringing and teaching. I cannot judge whether the argument is true or not, but it is essentially irrelevant. Freud's theories have to be tested by observation and experiment, and their truth or falsity objectively determined; his Jewish background does not influence this test at all. Historically and biographically Freud's background may be of interest, but from the point of view of the truth-function it is not! The situation may be different as far as Freud's own neurotic illness is concerned, and its background in his relations with his father and mother. If it is true that he framed his theory of the Oedipus conflict on his own infantile experiences, this is important and relevant to a judgement of the theory. As I shall argue, Freud's contribution is tied up with his personality in a unique way, and this relationship requires discussion, even though ultimately the truth of his theories is not dependent on their origins.

The same argument applies to recent publications suggesting that Freud consciously altered his theories, not because they were wrong, but because they might attract hostility. This is the burden of the book by J. M. Masson entitled *Freud: The Assault on Truth*. Masson had access to the Freud archives, and on the basis of Freud's correspondence with Fliess he argued that Freud consciously suppressed what he knew to be the evidence for actual child-molestation, deliberately falsifying his own clinical material and the witness of his patients, and instead invented the notions of traumatic 'sexual fantasies' and Oedipal impulses. According to Masson, Freud thus initiated that 'trend away from the real world that . . . is at the root of the present-day sterility of psychoanalysis and psychiatry throughout the world'.

Masson may be right, but certainly the evidence is not strong enough to prove this point, and in any case Freud's motives are not really relevant to the truth or falsity of his theories. The original 'seduction' theory is no more true than the later 'fantasy' theory; both have to be judged in terms of known facts, empirical studies and experiments, not in terms of hypothetical motivations on Freud's part.

The second great weapon in the scientist's *armamentarium* is the putting forward of alternative hypotheses. It is very rare indeed for science to find a situation where there is an obvious explanation of a given phenomenon; usually there are several possible explanations, and the experimentalist has to design empirical tests to decide between them. Crucial experiments may be rare in the history of science, but the constant attempt to decide between alternative theories is an essential element in scientific progress. Here too, psychoanalysts, and particularly Freud himself, have always been hostile and negative in their attitude. Instead of welcoming alternative hypotheses, such as those associated with Pavlov and the doctrines of the conditioned reflex, they have simply refused to recognize the existence of such alternative hypotheses, and have never seriously discussed them, or produced evidence to decide which theory could explain the facts better. Within the limited compass of this book I have tried to indicate, whenever relevant, the existence of theories alternative to the Freudian, and to point to evidence suggesting which theory may be better in accounting for the established facts. The continued hostility of Freudians to all forms of criticism, however well-informed, and to the formulation and existence of alternative theories, however well-supported, does not speak well for the scientific spirit of Freud and his followers. For any judgement of psychoanalysis as a scientific discipline, these points must constitute strong evidence against its acceptance.

There is one argument against the scientific status of psychoanalysis, often brought forward by philosophers of science like Karl Popper, which I think is mistaken, and should not be taken seriously. Popper proposed to distinguish between science and pseudo-science in terms of his criterion of 'falsifiability'; in other words, science is defined in terms of its ability to put forward testable hypotheses which can be falsified by experiment or observation. Popper instances psychoanalysis, Marxism and astrology as three pseudo-sciences, and argues that none of them have put forward testable hypotheses. There are, indeed, considerable difficulties in devising good tests of the theories in question, but these are no greater than the difficulties of devising suitable tests for Einstein's theory of relativity. No one acquainted with psychoanalysis, Marxism or astrology can doubt that all three make statements and predictions which can be experimentally tested, and I will show in later chapters that, with regard to psychoanalysis at least, Popper's objection must fail. I will also argue that when Freudian theories are subjected to experimental or observational tests, the results do not support them; they fail the test. Clearly, then, these theories are falsifiable, and if this were indeed the proper criterion for distinguishing between a science and a pseudo-science, then psychoanalysis should undoubtedly be regarded as a science. Modern philosophers of science, like Adolf Gruenbaum, have pointed out the irrelevance of Popper's criterion to psychoanalysis, and have suggested that the logical inadequacies of Freud's theory, and its failure to generate factual support, are much more cogent reasons for regarding psychoanalysis as a pseudo-science rather than a science.

The criticisms made of Freud extend, of course, in even stronger terms, to his many disciples, like Jung and Adler, who parted from him and set up shop for themselves. Most of them, in fact, abandoned the Freudian pretence at scientific rigour and determinism and turned, like Jung, to frank mysticism. In this book, however, I have concentrated mainly on Freud and his teachings.

One point should be made in this connection. It is sometimes said that Freudian theories do not require scientific proof of the ordinary kind, because they find their support 'on the couch'. As Gruenbaum has shown, this argument is unacceptable, but for those who favour it there remains the insoluble problem of deciding between very different theories, all of which claim to be supported in this manner. How, without proper controlled experiments, could we decide between the various 'dynamic' theories we are offered? Are we to rely on some kind of Dutch auction, or a buffet-type choice of whatever we happen to like? This would be the complete abandonment of all science, and the very existence of so many different theories makes it all the more important to find methods of testing their truth-value along proper scientific lines.

What essentially is the content of Freud's contribution? To put the matter briefly, it is usually agreed that psychoanalysis has three aspects. In the first place, it is a *general theory of psychology*. It attempts to deal with questions of motivation, personality, childhood development, memory and other important aspects of human behaviour. It is sometimes held (not entirely without good reason) that psychoanalysis deals with matters that are important and interesting, but in a non-scientific way, whereas academic psychology deals in a scientific way with matters that most people find esoteric and uninteresting. This is not quiet true; academic psychology also deals with personality, motivation, memory and other similar topics, but undoubtedly it does so in a less 'interesting' fashion than Freud.

In the second place, psychoanalysis is a *method of therapy and treatment*. Indeed, this is how it originated, when Freud collaborated with a friend, Josef Breuer, to cure a supposedly hysterical patient, Anna O. As we shall see later, Anna O. was not in fact a psychiatric patient; she suffered from a serious physical disease, and the alleged 'cure' was no cure at all. Nevertheless, it is as a system of therapy and treatment that psychoanalysis has become most widely known, and as this system depends very much on the general theory of psychology embraced by Freud's followers, the success or failure of this method of treatment is extremely important, theoretically as well as from a practical point of view.

In the third place, psychoanalysis may be regarded as a *method of enquiry or research*. Freud himself, at first enthusiastic about the possibilities of his methods of treatment, became more and more sceptical, and finally considered that he would be remembered more as the originator of a method of enquiry into mental processes than as a great therapist. The method of enquiry in question is that of free association, in which we start with a word or a concept or a scene, which may come from a dream, or from a certain slip of the tongue or pen, or from some other source. The patient or subject thus starts on a chain of associations which, according to Freud, invariably leads to areas of interest and concern, and frequently to unconscious material vital to an understanding of the subject's motivation, and crucial to the inauguration of a proper method of therapy. Actually, as we shall see, the method itself was originated by Sir Francis Galton, who recognized its powers long before Freud; certainly, something positive can be said for the method but it is woefully weak from the scientific point of view, for reasons which will be discussed later.

The psychology introduced by Freud has often been likened to a hydraulic system, diverting energy from one part of the psyche to another, as hydraulics diverts water. This rather Victorian analogue is relentlessly pursued by Freud, although it certainly does not fit what we know about the workings of the human mind. Freud believed that when an idea is liable to raise the excitation of the nervous system beyond tolerance, this energy is redistributed in such a way that the threatening elements cannot enter consciousness, and remain in the unconscious. This energy might be either sexual or self-preservative (in the earlier version), or might take either a loving or an aggressive and destructive form (in the later version). The unconscious in question is a highly speculative construct of Freud's, not in the sense that his theory originated it – on the contrary, unconscious processes had been recognized by philosophers and psychologists for over two thousand years (we shall mention many of these anticipations later on) – but rather because of the peculiar version of the unconscious that Freud presents. He attributes to it powers and tendencies which later research has conspicuously failed to detect, and of course his own theory has changed very much over the years, in such a complex fashion that it would be difficult to get any agreement as to the precise nature of Freud's 'unconscious'.

The whole psychic system attempts to preserve its equilibrium in the face of this distribution of energy, and of threats generated from within and without, by defending itself in a variety of ways. These defences have become quite widely known, and their names are almost self-explanatory. They are 'sublimation', 'projection', 'regression', 'rationalization', etc. Freud believed that these defences are used not only by neurotics or psychotics facing traumatic events with which the ego cannot cope, but also by normal persons when faced with emotional difficulties. In order to do this, an internal structure is developed as the child grows up, constituted of the id (the biological source of energy), the ego (the part of the system that relates it to reality) and the super-ego (the part embodying conscience and self-control).

Freudian psychology also posits certain stages through which the child goes in development to maturity; these will be discussed in more detail later. They are all 'sexual' in nature (the term is put in quotes because Freud often uses it in a manner which is much wider than would be customary in ordinary speech) and are related in turn to the mouth, the anus and the genitals. If this development is not accomplished in a proper manner, then the adult will probably exhibit neurotic or psychotic behaviour; this is particularly likely to happen when the defences which were used early in life to keep dangerous psyche elements at bay break down.

One particular feature of the development of the young boy is that he falls in love with his mother, and wishes to sleep with her; the father is regarded as an enemy, a powerful one who can frustrate and even castrate the child. This is the famous Oedipus complex, about which we will say a great deal more later on. According to Freud, the future sanity of the child depends on the ways in which he deals with this situation.

Freudian therapy is devoted to bringing repressed and unconcious material back to the surface and making it conscious. The therapist, using the method of free association, develops a special relationship with the patient, known as transference, which in essence involves a strong emotional attachment of the patient to the analyst, and which may be used to effect the cure; in some ways it resembles the bond between child and father. Whether it does indeed lead to a cure is, of course, a crucial question we shall have to look into later on; there is now practically unanimous agreement among experts that psychoanalysis does not in fact produce such cures.

These are the basic elements of psychoanalysis, over-simplified, but nevertheless outlining the general field which this book attempts to cover. Most readers will already be familiar with many aspects of the theory, and where relevant more detailed accounts will be given in the various chapters of this book. I will not, except very occasionally, refer to the many pupils who rebelled against Freud, and produced their own theories. Prominent among these, of course, was Jung, but the list of other figures, slightly less well known, like Melanie Klein, Wilhelm Stekel, Alfred Adler and many others, is too long to be given here. Their existence (it has been estimated that in New York at the moment there are about a hundred different schools of psychoanalysis, all engaged in internecine war!) indicates the major weakness of the Freudian credo; being entirely subjective in its method of proof, it cannot furnish any ways of deciding between alternative theories. However, this book is devoted to the Freudian theory, not to that of the rebels among his pupils, and will concentrate on Freud's own contribution.

CHAPTER ONE

Freud the Man

Doubt is not a pleasant condition,
but certainty is an absurd one.

VOLTAIRE

This book is about psychoanalysis, the psychological theory originated by Sigmund Freud almost a century ago. He believed that he laid the foundations for a science of psychology, and he also claimed to have originated a method for treating mentally ill patients which alone could lead to a permanent cure. This book assesses the present day status of Freud's theories in general, and evaluates his claims concerning the scientific status of these theories, and the value of his therapeutic methods, in particular. In doing so, we must begin with a chapter on Freud the man: that odd, contradictory and somewhat mysterious personality behind the theory and practice of psychoanalysis.

In many ways this must strike scientists as an odd beginning to a book of this kind. In discussing quantum mechanics, we do not normally begin with a description of Planck's personality; nor do we usually discuss the lives of Newton and Einstein in dealing with relativity theory. Yet in the case of Freud it is impossible to gain a proper insight into his life's work without paying due regard to the man himself. After all, much of his theory is derived from his own analysis of his neurotic personality; his discussion of the interpretation of dreams is often based on the analysis of his own dreams; and his ideas about treatment are largely derived from his attempts to psychoanalyse himself and cure his own neurosis. Freud himself, so it has been said, is the only man who has been able to impress his own neurosis on the world, and remould humanity in his own image.

This is certainly an achievement; whether it deserves to be regarded as a *scientific* achievement is another question, and one with which we will deal in succeeding chapters.

Certainly to many scientists psychoanalysis seems more a work of art than a work of science. In art, the vision of the artist is all-important; it is subjective, and unlike science it is not cumulative. Our science is greatly superior to that of Newton, but our drama is grossly inferior to that of Shakespeare or even the Ancient Greeks. Our poetry can hardly compare with that of Milton, Wordsworth or Shelley, yet our mathematics is vastly superior to that of Gauss or any of the ancient giants.

Just as the poet and the dramatist draw upon their own lives, so did Freud attempt to wrest insights from his own experiences, emotional upheavals and neurotic reactions. Psychoanalysis as an art form may be acceptable; psychoanalysis as a science has always evoked protests from scientists and philosophers of science.

Freud himself was, of course, aware of this fact, and proclaimed that he was not a scientist, but a *conquistador*. The conflict was deeply embedded in his mind, and he often voiced contradictory opinions about the scientific status of psychoanalysis, and his work generally. These doubts will be discussed later; here let us merely note that in many important, indeed fundamental, ways, psychoanalysis deviates from the tenets of orthodox science. 'So much the worse for orthodox science!' many people have exclaimed. 'What is so sacred about science that we should reject the wonderful insights of the sage and the prophet!' Such an attitude is indeed often shown by psychoanalysts themselves, who would wish to reinterpret the term 'science' so as to include psychoanalysis. Freud himself would not have agreed. He wanted psychoanalysis to be accepted as a science in the orthodox sense, and he would have regarded such efforts as unwarranted reinterpretation of his views. Such a way of looking at his life's work is incompatible with his own ideas. For him, psychoanalysis was science, or it was nothing. We will return to this question in the last chapter; here let us merely state that in this book we will investigate the claims of psychoanalysis to be a science, using the term in its orthodox sense, i.e. as *Naturwissenschaft* and not as *Geisteswissenschaft* (these two terms are widely used in German to discriminate between the natural sciences and literary and historical studies, *Wissenschaft* being used indiscriminately to describe any kind of academic investigation).

Freud was born on 6 May 1856, in the little town of Freiberg in Austria, some 150 miles north-east of Vienna in territory now ceded to Czechoslovakia. His mother was the third wife of a cloth merchant, and he was her first child; however, his father already had two grown-up sons from his first marriage. His mother was twenty years younger than her husband, and gave birth to seven more children, none of whom could compete with Sigmund who was for ever her 'undisputed darling'. This maternal preference led Freud to say that his later self-confidence in the face of hostility was due to the fact that he was his mother's favourite. The family was Jewish, but not Orthodox.

When Freud was four years old, his father's business began to fail, and the family finally settled in Vienna, where Freud went to the Sperl Gymnasium, where he was to prove a good pupil, being top of the class for seven years. He was particularly outstanding at languages, learning Latin and Greek and being able to read both English and French fluently; in addition he later taught himself Spanish and Italian. His major interests were in literature and philosophy, but he finally decided to study medicine, and at the age of seventeen he entered the University of Vienna. He graduated after eight years, having dabbled in chemistry and zoology, and finally settled down to do research in the physiological laboratory of Ernst Bruecke where he studied for six years, publishing various papers of a technical nature. Forced to earn a living, he finally took his degree and in 1882 entered the General Hospital in Vienna where, as a junior physician, he still carried on research and published on the topic of cerebral anatomy. Indeed, he was to continue this interest in neurology until he was forty-one, publishing monographs on aphasia and on cerebral palsy in children.

When he was twenty-nine he was appointed *Privatdozent* (lecturer) in Neuropathology; he was also awarded a travelling scholarship which enabled him to study for five months with Charcot in Paris. Charcot was famous for his studies in hypnosis, and it was through his association with Charcot that Freud became interested in psychological rather than physiological matters. On his return from Paris he married, and started in private practice, seeking to achieve fame as a scientist by studying the neurotic behaviour of his patients, and attempting to construct a theory which would account for neurotic disorders, thus enabling him to effect the cures that had been sought in vain by many of his predecessors. He was extremely ambitious; while still a student he wrote to his fiancée about his 'future biographers'. An early attempt to achieve fame led him to investigate the potential uses of the drug cocaine; he was particularly interested in its ability to reduce pain and create lasting exhilaration. He found that the drug helped him overcome periodic bouts of depression and apathy which frequently interfered with his work and seemed to overwhelm him. He failed to realize the addictive properties of the drug, and indiscriminately advocated its use to family and friends and also, in a paper he wrote on its uses, to the world at large. Cocaine was to play a vital role in his development, as we shall see later.

Following Charcot, Freud used hypnosis on his private patients, but was dissatisfied with it. Instead, he became interested in a new method of treatment which had been introduced by his friend Josef Breuer, who had developed 'talking therapy', a new technique for treating hysteria, one of the major neurotic disorders of the time. In this condition, paralyses and other physical disturbances appear without any apparent organic basis; this disorder seems very culture-bound, as it has almost completely disappeared in modern times – when one of my Ph.D. students wanted to investigate the ability of hysterics to form conditioned reflexes, he was unable over a period of years to find more than a very small number of patients showing even rudimentary signs of this classical disorder! Breuer had a patient called Bertha Pappenheim, a well-connected and talented young woman whose case was later written up under the pseudonym of 'Anna O.'. He relaxed her under hypnosis and encouraged her to talk about anything that came into her mind, the apparent fountain-head of all 'talking therapies'. After a long time the girl recounted a strong emotional reaction to a painful incident which she had apparently repressed from consciousness; as a consequence of this 'catharsis', her symptoms disappeared. (As we shall see later, this account, published jointly by Freud and Breuer in *Studies in Hysteria*, was seriously in error. The girl was suffering from a grave physical disease, not from a neurosis at all, and she was by no means 'cured' by the cathartic method used on her. The facts, as in many other cases published by Freud, were quite different from what he said.)

In any case, Breuer's wife became jealous of the attraction which developed between Breuer and Bertha, so Breuer broke off the treatment, taking his wife to Venice for a second honeymoon. Freud, however, continued to work with this method, replacing hypnosis with the technique of free association, i.e. taking as a starting point events in his patients' dreams, and getting the patients to say anything that came into their heads on thinking of particular items in the dreams. This method of free association had been originated by Sir Francis Galton, the celebrated English polymath and one of the founders of the London School of Psychology. Galton, like Jung forty years later, used a list of one hundred words and got his subjects (as well as himself) to say the first word that came into their mind, timing their reactions. He was very impressed with the meaningfulness of these associations. As he said:

They lay bare the foundations of a man's thoughts with curious distinctness, and exhibit his mental anatomy with more vividness and truth than he would probably care to publish to the world . . . perhaps the strongest impression left by these experiments regards the multifariousness of the work done by the mind in a state of half-consciousness, and the valid reason they afford for believing in the existence of still deeper strata of mental operations, sunk wholly below the level of consciousness, which may account for such mental phenomena as cannot otherwise be explained.

Here is another quotation from Galton, concerning his experiments with word association:

[The results] gave me an interesting and unexpected view of the number of the operations of the mind and of the obscure depths in which they took place, of which I had been little conscious before. The general impression they have left upon me is that which many of us have experienced when the basement of our house happens to be under thorough sanitary repairs, and we realise for the first time the complex system of drains and gas and water pipes, flues, bell-wires and so forth, upon which our comfort depends, but which are usually hidden out of sight, and with whose existence, as long as they acted well, we had never troubled ourselves.

C. T. Blacker, who was General Secretary of the Eugenics Society and wrote a book on Galton, commented: 'It is, I think, a remarkable fact that Galton, a shy man who had strong inhibitions about sex matters, should have been able to reach a conclusion of this sort through the determined application to himself of a system of investigation which he had himself devised. His achievement is a testimony to his candour and to his strength of will. For he overcame in himself the "resistances" which it is one of the tasks of the analyst to break down.' In Galton's own words, his self-imposed task 'was a most repugnant and laborious work, and it was only by strong self-control that I went through my schedule according to programme'. The later works of Jung and Freud certainly amplified Galton's conclusions, but did not really differ from them on any important point.

Galton published his observations in *Brain*, and as Sigmund Freud subscribed to the journal he would almost certainly have been familiar with Galton's work. However, he never referred to Galton's paper, nor did he credit Galton with priority in suggesting the existence of unconscious mental processes. This was typical of Freud, who was very chary in acknowledging contributions made by his predecessors, however directly they anticipated his own work. We shall find many other examples later on.

Beset by many neurotic symptoms, Freud undertook a protracted self-analysis; this, allied to his experiences with patients, led him to focus attention on childhood events, and to place particular emphasis on the importance of early sexual development in the formation of neuroses, and in the development of personality. Freud analysed his own dreams, and checked background details with his mother; he thought that he had found residues of repressed emotions from his early childhood;

both of destructive and hostile feelings towards his father and of intense affection for his mother. Thus was the Oedipus complex born.

In 1900 he published his first major work on psychoanalysis, *The Interpretation of Dreams*. He continued to publish, attracted a band of devoted followers who later became the Vienna Psychoanalytical Society, and achieved professorial rank. He ruled over his followers in a very dictatorial fashion, excluding those who did not wholeheartedly agree with him in every particular. The most famous to be exiled was probably C. G. Jung. Freud himself was vaguely aware of this tendency when, in 1911, he commented as follows in a letter: 'I have always made it my principle to be tolerant and not to exercise authority, but in practice it does not always work. It is like cars and pedestrians. When I began going about by car I got just as angry at the carelessness of pedestrians as I used to be at the recklessness of drivers.' Psychoanalysis has remained a cult ever since, hostile to all outsiders, resolutely refusing to accept criticism however well-founded, and insisting on initiation rites involving several years of analysis by members of the circle.

There would be little point in relating here the remaining events in Freud's life. Those relevant to points discussed in the later chapters will be described in the appropriate places. There are many biographies available but unfortunately most, if not all, of these are written by hagiographers – hero-worshippers who can see nothing wrong with their leader, and to whom any form of criticism is sacrilege. Even objective facts are often misinterpreted and misrepresented, and little credence can be given to these writings.

Much the same, alas, must be said about Freud's own writings. He was not what one might call a truthful witness; we have already noted that he was extremely reluctant to acknowledge priority in others, however obvious to the historian this priority might be. He was determined to create a mythology centring on himself and his achievements; he saw himself as the ancient hero, battling against a hostile environment and finally emerging as the victor in spite of persecution. Supported by his followers he was quite successful in impressing the world with this completely untruthful picture of himself and his battles, but anyone who is familiar with the historical circumstances will note the difference between Freud's account of the facts and the facts themselves. In reading and interpreting Freud's writings, and those of his followers, it may be useful to follow a number of rules. We will set down these rules in what follows, and will also give examples to illustrate the need for following them.

The first rule, and it is a very important one for anyone wishing to understand the truth about psychoanalysis and Freud, is the following: *Do not believe anything you see written about Freud or psychoanalysis, particularly when it is written by Freud or other psychoanalysts, without looking at the relevant evidence.* In other words, what is stated is often incorrect, and may even be the opposite of what actually happened. Let us consider for a moment what Sulloway has called 'the myth of the hero in the psychoanalytic movement'. He points out that 'few scientific figures, if any, are as shrouded by legend as is Freud'. As he goes on to say, the traditional account of Freud's achievements has acquired its mythological proportions at the expense of historical context. Indeed, he considers such a divorce between what actually happened and what is supposed to have happened to be a prerequisite for good myths, which invariably seek to deny history. Virtually all the major legends and misconceptions of traditional Freudian scholarship have sprung from the tendency to create the 'myth of the hero'.

Readers may wonder why they should believe Sulloway (or indeed the present writer) more than they do Freud. Ultimately the answer must, of course, be that the reader should go back to the original data. Fortunately this is made easier when historians of the Freudian movement, like Sulloway, actually reprint some of the necessary documents, as he has done. If anything said in these pages seems unlikely, the reader has the option of going back to the original sources on which I have based my account. Here we are dealing with the myth of the hero, and the documentation required is given in full in Sulloway's book.

There are two main features which characterize the myth of the hero in psychoanalytic history. The first is the emphasis on Freud's intellectual isolation during his crucial years of discovery, and the exaggeration of the hostile reception given to his theories by a world not prepared for these revelations. The second is the emphasis on Freud's 'absolute originality' as a man of science, crediting him with discoveries really made by his predecessors, contemporaries, rivals and followers. As Sulloway points out:

Such myths about Freud the psychoanalytic hero are far from being just a casual by-product of his highly charismatic personality or eventual life. Nor are these myths merely random distortions of the biographical facts. Rather, Freud's life history has lent itself to an archetypal pattern shared by almost all hero myths, and his biography has often been remoulded to fit this archetypal pattern whenever suggestive biographical details have first pointed the way.

What are the major characteristics of the traditional myth of the hero? This usually involves a dangerous journey which has three common motifs: isolation, initiation, and return. The initial call to adventure is often precipitated by a 'chance' circumstance – in the case of Freud, the remarkable case of Anna O. There may be a temporary refusal of the call – Freud did not take up the topic again for some six years; if so, its later acceptance may be initiated by a protective figure – i.e. Charcot, who caused Freud to return to the subject. The hero next faces a succession of difficult trials; he may be misled by women who act as temptresses, so that he blunders on the way. (Such a blunder may have been Freud's seduction theory, i.e. the notion that young children who developed neuroses had always been sexually seduced, a theory which temporarily prevented him from discovering infantile sexuality and the Oedipus complex.) At this stage a secret helper comes to the aid of the hero (in Freud's case his friend Fliess, who aided him during his courageous self-analysis).

The next stage of the hero's journey is the most dangerous, when he faces obscure inner resistances, and revives long-lost forgotten powers. Sulloway compares the story of Freud's heroic self-analysis with such equally heroic episodes as Aeneas' descent into the underworld to learn his destiny, or Moses' leadership of the Hebrews during the Exodus from Egypt. A well-known psychoanalyst, Kurt Eissler, illustrates the way in which this self-analysis has been made to fit into the heroic pattern:

The heroism – one is inclined to describe it so – that was necessary to carry out such an undertaking has not yet been sufficiently appreciated. But anyone who has ever undergone a personal analysis will know how strong the impulse is to take flight from insight into the unconscious and the repressed ... Freud's self-analysis will one day take a place of eminence in the history of ideas, just as the fact that it took place at all will remain, possibly for ever, a problem that is baffling to the psychologist.

After isolation and initiation, we have the return; the archetypal hero, having undergone his ordeal, emerges as a person possessing the power to bestow great benefits upon his fellow men. However, the path of the hero is not easy even now; he is faced by opposition to his new vision by people who cannot understand his message. Finally, after a long struggle, the hero is accepted as a guru and receives his appropriate reward and fame.

Sulloway has looked in detail at the reception Freud's original contribution received from scientific periodicals and reviewers in general. Ernest Jones, Freud's official biographer, tells us that Freud's most creative discoveries were 'simply ignored', that eighteen months after its publication *The Interpretation of Dreams* had yet to be reviewed by a scientific periodical, and that only five reviews of this classic work ever appeared, three of which were definitely unfavourable. He concludes that 'seldom has [such] an important book produced no echo whatever'. Jones goes on to say that while *The Interpretation of Dreams* had been hailed as fantastic and ridiculous, the *Three Essays on the Theory of Sexuality*, in which Freud questioned the sexual innocence of childhood, were considered shockingly wicked. 'Freud was a man with an evil and obscene mind ... this assault on the pristine innocence of childhood was unforgivable.'

Freud himself, in his *Autobiography*, attempted to give a similar impression. 'For more than ten years after my separation from Breuer I had no followers. I was completely isolated. In Vienna I was shunned; abroad no notice was taken of me. My *Interpretation of Dreams*, published in 1900, was scarcely reviewed in the technical journals.' And he tells us: 'I was one of those who had disturbed the sleep of the world . . . I could not reckon upon objectivity and tolerance.'

All this is in line with the beautiful myth of the isolation of the hero at the beginning of his journey, but a look at the actual historical record will show that the initial reception of Freud's theories was quite different from this traditional account. *The Interpretation of Dreams* was initially reviewed in at least eleven journal magazines and subject journals, including seven in the field of philosophy and theology, psychology, neuropsychiatry, psychic research, and criminal anthropology. These reviews were individualized presentations, not just routine notices, and together amount to more than 7,500 words. They appeared about a year after publication, which is probably quicker than usual. For the essay *On Dreams*, nineteen reviews have been found, all of which appeared in medical and psychiatric journals, with a total of some 9,500 words at an average time interval of eight months! As Bry and Rifkin, who undertook the research on which these findings are based, point out:

It appears that Freud's books on dreams were widely and promptly reviewed in recognized journals which included the outstanding ones in their respective fields. Furthermore, the editors of international annual biographies in psychology and philosophy selected Freud's books on dreams for inclusion . . . roughly by the end of 1901, Freud's contribution had been brought to the attention of medical, psychiatric, psychological, and generally educated circles on an international scale . . . Some of the reviews are thorough and highly competent, several are written by authors of major research on the subject, all are respectful. Criticism appears after a fair summary of the books' main contents.

Thus Freud's two books on dreams received at least thirty separate reviews totalling some 17,000 words; note the contrast between the facts and what is said about this period by Freud, Jones and Freud's biographers in general. Nor would it be true to say that these reviews were entirely hostile to Freud's new theory of dreams. The first one to appear described his book as 'epoch-making', and the psychiatrist Paul Naecke, who had an international reputation in the field and had reviewed many books in the German-speaking medical world, said *The*

Interpretation of Dreams was 'the most profound that dream psychology has produced thus far . . . in its entirety the work is forged as a unified whole and thought through with genius'.

It is interesting to consider the review written by the psychologist William Stern, which Jones had described, along with several others, as 'almost as annihilating as complete silence would have been'. This is what Stern actually said:

What appears to me valuable above all is [the author's] endeavour not to confine himself, in the explanation of the dream life, to the sphere of imagination, the play of associations, fantasy activity, [and] somatic relationships, but to point out the manifold, so little known, threads that lead down to the more nuclear world of the affects and that will perhaps indeed make understandable the formation and selection of the material of the imagination. In other respects, too, the book contains many details of high stimulative value, fine observations and theoretical vistas; but above all [it contains] extraordinarily rich material of very exactly recorded dreams, which must be highly welcome to every worker in this field.

Annihilating? How about the *Three Essays on the Theory of Sexuality*? It too was well received by the scientific world, and drew at least ten reviews which, while not without criticism, certainly welcomed Freud's contribution. Consider what Paul Naecke had to say:

The reviewer would know of no other work that treats important sexual problems in so brief, so ingenious, and so brilliant a manner. To the reader and even to the expert, entirely new horizons are opened up, and teachers and parents receive new doctrines for the understanding of sexuality of children . . . admittedly, the author certainly generalizes his theses too much . . . just as everyone especially loves his own children, so does the author love his theories. If we are not able to follow him here and in so many other matters, this detracts very little from the value of the whole . . . the reader alone can form a correct idea of the enormous richness of the contents. *Few publications might be so worth their money as this one!* [Naecke's italics]

And another well-known sexologist concluded that no work published in 1905 had equalled Freud's insight into the problem of human sexuality.

Sulloway points out that it is of particular historical significance 'that no one reviewer criticized Freud for his discussion of infantile sexual life, although some did question in this connection his more specific assertions about oral and anal erotogenic zones'. Indeed, as Ellenberger has said: 'Nothing is more remote from the truth than the usual assumption that Freud was the first to introduce novel sexual theories at a time when anything sexual was "taboo". In Vienna, where Sacher-Masoch, Krafft-Ebing and Weininger were widely read, Freud's ideas about sex were hardly found shocking by anyone.'

There is further evidence to show that what Freud and his biographers said about the development of psychoanalysis, and the personal fate of the hero, was contradictory to the actual events as they happened, but readers interested in this must be referred to Sulloway, Ellenberger, and other authors mentioned in my list of references. What has been said should be sufficient to show that statements made by Freud and his followers cannot be taken as factually accurate. The clear-cut intention is the development of a mythology which would show Freud as the traditional hero, and no facts are allowed to stand in the way of the myth. It is not only in relation to these early days that mythology has taken over; it extends in many other directions as well. This leads us to the second rule that should be followed by the reader interested in a truthful account of psychoanalysis: *Do not believe anything said by Freud and his followers about the success of psychoanalytic treatment.* As an example, let us take the case of Anna O. who, according to the myth, was completely cured of her hysteria by Breuer, and whose history is presented as a classic case of hysteria.

Anna was a girl of twenty-one when Breuer was called to attend to her. She had developed her illness while tending her sick father, and in Breuer's view the emotional trauma connected with his illness and eventual death was the precipitating cause of her symptoms. Breuer treated her with the new 'talking therapy', which was to be embraced later on by Freud. He and Freud claimed that the symptoms which afflicted Anna had been 'permanently removed' by the cathartic treatment, but recently her case notes were found in the Bellevue Sanatorium, in the Swiss town of Kreuzlingen. The case notes discovered there contained definite proof that the symptoms which Breuer had claimed had been removed were still present long after he had ceased to have her in his care. The symptoms had started with a 'hysterical cough', but soon there were muscular contractions, paralyses, fits, anaesthesias, peculiarities of vision, and many strange disturbances of speech. These were not cured by Breuer, but continued long after he had ceased to be involved.

Furthermore, Anna was not suffering from hysteria at all, but from a serious physical disease, namely *tuberculous meningitis*. Thornton gives a full account of the whole story:

The illness suffered by Bertha's father [Anna's true name was Bertha Pappenheim] was a sub-pleuritic abscess, a frequent complication of tuberculosis of the lungs then highly prevalent in Vienna. Helping with the nursing, and spending many hours at the bedside, Bertha would have been exposed to numerous occasions of infection. In addition, early in 1881 her father had had an operation – probably incision of the abscess and insertion of a drain; this was performed at home by a surgeon from Vienna. The changing of dressings and the disposal of the purulent secretions would have led to further dissemination of the infecting organisms. The father's death in spite of every care would indicate a virulent strain of the invading organism.

Thornton's detailed account should be consulted on the long-continued development of the disease, and the fact that Breuer's treatment was completely ineffective, unrelated to the disease itself, and based on an erroneous diagnosis. Thus all the claims made for the case by Freud and his followers are misconceived, and indeed Thornton makes it clear that Freud was aware of at least some of these facts. So were many of his followers; indeed it was Jung who was the first to point out that the alleged success of the treatment had in fact not been a success at all. This story should make us extremely cautious in accepting any claims made by Freud and his followers about alleged successes. We will encounter other examples of this tendency to claim success where none existed; the case of the Wolf Man is an obvious example that will be treated in some detail in a later chapter. Here again we have the myth of the hero, overcoming impossible obstacles and achieving success; unfortunately many of the successes in Freud's case were imaginary. Readers interested in the facts should go to the careful historical reconstructions of writers like Sulloway, Thornton, Ellenberger and others who have unearthed the details of these cases; the facts are quite unlike the stories told by Freud.

A third general rule which should be followed by anyone examining Freud's contribution is this: *Do not accept claims of originality, but look at the work of Freud's predecessors.* We have already noted, in connection with Galton's discovery of the method of free association, that Freud did not take kindly to having his 'discoveries' anticipated. Similarly, he used without acknowledgement the important work of the French psychiatrist Pierre Janet on anxiety; this anticipation too has been amply documented by Ellenberger. But perhaps the clearest and most obvious example is the doctrine of the unconscious. Freudian apologists make it appear that Freud was the first to enter the dark abyss of the unconscious, the solitary hero encountering grave dangers in his search for the truth. Nothing, unfortunately, could be further from the facts. As Whyte has shown in his book, *The Unconscious Before Freud*, Freud had hundreds of predecessors who postulated the existence of an unconscious mind, and wrote about it in great detail. Indeed, it would have been very difficult to find any psychologist who did not postulate some form of unconscious in his treatment of the mind. They all differed in the precise nature of the unconscious mind which they postulated, but Freud in his version came very close to that of E. von Hartmann, whose *Philosophy of the Unconscious*, published in 1868, was devoted to the presentation of an account of unconscious mental processes. As Whyte makes clear:

Around 1870 the 'unconscious' was not merely topical for professionals, it was already fashionable talk for those who wished to display their culture. The German writer, von Spielhagen, in a period novel written about 1890, described the atmosphere in a salon in Berlin in the 1870s, when two topics dominated the conversation: Wagner and von Hartmann, the music and the Philosophy of the Unconscious, Tristan and instinct.

The *Philosophy of the Unconscious* is a huge book, filling 1100 pages in its English translation; it gives an excellent review of von Hartmann's predecessors, including a discussion of the ideas contained in the Indian Vedas, and the writings of Leibniz, Hume, Kant, Fichter, Hamann, Herder, Schalling, Schubert,

Richter, Hegel, Schopenhauer, Herbart, Fechner, Carus, Wundt, and many others. As Whyte points out, 'by 1870, Europe was ready to discard the Cartesian view of mind as awareness, but not prepared to wait any longer for physiology to take over the problem'. Whyte states that Freud had not read von Hartmann, but this is unlikely, and in any case he is known to have had in his library a book explaining in great detail the ideas expressed by von Hartmann.

A few quotations from orthodox psychiatrists in England may give an idea of the degree to which the importance of the unconscious had been accepted well before Freud came on the scene. Here is a quotation from Laycock, published in 1860: 'No general fact is so well established by the experience of mankind or so universally accepted as a guide in the affairs of life, as that of unconscious life and action.' And Maudsley expressed the idea of the English school of psychiatry in his *Physiology and Pathology of the Mind*, published in 1867, in the following words: 'The most important part of mental action, the central process on which thinking depends, is unconscious mental activity.' Many other examples could be given from the writings of W. B. Carpenter, J. C. Brodie, and D. H. Tuke.

One last quotation must suffice. It comes from Wilhelm Wundt, the father of experimental psychology, and a keen introspectionist – hardly the man one would have imagined to have been interested in the unconscious! This is what he had to say: 'Our mind is so fortunately equipped, that it brings us the most important bases for our thoughts without our having the least knowledge of this work of elaboration. Only the results of it become conscious. This unconscious mind is for us like an unknown being who creates and produces for us, and finally throws the ripe fruits in our lap.'

Clearly there can be no question of the fact that many professional philosophers, psychologists and even physiologists postulated an unconscious mind long before Freud, and the notion that he invented 'the unconscious' is simply nonsensical. In relation to these theories of the unconscious, the famous German psychologist H. Ebbinghaus, who singlehandedly introduced the experimental study of memory into the field, complained: 'What is new in these theories is not true, and what is true is not new.' This is the perfect epitaph, not only on Freud's theories of the unconscious, but on his whole work, and we will have opportunity to return to it many times. Unconscious activity there certainly is, but the Freudian unconscious, populated like a medieval morality play by such mythological figures as the ego, the id and the super-ego, the censor, Eros and Thanatos, and imbued by a variety of complexes, among them the Oedipus and Electra complexes, is too absurd to deserve scientific status.

Let us now turn to our fourth suggestion to readers of Freud. It is this: *Be careful about accepting alleged evidence about the correctness of Freudian theories; the evidence often proves exactly the opposite.* The rest of the book will contain much material to support this notion, but we will give just one example to illustrate our meaning. The example is taken from Freud's theory of dreams, where he posits that dreams are always wish-fulfilments, the wishes relating to repressed infantile material. As we shall show in the chapter devoted to dream interpretation, Freud in his book gives many examples of the way in which he would interpret dreams, but astonishingly enough not one of these dreams deals with repressed infantile material! This is, of course, widely acknowledged by psychoanalysts themselves. Here is what one of Freud's most ardent followers, Richard M. Jones, has to say in *The New Psychology of Dreaming*: 'I have made a thorough search of *The Interpretation of Dreams* and can report that there is not one illustration of wish-fulfilment which meets the criterion of reference to a repressed infantile wish. Every illustration posits a wish, but every wish . . . is either a wish of out-and-out conscious reflection, or is a suppressed wish of post-infantile origin.' We will return to this point later.

Let us take an example from a well-known American psychoanalyst, to illustrate the difficulties attending the proper interpretation of dreams as supporting Freudian theory. This is the dream. A young woman dreamt that a man was trying to mount a very frisky small brown horse. He made three unsuccessful attempts; at the fourth he managed to take his seat in the saddle and rode off. In Freud's general symbolism, horse-riding often represents coitus. But the analyst based his interpretation on the subject's associations. The horse reminded the dreamer, whose mother-tongue was English, that in her childhood she had been given a nickname, the French word *cheval*, and that her father had told her it meant 'horse'. The analyst observed too that his client was a small and very lively brunette, like the horse in the dream. The man who was trying to mount the horse was one of the dreamer's most intimate friends. She admitted that in flirting with him she had gone to such lengths that three times he had wished to take advantage of her, and that each time her moral sentiments had gained the upper hand at the last moment, and she had been saved. Inhibitions are not as strong in dreams as in life; in her dream a fourth attempt took place which ended in a wish-fulfilment. The interpretation of the associations therefore supports the symbolic interpretation of the dream.

A French psychoanalyst, Roland Dalbiez, who wrote a very highly regarded book, *Psychoanalytical Method and the Doctrine of Freud*, states that:

> In all the literature of psychoanalysis which I have examined, I do not know of a more highly illustrative case ... If the psychoanalytic theory is rejected, it becomes necessary to assert that there is no causality whatever between the two series of the waking and the dream life, but only fortuitous coincidence. Between the nickname of 'cheval' given the dreamer in her childhood and the three unsuccessful attempts by her friend to seduce her on the one hand, and the three unsuccessful attempts made by this man to mount the horse in the dream on the other hand, there is no dependent link whatever: this is precisely what those who refuse to accept psychoanalytic interpretation are obliged to maintain.

Many readers of dream interpretations such as this have been convinced that they do support Freudian theories, but surely this is not so. In Freudian theory the wishes involved are *unconscious*, but it can hardly be claimed that a woman who is almost seduced successfully three times is unconscious of her desires for intercourse with the man in question. Furthermore, the wish involved is not an infantile one, but a very real and present wish. In other words, the interpretation of the dream owes nothing to the Freudian theory of dream interpretation, but rather disproves it. The wish involved in the dream is a perfectly conscious and present one, and this goes completely contrary to Freud's hypothesis. Thus we have the odd but often repeated situation that facts are offered us as proof of the correctness of Freudian theories when in fact they serve to disprove them.

Nor is it true to say that critics of psychoanalysis would be obliged to deny any dependent link between the dream and reality. Symbolism, as we shall show in the chapter on dreams, has been employed for thousands of years, and has often been made use of in the interpretation of dreams. The common-sense interpretation of the dream and its symbolism would appear to be far more correct than the Freudian one, which involves non-existent unconscious infantile wishes. We will deal in more detail with this whole problem later on; here the example is merely quoted to illustrate a stratagem frequently used by Freud and his followers to mislead the reader into believing that a particular case supports Freud's views although in actual fact it disproves it. The interpretation of a dream is accepted because it makes sense on common-sense grounds, and the reader is thus prevented from thinking deeply about the actual relevance of the dream to Freudian theory, which is much more complex and convoluted than the straightforward interpretation would suggest.

We now come to the last piece of advice to readers in evaluating the psychoanalytic theory, and the personality of its originator. It is: *In looking at a life history, don't forget the obvious.* We shall illustrate the importance of this advice by reference to Freud's life history, and try to explain the great paradox which it presents. This paradox is the sudden and unexpected change that took place in Freud at the beginning of the 1890s. By the end of the 1880s, Freud was a lecturer at the university, an honorary consultant to the Institute for Children's Diseases, and director of its neurology department. He had published widely on matters concerning neurology and was a very accomplished neuroanatomist whose technical mastery was widely acclaimed. He was happily married with a rapidly growing family to support, and was engaged in a lucrative private practice concerning diseases of the nervous system. He was a nonconformist member of the bourgeoisie, conservative and orthodox. All of this changed abruptly in the early 1890s.

This change became very clear in his general philosophy; where previously he had been extremely strait-laced and Victorian in his sexual attitudes, he was now advocating the complete overthrow of all conventional sexual morality. His style of writing changed, as shown in his published papers. Until the change, his scientific contributions had been lucid, concise, and conforming to the state of knowledge as it existed at the time, but now his style became extraordinarily speculative and theoretical, strained and contrived.

Ernest Jones, Freud's official biographer, also tells us that during this period (roughly from 1892 to 1900) Freud underwent a marked personality change, and suffered from a 'very considerable psychoneurosis, characterized by swings of mood from extreme exhilaration to profound depression and twilight states of consciousness'. Over the same period he developed unexplained symptoms of cardiac irregularity and rapidity of heart movement. He suffered from a strange disorder called the 'nasal reflex neurosis', and conceived a violent hatred for his old friend and colleague Breuer, while at the same time conceiving an intense admiration for and devotion to another friend, Wilhelm Fliess. And the last great change that occurred was that the more the sexual impulse became the corner-stone of his general theory, the less he practised it, so that by the turn of the century he had virtually ceased to have intercourse with his wife.

Other symptoms of a personality change which appeared around this time were the Messianic conviction of a mission, the acceptance of the myth of the hero (already mentioned), and the general dictatorial tendency to rule over his followers and expel them for any slight doubts about the complete and general truth of his theories. This, too, is very different from the behaviour of the early Freud, who did not show any of these odd and unacceptable character traits.

Thornton, on the basis of Freud's correspondence with Fliess, has put forward a very clear-cut hypothesis which would explain all these sudden changes in terms of an addiction Freud developed to cocaine. Freud had worked with cocaine, had used it to contain his frequent headaches, and had advocated it enthusiastically to all who wished to control their mental states.

Fliess had worked out a rather absurd theory about the action of cocaine producing a dramatic amelioration of the pains of migraine and other disorders by nasal application. What happens in effect is that the application of the drug to mucous membranes, such as those inside the nose, results in extremely speedy absorption, so that the drug enters the bloodstream and reaches the brain rapidly and practically unchanged. There is no doubt about the fact that Freud was induced by Fliess to use cocaine for the purpose of curing his migraine, and improving his 'nasal reflex neurosis'. This is what Ernest Jones has to say about it:

Then, as was fitting in his relation to a rhinologist, Freud suffered badly from nasal infection in those years. In fact, they both did [i.e. Freud and Fliess] and an inordinate interest was taken on both sides in the state of each other's nose, an organ which, after all, had first aroused Fliess's interest in sexual processes. Fliess twice operated on Freud, probably by cauterisation of the turbinate bones; the second time was in the summer of 1895. Cocaine, in which Fliess was a great believer, was also constantly prescribed.

Unfortunately, of course, this use of cocaine set up a vicious circle producing real nasal pathology and making worse what it was supposed to cure. As Thornton points out, 'such pathology is concomitant with chronic regular use of cocaine. Necrosis of the membranes, crusting, ulceration and frequent bleeds with resultant infections are invariable sequelae of such usage . . . Infection of the ulcerated tissues leads to severe sinus infections from which, in fact, Freud suffered badly in the second half of the decade.' This, then, was the reason for the 'inordinate interest' in each other's noses which so amused Jones in his account of Freud and Fliess. 'Both men had begun to suffer from the effects of cocaine on the brain. Hence the progressively bizarre quality of the theories of both men as the decade progressed.'

There is direct evidence for this theory in Freud's own writings. Thus in *The Interpretation of Dreams* he recalled the worry about his own state of health, when writing about some of the patients. This is what he wrote: 'I was making frequent use of cocaine at that time to reduce some troublesome nasal swellings, and I had heard a few days earlier that one of my women patients who had followed my example had developed an extensive necrosis of the nasal mucous membrane.' Thornton comments: 'Freud's use of cocaine was not merely for the relief of an occasional attack of migraine. He was trapped in a vicious circle of using it to reduce nasal swellings which had actually been caused by the drug itself and which would inevitably recur more intensely as its effects wore off. Almost continuous usage would be the result.'

Can the case be regarded as proven? The evidence is largely circumstantial, but any reader of Thornton's very detailed and carefully annotated analysis will find the evidence very strong indeed. Conclusive additional material might be obtained from Freud's correspondence with Fliess, but Freud's family have refused to allow Thornton and other academic investigators to read the material. What is beyond any doubt is that the odd changes that took place in Freud correspond very precisely to the kind of changes, both physical and psychological, which have been noted many times in patients suffering from cocaine addiction. We might thus be on the wrong track (as Freud and Breuer were in the case of Anna O.) in ascribing behavioural symptoms to psychological causes and neurosis; in both cases there may have been a physical cause. Orthodox doctors often miss psychological illness and attribute it to physical causes; psychoanalysts make similar mistakes in the opposite direction. Only detailed investigation free of preconceived notions can tell us in any given case what the true causes of a disorder might be.

We have now said enough about Freud the man, and the dangers in taking too seriously anything he and his followers may say. The reader may by now have felt worried and uncertain on a number of issues. How can it be that Freud could illustrate his theories about dreaming and the unconscious, in *The Interpretation of Dreams*, using exclusively as his examples dreams which departed completely from his own theory? How can it be that so many of the critics he considered overtly hostile failed to see the obvious? How is it that psychoanalysts who now acknowledge this defect still claim *The Interpretation of Dreams* as a work of genius? There are many such questions which arise from the material surveyed here; the main answer must surely be that Freud's theory is not a scientific one in the ordinary sense, and that it has been put over as a piece of propaganda, irrespective of the facts of the case, rather than in terms of proof for a scientific theory.

This propaganda effort has taken an extraordinary form. Critics, however knowledgeable, were never answered in scientific terms; they were accused of hostility towards psychoanalysis, produced by neurotic and other infantile repressed wishes and feelings. Such an *argumentum ad hominem* is abhorrent to science, and cannot be taken seriously. Whatever the motives of a critic, the scientist still has to answer the rational parts of the critique. This psychoanalysts have never done; neither have they ever considered alternative hypotheses to the Freudian, as we shall document in succeeding chapters. These are not the characteristics of science, but of religion and politics. Freud's mythological hero departs completely from the role of the serious scientist, and takes on the role of the religious prophet or political leader. It is only in those terms that we can understand the facts surveyed in this chapter. An understanding of Freud the man is necessary before we can understand psychoanalysis as a movement. In all art, there is a close relationship between the artist and the work he produced. Not so in science. Calculus would have been invented even without Newton, and indeed Leibniz invented it about the same time, and quite independently. Science is objective and largely independent of personality; art and psychoanalysis are subjective, and intimately related to the personality of the artist. As we shall see in more detail later, the psychoanalytic movement is not a scientific one in the ordinary sense, and all the oddities mentioned in this chapter stem from this simple fact.

CHAPTER TWO

Psychoanalysis as a Method of Treatment

The only standard by which truth can be assessed
is its practical results.

MAO TSE-TUNG

To the layman, psychoanalysis is mainly known as a method of treatment for neurotic, and possibly psychotic, mental disorders. Freud certainly elaborated the theory and methods of psychoanalysis originally in order to treat patients, and he made far-reaching claims for these methods. The first of his claims was that psychoanalysis could cure mental patients of their troubles: the second was that *only* psychoanalysis could do this. His theory of neurosis and psychosis essentially states that the complaints with which the patient comes to the psychiatrist or psychologist are merely symptoms of some deeper, underlying disease; unless this disease is cured, there is no hope for the patient. If we try to eliminate the symptoms, either they will return, or we will have a symptom substitution, i.e. the emergence of another symptom, as distressing as, or even more disabling than, the original one. Hence Freud's disdain for what he called 'symptomatic cures', a disdain shared by his modern successors.

Freud believed that the 'disease' underlying the symptoms shown by the patient was due to the repression of thoughts and feelings which were in conflict with the patient's morality and conscious attitude; the symptoms were the eruption of these repressed and unconscious thoughts and wishes. The only way to cure the patient was to give him 'insight', by interpreting his dreams and the accidental slips of the tongue, memory lapses and inappropriate actions which, being caused by the repressed materials, could be used to trace their origin. Once 'insight' was achieved, and by this Freud meant not only cognitive agreement with the therapist but emotional acceptance of the causal nexus, the symptoms would vanish and the patient would be cured. Without such insight, some treatments might succeed in banishing the symptoms for a while, but the disease would remain.

This model, taken from the medical view of disease, was very appealing to medical men; they are used to being told that you should not treat the fever directly, because it is only a symptom. What you should do is to attack the disease which causes the fever, for the fever will vanish once the disease itself is eliminated. Of course, even in general medicine the distinction between disease and symptom is not always clear; is a broken leg a symptom, or is it a disease? Freud and his followers never doubted the applicability of the medical model to mental disorders, but as we shall see, their view is not obviously true, and alternative views have been put forward.

In later years Freud became distinctly pessimistic about the possibility of using psychoanalysis as a method of treatment; shortly before his death he declared that he would be remembered as a pioneer in a new method of investigating mental activity, rather than as a therapist, and as we shall see, many grave doubts have arisen about the efficacy of psychoanalysis as a method of treatment. However, most of his followers, having to earn a living as psychotherapists, have refused to follow him in this pessimistic conclusion, and strong claims are still being made for the efficacy of psychoanalysis as a method of treatment. Few psychoanalysts would nowadays advocate its use as a treatment for psychosis, such as schizophrenia and manic-depressive disorder. Here there is practically universal agreement that psychoanalysis has little to offer; it is in relation to neurotic disorders, such as anxiety states, phobic disorders, obsessional and compulsive neuroses, hysteria and so forth, that the most far-reaching claims are made. Clearly, patients would not spend many years under treatment, paying exorbitant fees, unless they were convinced that psychoanalysis could ameliorate their condition, or indeed cure them of their illness. Psychoanalysts have always played up to these hopes, and still claim to be successful in treating neurotic disorders, a claim which has never been proved.

This is a serious charge, and it will be the aim of this chapter and the next to discuss the facts in detail, and to justify our conclusion. Before doing so, however, let us briefly consider why the question is such an important one. It is important for two reasons. In the first place, if it were really true that psychoanalysis as a method of treatment cannot do what it is supposed to do, then surely public interest in it would wane to a considerable extent. Governments would cease to allocate resources to psychoanalytic treatment, and to the training of psychoanalysts. Public consideration of the psychoanalyst as a successful 'healer' would evaporate, and his views on many other issues would perhaps be received with less enthusiasm once it was clear that he could not even succeed in his first duty, the curing of his patients. Another important consequence would be that we would look around for better methods of treatment, and we would no longer feel obliged to relegate the so-called 'symptomatic cures' to oblivion, simply because Freud advocated a theory which suggested that these methods could not work. These are important practical consequences, and considering the very large number of patients suffering from neurotic disorders (something like one person in six of the population is seriously troubled by neurotic symptoms and needs treatment), we should not underrate the degree of unhappiness and downright misery which waits to be eliminated by successful treatment. Holding out false hopes of such successful treatment, charging large sums of money for unsuccessful treatment, and causing patients to spend long periods of time, sometimes four or more years of daily visits to the psychoanalyst, cannot be taken lightly.

From the scientific point of view, there are other theoretical consequences of the failure of psychoanalytic treatments which are even more important. According to the theory, the treatment *should* work; if the treatment does not work, this suggests very strongly that the theory itself is not sound. This argument has often been dismissed by psychoanalysts who believe that the treatment is to some degree independent of the theory, and that the theory might be correct, even though the therapy might not work. Logically this is, of course, possible; there may be reasons, unknown to Freud, which would cause his treatment to fail, although the theory was in fact correct. However, this does not seem a very likely contingency, particularly as no such obstacles have been specifically suggested by psychoanalysts, and no research seems to have been done by them to unearth such obstacles. Certainly at the beginning Freud regarded the alleged success of his therapy as the most powerful support for his theory. The failure of the therapy should therefore have alerted him to possible errors in the theory; it did not do so.

However, even more impressive than the failure of Freudian therapy is the success of alternative methods, which are discussed in the next chapter. These alternative methods are based on what Freud dismissed as 'symptomatic treatment', and according to his theory they should be unsuccessful or, if successful in the short run, should encounter either a return of the symptom, or some kind of symptom substitution. The fact that these dire consequences are not found is, as we shall point out, truly a death-blow to the whole Freudian theory. Freud was quite clear in his prediction that on the basis of his theory these consequences should follow: the consequences do not in fact follow, and it is therefore difficult not to argue that the theory was incorrect. This is one of the few cases where Freud made a very clear prediction on the basis of his theory, and indeed he was right in doing so: clearly the theory demands the consequences he predicted, and the failure of these consequences to occur must seriously undermine the theory. It is sometimes possible to rescue a theory from the consequences of erroneous prediction, either by making slight changes in the theory, or by pointing out certain factors which caused the prediction to go wrong; nothing of the kind has been attempted by Freudians, and it is difficult to see how such a rescue could be accomplished.

I would contend, therefore, that the study of the effects of psychoanalytic psychotherapy is of major importance in an evaluation of Freud's contribution. It is not absolutely conclusive; the therapy might work, even though the theory might be wrong, or the therapy might not work, although the theory might be correct. As far as the theoretical issues are concerned, caution is necessary to avoid arriving at premature and possibly unjustified conclusions. On the practical side, however, there can be no doubt that if the therapy does not work, then it is wrong that people should still be persuaded to undergo treatment, spend money on it, and waste considerable time on the couch.

It is a curious feature of psychoanalysis that until relatively recently very little attempt was made to demonstrate its effectiveness. Right from the beginning Freud himself opposed the usual medical practice of instituting clinical trials to assess the efficacy of a new method of therapy, and his followers have slavishly adopted the same stand. He argued that statistical comparisons between groups of patients treated by psychoanalysis and those not so treated would give false results, because no two patients were ever alike. This is perfectly true, of course, but it is equally true when we consider clinical trials to assess the efficacy of a given drug. This has not prevented medicine from advancing by using such clinical trials, and most if not all of our knowledge of pharmacology is based on the demonstrable fact that individual differences will cancel out if large enough groups are employed, and the effects of the drugs, or other treatment, will emerge *on the average*. If psychoanalysis helps some, most, or all patients in the experimental group, while the absence of psychoanalysis leaves the patients in the control group unimproved, then surely an overall success rate for the experimental over the control patient should emerge from such a trial.

This is what Freud actually said:

Friends of analysis have advised us to counterbalance a collection of failures by drawing up a statistical enumeration of our successes. I have not taken up this suggestion either. I put forward the argument that statistics would be valueless if the units collated were not alike and the cases which had been treated were in fact not equivalent in many respects. Further, the period of time that could be reviewed was short for one to be able to judge of the permanence of the cures; and of many cases it would be impossible to give any account. They were persons who had kept both their illness and their treatment secret, and whose recovery in consequence had similarly to be kept secret. The strongest reason against it, however, lay in the recognition of the fact that in the matter of therapy, humanity is in the highest degree irrational, so that there is no prospect of influencing it by reasonable arguments.

To this, one can only say that humanity is quite prepared to pay attention to well-documented accounts of successful therapy; people may be irrational, but not so irrational as to prefer theories presented without proof to theories which carry with them well-designed experimental support!

If we were to take Freud's pessimism seriously, we should realize that it would not be confined to psychoanalytic treatment. The argument would apply equally to any form of psychological treatment, and also to the effects of drugs on psychological or medical disorders. This really is not so, as the history of psychiatry clearly shows. For those who agree with Freud, the only conclusion to be drawn would be that psychoanalysis is a treatment of unproven value (indeed of *unprovable value*), and this should in future lead analysts to refuse to offer it as a form of therapy for psychological disorders, or even to insist that it is the *only* treatment that is suitable. Only proper clinical trials, using an untreated control group and comparing its progress with that made by an experimental group treated by psychoanalysis, can solve the problems of establishing effectiveness.

Freud instead relied on individual case histories, suggesting that the fact of an improvement or a cure *after* the patient had undergone psychoanalysis would be sufficient proof for his contentions. There are three major reasons for not accepting this argument. In the first place, neurotic and psychotic patients are known to have their ups and downs; they might show apparently spontaneous improvements over a period of weeks, months, or even years; then they might suddenly fall ill again, only to renew the cycle once more after a period of time. Most frequently they would come to the psychiatrist when they were particularly low on this cycle, and while it is possible that his therapeutic efforts improved their status, it is also possible that they were simply on the upswing which would have occurred in any case. This is sometimes known as the 'Hallo–Goodbye' phenomenon; the therapist says hallo when the patients come to him with their trouble, and says goodbye to them when they have improved; to argue that the improvement is due to the therapist's efforts is a typical *post hoc ergo propter hoc* argument, which has no logical significance. Because Event *B* follows Event *A*, it cannot be argued that *A* has caused *B*! We would need a stronger reason than this to argue for the efficacy of a method of therapy.

This is the reason why we need a control (no treatment) group to compare with our experimental (treatment) group. All our patients might get better, but they might have got better in any case, even without our treatment. We can check on this possibility only by having a control group of patients who do not receive the treatment; if they do not get better, but the experimental group does, then we have at least some reason to believe that our treatment has been efficacious. If the control group gets better just as much and as quickly as the experimental group, then we have no reason to believe that our treatment had any effect at all. As we shall see, this seems to be the fact as far as psychoanalysis is concerned.

The second point that is relevant, and often neglected, is the need for a follow-up. The 'Hallo–Goodbye' phenomenon suggests that the therapist may dismiss a patient who is at the top of an upswing, when it is quite likely that a downswing will follow; unless we keep track of the patient's progress over a period of years, we are not likely to know if our treatment had, in fact, had no long-term therapeutic effect at all! It might, of course, have slightly hastened the advent of the upswing, but it would then not have prevented the following downswing; in other words, it would not have effected a cure. As we shall see presently, in the case of Freud's treatment of the 'Wolf Man', this possibility never seems to have occurred to Freud, and he claimed as successes cases which were clearly unsuccessful. Follow-ups are an absolute necessity for the evaluation of any kind of treatment.

The third difficulty, which arises from the simple-minded proposition that a physician should himself decide in each case whether treatment has been successful or not, is that the physician has a high motivation for declaring his treatment to be successful. He, just like the patient, has such an investment in the treatment that he may be persuaded to look at the results through rose-coloured spectacles. Unsupported testimony by patient or therapist alike cannot be regarded as persuasive. We would need some objective criteria to make it reasonably clear that an actual, sizeable and meaningful improvement in the condition of the patient had occurred. This is never offered by psychoanalysts, who rely stubbornly on their own evaluation of their patients' alleged improvement. Such subjectivity is not scientifically acceptable.

One reason sometimes given by psychoanalysts for not conducting a clinical trial, with an experimental and a control group, and a long-term follow-up, is the difficulty of such an undertaking. There is no doubt about the difficulties involved, and we shall deal with these presently; it is, however, necessary to make a very important point here. In science, when someone makes a claim to have accomplished something – to have invented a new cure, for example – the onus of proof is clearly on him. Indeed, it is far more difficult for the scientist to *prove* his theory than to *invent* it in the first place; difficulties of that kind are inherent in the scientific process, and are not confined to psychoanalysis. One of the deductions made from Copernicus' heliocentric theory was that stellar parallax would be observed, i.e. that the relative positions of the stars would look different in December from the way they would look in June, because the earth had moved round the sun. Such proof was extremely difficult, because of the immense distances involved; changes in angles of observations were so small that it took two hundred and fifty years before they could be observed. Difficulties of this kind are commonplace, and must be overcome before a theory is accepted. Psychoanalysts often scoff at attempts to conduct clinical trials of psychoanalytic treatment, citing these difficulties; yet until successful trials are completed, psychoanalysts have no right to make any claims. The fact that they have hitherto completely shunned this duty is a sad reflection on their responsibility as scientists and doctors.

What are the problems in the way of conducting a meaningful clinical trial? To most people it might seem simple to assemble a large group of patients, divide them on a random basis into an experimental group and a control group, administer psychoanalysis to the experimental group and either no treatment at all, or placebo treatment, to the control group, and study the effects after a number of years. Of the difficulties that arise, the most important is perhaps the question of the criterion to be accepted for improvement or cure. The patient usually presents with certain fairly definite symptoms; thus he may have a severe phobia, suffer from attacks of anxiety, have depressive episodes, complain of obsessions or compulsive actions, or have hysterical paralysis of a limb. We can certainly measure the degree·to which the symptoms are improved or eradicated after therapy, and to most people this would constitute a very real and desirable effect of the treatment. Psychoanalysts would say that this is not enough, and that we might not have succeeded in eradicating the 'disease' underlying and giving rise to the symptoms. For many psychologists holding other views about the nature of neurosis, the abolition of the symptoms would be quite sufficient; they would not ask for anything more, provided the symptoms did not return, and no other symptoms took their place.

In the nature of things, these questions cannot be resolved without coming to grips with the problem of the theory underlying neurotic disorder, and up to now there is no indication that any agreement has been reached on this point. What we can perhaps say, to accommodate both sides, is that the abolition of the symptoms is a *necessary* but may not be a *sufficient* condition for a complete cure. Research has been concerned mainly with the abolition of symptoms as a necessary condition for a cure, leaving aside the possibility that some underlying complex may remain. As long as this does not give rise to a renewal of the symptom, or to substitute symptoms, the debate is probably largely academic, and of little practical interest; it is doubtful whether it is of very great scientific interest either, because in such a condition there is absolutely no way of proving the existence of this alleged 'complex'. Psychoanalysts would disagree, however, and we will leave this particular question open. The more crucial question is whether in fact psychoanalysis succeeds in abolishing the 'symptoms' – the word is put in quotes because for many psychologists the manifestations of neuroses are not really symptoms of any 'disease' underlying them; as we shall see, the symptom is the disease!

If we can thus overcome the difficulty of the criterion, we must next consider the question of the make-up of the experimental and control groups. Psychoanalysts are very definite that their treatment is only suitable for a very small percentage of neurotic patients; they are very careful in their criteria for selection. In preference a patient should be young, well educated, not too seriously ill, and reasonably well-off – in other words, the subjects who are preferred as patients are the ones most likely to benefit from treatment. It is important always to remember this, since from the social point of view psychoanalysis would be very largely useless as a therapeutic technique because a vast majority of people would be unlikely, on the psychoanalysts' own showing, to benefit from it. Indeed, very few patients are treated by psychoanalysis at the moment; most psychoanalyses done are *training analyses*, by practising analysts on psychiatric registrars and others aspiring to become psychiatrists or psychoanalysts!

The seriousness of the selection problem is underlined by the fact that in one typical study, 64 per cent of patients undergoing analysis had received postgraduate education (as compared with no more than 2 per cent or 3 per cent of the general population), 72 per cent were in professional and academic work, and approximately half of all the cases were 'engaged in work related to psychiatry and psychoanalysis'. In addition, the very high rejection rate of patients by psychoanalysts is compounded by the unacceptably large number of patients (roughly half) who terminate treatment prematurely. Rightly or wrongly, psychoanalysts appear to believe that their method is suitable for only a tiny fraction of the cases of psychological disorder, and those chosen usually have the best mental and economic resources to achieve recovery. Thus, even if psychoanalysis were an important source for good mental health, it would be least available to those most in need.

Another difficulty is the control group. If denied treatment, are they not likely to seek help elsewhere – either by going to a general physician or a priest, or by discussing their problems with friends or members of the family, thus seeking some kind of therapy, even though not of a medically recognized type? The practice of confession used in the Catholic religion is well known to have therapeutic properties, and is indeed a kind of psychotherapy; how can we prevent members of our control group from making use of such facilities, unlike psychoanalysis as they might be?

A further problem that arises is the following. Psychoanalysis may succeed because Freud's theories are correct; it might also succeed because it contains certain elements, quite unrelated to Freudian theories, which are beneficial to neurotic patients, such as sympathetic attention on the part of the analyst, helpful advice given by the analyst, an opportunity for the patient to discuss problems, etc. These are called 'non-specific' parts of psychotherapy – non-specific because they do not derive from a particular theory about neurosis or treatment but are common to *all* types of psychiatric treatment and are not confined to one particular type of therapy. How can we distinguish between effects produced by specific and non-specific causes? The answer seems to be: by administering a placebo type of treatment to the members of the control group, i.e. giving them a relatively meaningless kind of treatment which leaves out all the theoretically relevant and important parts of the treatment derived from psychoanalytic theory. Placebo treatment is regarded as absolutely essential in clinical drug trials, because an inert substance administered as a placebo under conditions where the patient expects some effects usually produces quite strong effects, due to the suggestibility of the patient. Indeed, sometimes the placebo effects are as strong as the drug effects themselves, suggesting that the drug had no specific effect on the disease whatsoever.

Much of this might be true in treatment trials for psychotherapy and, consequently, a placebo control group is really essential if the trial is to be taken very seriously. However, it is, of course, difficult to design a treatment which fulfils the function of the placebo in not containing any of the specific parts of the experimental treatment, but is also acceptable as meaningful to the patients involved! It is not impossible to devise such placebo treatments, but it obviously needs a good deal of thought and experience.

There are many other difficulties, but we will deal only with the one which is often suggested as extremely important by psychoanalysts. The problem involved is an ethical one – how can we really justify the withholding of a successful treatment from the control group of patients, simply because of our scientific curiosity? This question, of course, assumes that the treatment is successful, when we are really trying to find out whether it is or is not successful. The assumption that the treatment is successful simply because it has been widely used is not uncommon in medicine. Until quite recently, the efficacy of intensive care units for certain purposes was unquestioned, but then some critics doubted the usefulness of the system and suggested that ordinary care in the patient's home might be just as efficacious. Clinical trials were fiercely resisted by proponents of the intensive care unit system, on the grounds that to deny it to the patients in the control group would put their lives at risk. Eventually the experiment was done, and it was found that intensive care units were certainly no better, indeed slightly worse, as far as saving life was concerned, than ordinary care in the patient's home! Once a particular method of treatment has been found efficacious by clinical trial, it may be unethical to deny it to patients; while it is still questionable whether it has any effect at all, or arguable that it may instead have a negative effect, i.e. make the patient worse, as has been suggested for psychoanalysis, no ethical problem arises. Indeed, it may then be said that it is unethical *not* to submit a new method of treatment to proper clinical trials, because if this is not done, inefficient and possibly dangerous types of treatment might be inflicted on patients. Furthermore, the widespread use of such methods might prevent the emergence of new and better methods, and the undertaking of research leading to the discovery of such methods.

Before turning to a consideration of the outcome of the clinical trials that have been carried out in recent years to establish the relative successes and failures of psychotherapy and psychoanalysis, it will be interesting to look at a typical case history presented by Freud in support of his claim that psychoanalysis is a uniquely successful technique for treating mental patients. It should be noted, however, that Freud in fact reported very few case histories, and usually not in sufficient detail to come to any kind of conclusion about their relative success. Vital information is usually withheld, often on grounds of confidentiality, and there is never any follow-up to enable one to see whether or not the patient derived any lasting benefit from the analysis. The story of 'the Wolf Man' is of particular interest here because it is usually cited as one of Freud's outstanding successes, and was so regarded by himself. Sixty years after his treatment by Freud, the Wolf Man was interviewed over a lengthy period of time by an Austrian psychologist and journalist, Karin Obholzer, and the book which was the outcome of these interviews is of absorbing interest to anyone who wishes to judge Freudian claims for himself. One must remember that Freud published only six extensive case histories, and analysed only four of the patients involved himself.

The Wolf Man derived his name from a dream extensively analysed by Freud:

I dreamt that it was night and that I was lying in my bed. My bed stood with its foot towards the window; in front of the window there was a row of old walnut trees. I know it was winter when I had the dream, and night time. Suddenly, the window opened of its own accord, and I was terrified to see that some white wolves were sitting on the big walnut tree in front of the window. There were six or seven of them. The wolves were quite white, and looked more like foxes or sheepdogs, for they had big tails like foxes and they had their ears pricked like dogs when they pay attention to something. In great terror, evidently of being eaten up by the wolves, I screamed and woke up.

The patient had this dream at the age of four, and from it Freud derived the cause of the neurosis. According to Freud, the dream is inspired by an experience from early childhood that provided the basis for the patient's castration fears; at the age of eighteen months, he had fallen ill with malaria and slept in his parents' room, instead of his nanny's as was customary. One afternoon, 'he witnessed a coitus *a tergo*, 3 times repeated', where he could see 'his mother's genitals as well as his father's organ'. In Freud's interpretation of the dream derived from this primal scene, the white wolves stand for the parents' white underwear.

According to Freud, the primal scene produced a deterioration in the patient's relations with his father. He identified with his mother, the woman whose 'castrated' state he observed at this early stage of his development. However, the patient repressed his homosexual inclinations, and this complex condition manifested itself in the malfunctioning of the anal zone. 'The organ by which his identification with women, his passive homosexual attitude to men, was able to express itself was the anal zone. The disorders in the fuctioning of this zone had acquired a significance of feminine impulses of tenderness, and they retained it during the latter illness as well.' This was also supposed to be the cause of the patient's long-continued 'intestinal difficulties', which prevented spontaneous evacuations for periods of months at a time. They were connected by Freud with the difficulties and problems the patient had with money:

> In our patient, at the time of his later illness, these relations [with money] were disturbed to a particularly severe degree and this factor was not the least considerable element in his lack of independence and his incapacity for dealing with life. He had become very rich through legacies from his father and uncle; it was obvious that he attached great importance to being taken for rich, and he was liable to feel very much hurt if he was undervalued in this respect. But he had no idea how much he possessed, what his expenditure was, or what balance was left over.

The second problem Freud saw was the Wolf Man's disturbed relation to women; the Wolf Man felt drawn to servants and fell in love obsessionally when he saw a woman in a certain position (that assumed by his mother in the primal scene described above). Altogether, Freud concluded that the Wolf Man was suffering from obsessional neurosis, and he was treated for this disorder as well as for depressive and other features described in Freud's book. After four years of analysis, and a reanalysis undertaken some time later because of a recurrence of symptoms, the Wolf Man was discharged by Freud as cured. Yet only a little later he was again feeling in need of analysis, and was treated by Ruth Mack Brunswick, for five months in the first instance, and then, after about two years, irregularly for a number of years. For psychoanalysts, the treatment and its outcome are seen as outstanding and impressive successes of psychoanalysis. What does the Wolf Man himself have to say about this?

Obholzer begins the set of conversations with the Wolf Man by quoting him: 'You know I feel so bad, I have been having such terrible depressions lately . . . you probably think that psycho-analysis didn't do me any good.' This does not sound like a great success for the therapy adopted, and reading the book in detail makes it very clear that effectively Freud's treatment did nothing whatsoever for the patient's mental health, or his symptoms; they continued up and down over the sixty years after he was dismissed as 'cured' by Freud, very much as if he had had no treatment at all. This case illustrates beautifully the necessity of having a long-term follow-up; no success can be claimed unless it is demonstrated that the symptoms have not only disappeared, but *continue* to be absent over a long period of time. It is well known that Freud accused therapists favouring other methods of treatment of inviting relapses, and declared that his method was the only one which, by eliminating the underlying complexes, was not subject to such relapses. Yet the case he was particularly proud of, and quoted repeatedly as an instance of the therapeutic value of psychoanalysis, was beset by repeated recurrences of the original symptoms, by relapses of a very serious kind, and generally by a continuation of the disorder of which Freud declared his patient had been 'cured'.

In the case of 'Anna O.' another great success was claimed by Freud and his followers, but as H. F. Ellenberger has pointed out in his book *The Discovery of the Unconscious*, this is a completely erroneous view of the matter. Jung, who was well acquainted with the facts, has been quoted as revealing that this famous case, 'so much spoken about as an example of brilliant therapeutic success, was in reality nothing of the kind . . . There was no cure at all in the sense of which it was originally presented.' Indeed, as already pointed out earlier, Anna O. was not suffering from a neurosis at all, but from *tuberculous menin-gitis*; the interpretation of this very real disease in psychological terms, and the claim to have cured it, is an absurdity illustrating the irresponsibility that can go on under the name of psycho-therapy. Thornton, in her book *Freud and Cocaine*, devotes many pages to this case, and makes it perfectly clear that Freud gave a completely deceptive account of this affair, and that he concealed the fact that the girl had not been cured by the 'carthartic' method – a fact well known to him. This fact alone must make one think: case histories, though insufficient to prove a theory, can illustrate the application of a method of treatment. But when the author quite consciously deceives the reader about vital facts of the case, such as the outcome, how can one take these case histories seriously – and above all, how can we ever believe him again?

The quite excessive degree of speculation which Freud brought to the task of interpreting the dreams, words and actions of patients is most clearly revealed in his study of a German magistrate, Daniel Paul Schreber. This is of interest, not only because of the fame it has achieved in suggesting homosexuality as the causal feature in paranoia, but also because it shows how readily Freud neglected his own precepts. For the understanding of the symptoms and the illnesses of patients he required the detailed analysis and interpretation of dreams and other material, along the lines of free association; yet in this case he never saw the patient, and relied exclusively on the latter's own written memoir! Schreber, a man of very high intelligence and ability, spent ten years in mental institutions on account of a severe mental illness. After recovery he published a long narrative of his delusions, but it lacked data about his family, his childhood, and his life history before his committal – all material which one would have thought essential from the point of view of a psychoanalytic interpretation. The account of the illness itself did not set out its chronological development but showed only the final shape it took. Even more damaging is the fact that the editors had cut out from Shreber's writings those parts that would have been the most important from the psychoanalytic point of view!

Nevertheless, a great many illusional ideas do, of course, remain in these writings. Thus Schreber told how he conversed with the sun, the trees, and the birds; how God spoke to him in High German; how nearly all the organs of his body had been changed; how the end of the world was coming; and how God had chosen him to save mankind! Freud concentrated on two particular illusions which he thought to be fundamental; Schreber's belief that he was in the process of being changed from man to woman, and his complaint of having suffered homosexual assaults on the part of the neurologist Flechsig who first took on his treatment.

From the basis of these very precarious supports, Freud assumed that repressed homosexuality was the cause of Schreber's paranoid illness, and he went on to apply this to *all* paranoid illnesses, which he declared to be due to repressed homosexuality. According to Freud, the role of the homosexual love object that was responsible was filled first by Schreber's father, then by Flechsig, and finally by God, or the sun. Freud argued that the origins of the condition lay in a childhood Oedipal conflict in which Schreber, due to fear of castration, had become fixated on the notion of sexual submission to his father. This unconscious desire was kept from the adult Schreber by a series of psychoanalytic defence mechanisms. These involved converting it into its opposite – hatred; and then projecting and displacing this hatred, which resulted in his coming to believe that other people hated him. Thus we have a complex chain of what psychoanalysts call projections. The patient denies the sentence 'I love him', and replaces it by 'I do not love him', 'I hate him', 'Because he hates and persecutes me'.

Critics have pointed out that Schreber's sexual deviation was transsexuality, rather than homosexuality, and his mental illness was schizophrenia, not paranoia. My interest here is not so much in an alternative diagnosis or explanation of Schreber's conduct and illness. It is rather to point out how Freud constructed grandiose schemes and theories on such a small and unreliable factual basis – how could one take as fact the vague recollections of a schizophrenic, amended as they were, in any case, by an editor who removed much of the most important material, and not going back to the stages of the illness which had preceded the breakdown? Furthermore, how would one ever test a theory of this complex kind? Scientists have a right to speculate, and to formulate novel theories, but in Freud's case the ratio of fact to speculation is unreasonably small, and the Schreber case illustrates better than most the gap between facts and theory.

When closely examined, the other cases treated by Freud do not fare any better, but I will not go into details which are discussed at great length elsewhere by competent medical and psychiatric historians, such as Thornton. We will, however, deal in Chapter 4 in some more detail with one other case, that of little Hans, which is supposed to have established the psycho-analytic practice of child therapy. For the present, we will merely conclude that even if single cases could establish the value of a given treatment, the few cases extensively discussed by Freud must be regarded not as outstanding successes but as therapeutic and probably diagnostic failures. If this is the best that can be said for psychoanalytic treatment, we may wonder what an experimental and critical reviewer might have to say!

There is one possibility, however, which we have not men-tioned yet but which is very relevant to an evaluation of Freudian psychotherapy. If the theory were true, then it would seem to follow that partial or complete insight gained by the patient should be immediately followed by the disappearance of the symptoms, and indeed psychoanalysts often make the claim that this is so. Freud himself soon realized that there was no such correspondence. There was, indeed, little correlation between the improvement (and frequently the worsening) of the condition of the patient, and the alleged 'insights' mediated by the psychoanalytic therapy. He did not let this bother him too much, and tried to argue that perhaps this lack of relationship was not too serious. However, from the point of view of the evaluation of the therapeutic process, it removes the last possible way in which the treatment of the individual patient could prove the efficacy of a given theory in mediating a particular type of treatment. Spectacular congruence between insight and recovery might serve as a strong indication of the correctness of the theory; its almost complete absence must throw severe doubts on it.

Before turning, in the next chapter, to a consideration of the clinical trials that have been undertaken of psychotherapy in general, and of psychoanalysis in particular, it may be useful to comment on one further argument that is often put forward by psychoanalysts to justify their procedures. They argue that possibly the method does not remove the symptoms, but that it enables the patient to live more happily with his symptoms. Furthermore, they claim that the analysis makes him a 'better person', although in what way he is in fact 'better' is usually left undefined, and therefore impossible to measure. These claims may or may not refer to some real kind of improvement of the patient, but they too have received no serious support; indeed, there is no evidence that psychoanalysts have attempted to provide experimental or circumstantial support for their claim. As in the case of symptoms, all that we have is a barrage of unsupported claims of the wonders psychoanalysis can perform, but not a tittle of proof that it actually does what it is claimed to do.

It might be argued that if there were no alternatives to psychoanalysis and psychotherapy, then the good that it did might outweigh the money and the time spent on it; even though the patient may not be healed, he may nevertheless derive some reassurance and other benefits from the treatment. However, there *are* alternative methods of treatment, much shorter and demonstrably more successful, which can be used to remove symptoms and improve the condition of the patient; these will be mentioned in the next chapters. Under the circumstances, therefore, these alternative pleas on the part of the psychoanalysts are not acceptable; they do nothing to rescue psychoanalysis from the accusation that it is ineffective.

One problem not often mentioned by psychoanalysts, but becoming more and more prominent, is that psychoanalysis may have very pronounced *negative* effects, i.e. it may make the patient worse rather than better. Hans Strupp and his colleagues, in a book entitled *Psychotherapy for Better or Worse: The Problem of Negative Effects*, give a thorough discussion of the problems, and reveal that there is considerable evidence that psychoanalysis can produce negative effects, and that most analysts and psychotherapists are well aware of this fact. It is suggested that perhaps the apparent lack of effectiveness of psychoanalysis may be due to the fact that it has strong positive, but also strong negative, effects, and these may cancel out. If this were true, it would certainly not be a good advertisement for psychoanalysis as a method of treatment; few patients would be willing to take a pill which would either make them much better or much worse! (It should be noted that Strupp has always been an outspoken advocate of psychotherapy and is by no means to be construed as a hostile critic; to those who believe that all criticism is just a matter of psychological resistance to the revealed truth, this may be an important item of information!)

How is it that a treatment designed to remove fears and anxieties, and alleviate the depression and complexes supposed to underlie these symptoms, can, on the contrary, make patients more anxious and depressed? The answer is a complex one, but it probably relates to the personality of the therapist, and to his manner. In the next chapter we will discuss an alternative theory to the Freudian, which demonstrates that one can cure neurotic patients quite readily by certain methods aimed at the direct reduction of anxiety, tension and worry. It has been demonstrated empirically that a sympathetic, friendly, and optimistic therapist, who is ready to support and advise the patient, is likely to reduce the anxieties that the patient may have, and thus be conducive to a successful treatment. Such tests will also show that different and opposite personalities – cruel, obsessional, pessimistic, lacking in interest or warmth – whose interest lies in the field of Freudian interpretation of dreams and behaviour, rather than in giving advice and help, are likely to increase the patient's anxieties to a catastrophic extent. Thus the very training that psychoanalysts receive, and the kind of role they are taught to play, stand in the way of therapeutic success, and are likely to have the opposite effect on their patients.

The facts about the negative effects of psychoanalysis are well documented, but for non-technical readers actual case histories may be more impressive, and easier to read. Two books have been written from the patient's point of view, portraying the behaviour of psychoanalysts and its effects on the patients. The first of these accounts, simply entitled *Breakdown*, is by an outstanding experimental psychologist, Stuart Sutherland, who recounts the history of his nervous breakdown and his disastrous adventures with several psychoanalysts. Sutherland is not only a very experienced and well-read psychologist, but he also writes extremely well; his detailed exposition of what happened to him in these encounters will give the reader who has not been psychoanalysed an idea of the terrible effects that the typical psychoanalytic attitude to patients can have on someone who is driven to extremes of anxiety and depression by his neurotic worries, which are not at all alleviated by the cold, interpretive attitude of the therapist. The account is harrowing but salutary; it illustrates in brilliant narrative detail the stark scientific facts set down in the preceding paragraphs.

Another interesting tale devoted entirely to encounters with five psychiatrists is *If Hopes Were Dupes* by Catherine York, a pseudonym which hides the identity of a well-known actress. The book contains the true description of one woman's efforts with the aid of psychiatry to rid herself of mental illness. It shows the agony and confusion experienced by someone who enters this world of psychoanalysis in almost total ignorance of its implications. The title of the book is, of course, taken from a poem by Arthur Hugh Clough; the full quotation is, 'If hopes were dupes, fears may be liars.' The reader will be struck by the similarity of the experiences of Mrs York and Stuart Sutherland in their encounters with psychoanalysts. Among the common factors are the apparent lack of sympathy on the part of the analyst, his coolness, and his lack of simple human feeling. It is not important in this context whether the attitudes are assumed in obedience to Freudian rules, or whether they are natural; the effect on the patient is equally disastrous. When we talk about the effect of psychoanalysis and psychotherapy, we should never forget that quite frequently the alleged 'treatment' may in fact severely increase the suffering of the patient. This is a chill warning to anyone already weakened by the anxieties and feelings of depression that lead him or her to the analyst; the hopes with which the patient enters the analyst's study are very likely to be dupes, but his or her fears are unlikely to be liars. Whether it is ethical to allow medical practitioners to inflict such suffering on patients already in despair is a question I will leave to the reader.

Readers who regard the Freudian psychotherapist as a benign, well-meaning, kindly uncle who helps his patients in their difficulties, calms their fears and is generally supportive, may like to consider a particular case reported by Freud himself, namely that of 'Dora'. The patient, whose real name was Ida Bauer, was a bright and attractive young woman who came to Freud at the age of eighteen suffering from fainting fits, with convulsions and delirium, catarrh, occasional loss of voice, shortness of breath, and a dragging leg. The symptoms suggest an organic syndrome, and indeed Dora had grown up with a tubercular father who had contracted syphilis before her conception, and both father and daugher manifested virtually identical asthmatic troubles. Freud agreed with Dora when she implored him to consider the syphilitic basis of her troubles. He explained to her that every neurosis finds a 'somatic compliance' in some underlying condition, and he claimed that in his clinical experience a father's syphilis is regularly 'a very relevant factor in the aetiology of the neuropathic constitution of children'. In spite of this presumed organic origin of her troubles, he regarded Dora as yet another weak-willed woman exhibiting 'intolerable behaviour' and 'a *taedium vitae* which was probably not entirely genuine'. Without any proper examination, Freud had diagnosed Dora as a neurotic as soon as she had recounted her symptoms, and the organic aspect of Dora's coughing, according to him, was only its 'lower stratum', acting 'like the grain of sand around which an oyster forms its pearl'. As a consequence he didn't bother with the organic symptoms or indications at all but proceeded on the assumption that the only hope of cure lay in undoing the patient's evasions. Freud apparently did not even take the trouble to put Dora through a routine physical examination, but rather subjected her to an extraordinary campaign of mental harassment.

As Janet Malcolm pointed out in her book on *Psychoanalysis: The Impossible Profession*, 'Freud treated Dora as a deadly adversary. He sparred with her, laid traps for her, pushed her into corners, bombarded her with interpretations, gave no quarter, was as unspeakable, in his way, as any of the people in her sinister family circle, went too far, and finally drove her away.' (Dora escaped from analysis after three months.) As an example, consider Freud's action when Dora claimed she had recently suffered an attack of appendicitis. He brushed aside this view and peremptorily decided that the appendicitis had really been a hysterical pregnancy expressing her unconscious sexual fantasies. He considered that her asthmatic symptoms were indeed linked to her father's identical condition, but only in the sense that she must have overheard him wheezing in an act of copulation! Her coughing, according to Freud, was just another timid female love-song. As Frederick Crews put it in an essay on 'The Freudian Way of Knowledge', 'in Freud's now prurient mind, steaming erotic speculations were of greater diagnostic interest than manifest signs of disease'. He goes on to say:

Freud's novelistic case history, in which he plays Poe's infallible detective Dupin, is full of vindictive touches at Dora's expense. One of her complaints, evidently justified, was that her philandering father was tacitly encouraging advances to her by the husband of the same father's mistress – a state of affairs in which the least culpable party would surely have been the bewildered and frightened teenage girl. But Freud set about to prove that Dora's troubles were produced chiefly by her own mind. When he learned, for example, that years earlier she had felt disgust at being sexually assailed by this 'still quite young' and 'prepossessing' man, he concluded: 'In this scene . . . the behaviour of this child of fourteen was already entirely and completely hysterical. I should without question consider a person hysterical in whom an occasion for sexual excitement elicited feelings that were preponderantly or exclusively unpleasurable; and I should do so whether or not [sic] the person were capable of producing somatic symptoms.'

Freud was convinced that women with neurotic problems were almost certainly masturbators, and that no progress could be expected until a confession on that point had been extracted. Accepting as axiomatic Fliess's law that recurrent enuresis is caused by masturbation, he forced Dora to admit that in childhood she had been a late bed-wetter, and he suggested to her that catarrh, too, 'pointed primarily to masturbation', as did her stomach troubles.

Another example of Freud's obsessive need to find a sexual explanation for every item of behaviour occurred when he remarked that her dragging leg must indicate a worry that her fantasized pregnancy (fantasized only by Freud under Dora's strenuous protest) was a 'false step'. Many other similar absurdities can be found in Freud's account of the case, where he clearly forces on Dora interpretations that lead back to his own complexes, rather than to hers. These are just a few instances of the way Freud treated Dora. The reader can imagine how such behaviour on the part of the analyst would affect an emotionally unstable girl of eighteen, growing up in a bizarre family circle, without assistance from her father, and lusted after by a lecherous and aggressive man who was her father's friend. Instead of finding the promised help and sympathy, she encountered a hostile, determined adversary whose only aim seemed to be to humiliate her and attribute to her motives and behaviours which were quite alien to her. If that, indeed, is a prototype of Freudian therapy, then no wonder that it often makes a patient worse, rather than better!

In conclusion, we may note that the existence of alternative theories and methods of treatment is very important for an evaluation of psychoanalysis, both as a theory and as a method of treatment. In science, even a bad theory is better than no theory at all. You can improve a bad theory, but if you have no theory at all you are lost in a welter of unconnected facts. Similarly with treatment; any kind of treatment is probably better than no treatment at all, because at least it arouses hope in the patient, reassures him that something is being done for him, and makes him believe in the possibility of a cure. When we have alternative theories and treatments, however, we have a much more powerful method of evaluation of both. One theory can be pitted against another, and experiments arranged to see which is supported by their outcome. Similarly, the existence of alternative treatments makes it possible to compare one with the other, and to see to what extent one is superior. It is for this reason that in the next chapters we will discuss alternative theories to the Freudian, and look briefly at the type of treatment suggested by these. In an evaluation of psychoanalysis, such comparisons are vital. They increase our knowledge and enable us to form a more secure judgement of the value of psychoanalysis than would be possible in the absence of such alternatives.

CHAPTER THREE

Psychoanalytic Treatment
and its Alternatives

> If a man will begin with certainties, he shall end in doubts;
> but if he will be content to begin with doubts, he shall end in
> certainties.
>
> FRANCIS BACON

Until about 1950 the claims of psychoanalysts to be able to treat neurotic patients successfully, and indeed to be the only ones who could effect permanent cures, were widely accepted by psychiatrists and psychologists. There were critical voices concerning the general psychoanalytic theory, but even these were somewhat muted, and it could be said that psychoanalysis was in the mainstream of psychological thinking where personality, neurosis, and social psychology generally were concerned. This position changed when a number of critics began to look at the available evidence concerning the efficacy of psychoanalysis and psychotherapy, and failed to find any data to support the psychoanalytic claims. Among those who put forward the view that psychoanalysts had failed to prove their case were men like P. G. Denker, C. Landis, A. Salter, J. Wilder, and J. Zubin; perhaps the most prominent was Donald Hebb, later to become President of the American Psychological Association. The growth of this movement is well told by Alan Kazdin, in his book *History of Behaviour Modification*.

Kazdin singles out an article along these lines which I published in 1952 as 'the most influential critical evaluation of psychotherapy', and it may be useful to look at the precise arguments employed in that article.

To begin with, I looked at the very important question of what happens to neurotics who do not receive any kind of psychiatric treatment. The answer, surprisingly enough, was that apparently neurosis is a self-terminating disorder; in other words, neurotics tend to get better without any treatment! After a period of about two years, something like two-thirds will have improved so much that they consider themselves cured, or at least very much improved. This is a very important figure to remember, because it sets a baseline for any comparison; any treatment worth its salt must do better than that in order to be considered successful. This rate of improvement was even found in insurance cases, i.e. where people were in receipt of moneys which would stop the moment they acknowledged that they had recovered – in other words, for them there was a considerable incentive to retain their neurotic symptoms! This process of improvement without therapy has been called 'spontaneous remission', and it resembles in its form the sort of thing that happens to sufferers from the common cold – after three or four days the cold will go away, whatever you may do, or even if you do nothing at all. To attribute the cure to the fact that you have taken Vitamin C tablets, or aspirin, or whisky, is an obvious case of *post hoc ergo propter hoc*; no matter what you do in the first day or two, the cold will cease to plague you very soon afterwards, but not necessarily because of any treatment you may have tried. Clearly it would have gone away anyway, and much the same happens with neurosis; in a large number of cases the neurosis remits spontaneously within two years. We will have to look carefully at what happens during these two years in order to find out whether the neurosis disappears of its own accord, or whether its disappearance is due to something that happens to the person during the period before the spontaneous remission occurs. Spontaneous, in this context, simply means 'without benefit of psychiatric help'; it does not mean some miraculous event without any cause at all.

When I compared the reported successes of psychoanalysts and psychotherapists with this baseline success rate, the answer turned out to be that there was no real difference; in other words, patients who underwent psychoanalysis, or psychoanalytic-type psychotherapy, did not get better any more quickly than did patients suffering from severe neuroses who received no treatment at all. I concluded from the examination of the literature covering something like 10,000 cases that there was no real evidence for the efficacy of psychoanalysis here. It is important to note the precise framing of this conclusion. I did not say that psychoanalysis or psychotherapy had been proven to be useless; that would have been to go far beyond the evidence. I simply stated that psychoanalysts and psychotherapists had not *proved* their case, namely that their methods of treatment were better than no treatment at all. It is difficult to see how this conclusion could be countered, because the figures were very clear. Nevertheless, a whole host of attempted refutations appeared in the psychological and psychiatric journals in the years following my article.

The critics pointed out, quite rightly, that the quality of the evidence was not really very good. Too little information was given about the precise diagnoses of the patients involved; the living conditions of treated and untreated patients were quite different; the criteria used by the various writers might not have been identical; and there were differences in age, social status and other factors between the groups. In my article I had in fact pointed out the poverty of the evidence, and it was because of these various weaknesses that I did not conclude that the studies quoted by me proved psychoanalysis to be valueless; that would have been over-interpreting the weak evidence available. But the more subject to criticism the evidence turned out to be, the stronger my conclusion appeared: namely, that the evidence failed to prove the value of psychoanalysis. Logically, you need strong evidence to prove the value of a given treatment; if the only available evidence is subject to severe criticism, then clearly it cannot prove the value of the treatment.

Most, if not all, of the critics took me to task for having concluded from this weak evidence that psychoanalysis had been disproved as a successful method of treatment. I was somewhat surprised at these criticisms, because I had been very careful not to make this claim; I wrote an answer pointing out that I had been misquoted, but even nowadays critics will still come up with this erroneous interpretation of what I actually said. This is perhaps not surprising; to many people psychoanalysis is a way of life, and any criticism arouses strong emotions which make it impossible for them to see the logic of a given argument, or to read carefully a criticism of their cherished beliefs.

The years that followed have seen a great increase in studies of the effects of psychotherapy, many of them a good deal better than the ones on which I had based my original paper. In 1965 I published another review, from which I drew eight conclusions which are reproduced below.

1. When untreated neurotic control groups are compared with experimental groups of neurotic patients treated by means of psychotherapy, both groups recover to approximately the same extent.

2. When soldiers who have suffered a neurotic breakdown and have not received psychotherapy are compared with soldiers who have received psychotherapy, the chances of the two groups returning to duty are approximately equal.

3. When neurotic soldiers are separated from the service, their chances of recovery are not affected by their receiving or not receiving psychotherapy.

4. Civilian neurotics who are treated by psychotherapy recover or improve to approximately the same extent as similar neurotics receiving no psychotherapy.

5. Children suffering from emotional disorders and treated by psychotherapy recover or improve to approximately the same extent as similar children not receiving psychotherapy.

6. Neurotic patients treated by means of psychotherapeutic procedures based on learning theory improve significantly more quickly than do patients treated by psychoanalytic or eclectic psychotherapy, or not treated by psychotherapy at all.

7. Neurotic patients treated by psychoanalytic psychotherapy do not improve more quickly than patients treated by means of eclectic psychotherapy and may improve less quickly when account is taken of the large proportion of patients breaking off treatment.

8. With the single exception of psychotherapeutic methods based on learning theory, results of published research with military and civilian neurotics, and with both adults and

children, suggest that the therapeutic effects of psychotherapy are small or non-existent and do not in any demonstrable way add to the non-specific effects of routine medical
treatment, or to such events as occur in the patient's everyday
experience.

Two points may be made in relation to these conclusions. The
first one is that they are rather surprising. Patients who undergo
psychoanalysis are nearly always of the type classified as YAVIS
(young, attractive, verbal, intelligent and successful), and such
people tend to have a favourable prognosis regardless of treatment. Selection criteria adopted by psychoanalysts result in the
exclusion of extremely disturbed clients (including sexual
deviants and alcoholics), of clients who do not request 'talking
therapy', and of clients whom the assessor would not normally
have considered suitable for psychotherapy. By thus excluding
the most difficult and recalcitrant neurotic patients, and concen-
trating on those most likely to improve in any case, psychoanalysts would seem to have loaded the dice in their favour;
failure to do better than no treatment or eclectic forms of psychotherapy, where no or few patients are excluded, seems to
suggest, if anything, that psychoanalysis does less well than
eclectic psychotherapy or no treatment at all.

Another point that must be noted is the large number of psychoanalytically treated patients who opt out of treatment before
it is finished. This has led to some dispute about the statistics of
recoveries after psychoanalytic treatment. Should the 50 per cent
or more of patients who terminate treatment before they have
shown much improvement be counted as failures, or should they
be omitted? My own view has always been that they should be
counted as failures. A patient comes to a doctor in order to be
treated and cured; if he goes away without any great improvement, then the treatment clearly has been a failure. This argument is strengthened by the peculiar logic often used by
psychoanalysts. According to their beliefs, there are three groups
of patients. The first group contains patients who are treated
successfully and are cured. The second group contains patients
who are still in treatment, a treatment that may have gone on for
several years, and indeed may continue for up to thirty years or
more. The third group contains the patients who break off treat-

ment. Now, psychoanalysts argue that treatment is always successful, so that the second group cannot be regarded as failures; they must simply continue to receive treatment for as long as it takes – another ten or twenty or thirty years – or until they die. If they opt out of treatment, and join the third group, then the psychoanalysts argue that these patients would have been cured if they had continued, and should therefore not be counted as failures. But on this kind of argument no patient could ever be a failure; either he is discharged as cured (and we know from the case of the Wolf Man just what that means!), or he continues in treatment. By definition there can be no failures, and consequently it is impossible to disprove the psychoanalytic hypothesis that treatment is always successful. The arguments used by the psychoanalysts resemble a proposition by Galen, a Greek physician living in the second century AD, who wrote the following in support of a particular medicine: 'All who drink this remedy recover in a short time except those whom it does not help, who all die and have no relief from any other medicine. Therefore it is obvious that it fails only in incurable cases'! This may be a slight caricature of the argument presented by psychoanalysts, but it contains the essence of what is suggested by so many of them in reply to criticisms based on the published failure rates.

There is another reason which may lead us to wonder why psychoanalysis does so poorly, and which may help to explain this. As already explained, psychoanalysts tend to screen out their patients in such a way that only those most likely to benefit, and least seriously ill, are accepted for treatment. It would also seem, however, that many of those who go to the psychoanalyst are not in fact neurotically ill at all. For the majority of them, psychoanalysis constitutes what one critic once termed the 'prostitution of friendship'. In other words, unable because of defects of personality and character to make and keep friends in whom they can confide, they pay the psychoanalyst to serve this function, just as men buy sex from prostitutes because they are unable or unwilling to pay the necessary price of affection, love and tenderness which is needed to achieve a sexual relation on a non-commercial basis. Other patients, particularly in America, tend to visit psychoanalysts because it is (or used to be – the habit is dying out!) the 'done thing'; to be able to speak about 'my psychoanalyst' is to be one up on the Joneses, and the patient can dine out on the 'insights' gained in analysis. All these people, not being ill, cannot of course be cured; the habit of relying on the psycho-analyst (like the habit of relying on priests, or astrologers, or witch-doctors) becomes self-perpetuating, and while the money lasts can be quite amusing. But all this has nothing to do with serious mental disorders of the kind we are considering. The psychoanalyst as prostitute or entertainer may not fit the self-important concept of the 'healer' developed by Freud and his successors, but it applies only too often.

After the second summary I published in 1965, the number of published articles on the problem of effectiveness of psycho-therapy increased dramatically, and a huge amount of material has been critically examined in a recent book by S. Rachman and T. Wilson, entitled *The Effects of Psychological Therapy*. Here I will only quote the conclusions they reach, after a careful analysis of all the available evidence.

The occurrence of spontaneous remission of neurotic disorders provided the foundations for Eysenck's sceptical evaluation of the case for psychotherapy. His analysis of the admittedly insufficient data at the time led Eysenck to accept as the best available estimate the figure that roughly two-thirds of all neurotic disorders will remit spontan-eously within two years of onset. Our review of the evidence that has accumulated during the past twenty-five years does not put us in a position to revise Eysenck's original estimate, but there is a strong case for refining his estimate for each of a group of different neurotic disorders; the early assumption of uniformity of spontaneous remission rate among different disorders is increasingly difficult to defend. Given the widespread occurrence of spontaneous remissions, and it is difficult to see how they can any longer be denied, the claims made for the specific value of particular forms of psychotherapy begin to look exaggerated. It comes as a surprise to find how meagre is the evidence to support the wide-ranging claims made or implied by such analytic therapists. The lengthy descriptions of spectacular improvements achieved in particular cases are out-numbered by the descriptions of patients whose analyses appear to be interminable. More important, however, is the rarity of any form of controlled evaluation of the effects of psychoanalysis. We are unaware of any methodological study of this kind which has taken adequate account of spontaneous changes or, more importantly, of the contribution of non-specific therapeutic influences such as placebo effects, expectancy, and so on. In view of the ambitiousness, scope, and influence of psychoanalysis, one might be inclined to recommend to one's scientific colleagues an attitude of continuing patience, but for the fact that insufficient progress has been made either in acknowledging the need for stringent scientific evaluations or in establishing criteria of outcomes that are even halfway satisfactory. One suspects, however, that consumer groups will prove to be far less patient when they finally undertake an examination of the evidence on which the claims of psychoanalytic effectiveness now rest.

It appears that the main change has been a closer look at the rates of spontaneous remission for different types of neurotics, and it is indisputable that such differences exist. For instance, obsessional disorders appear to have a much lower rate of spontaneous remission than anxiety conditions, with hysterical symptoms intermediate. Rachman and Wilson point out: 'Future investigators will be well advised to analyse the spontaneous remission rates of the various neuroses within, rather than across, diagnostic groupings. If we proceed in this manner it will be possible to make more accurate estimates of the likelihood of spontaneous remission occurring in a particular type of disorder, and, indeed, for a particular group of patients.'

Before discussing alternative methods of therapy, and in particular the therapies based on learning theory already mentioned in the summary of results obtained in studies of the effectiveness of therapy, it will be necessary to consider views of other psychologists who have reviewed the evidence, and have come to conclusions different from those of Rachman and Wilson. Thus, for instance, A. E. Bergin proposed (in A. E. Bergin and S. L. Garfield, eds., *Handbook of Psychotherapy and Behaviour Change*, 1971) that a spontaneous remission rate of 30 per cent is a much closer approximation to the truth than my suggested estimate of 66 per cent. However, as Rachman and Wilson point out in a lengthy critique, Bergin's work contains many curious features which render it quite unacceptable. In the first place, Bergin averages results from several new studies, but he forgets to include the older studies on which my own estimate was based! Rachman and Wilson point out that 'the new data . . . should have been considered in conjunction with, or at least in the light of, the existing information'. Another point made is that in his review Bergin missed a number of studies which were more satisfactory and pertinent to the question of spontaneous recovery rate than those actually included. Last but not least, some of the studies Bergin uses to bolster up his estimate of 30 per cent do not actually deal with spontaneous remission of neurotic disorders at all! The point may be illustrated by looking at one or two of the studies he uses. Thus Bergin gives a spontaneous remission rate of 0 per cent for a study by D. Cappon, but a closer look provides a number of surprises. The first is the title of the study – 'Results of Psychotherapy'. Cappon in fact reports on a population consisting of 201 consecutive private patients who underwent therapy; he reports that some patients got better and others got worse, but he does not provide any figures on which to calculate the rate of spontaneous remission. Bergin's figure of 0 per cent spontaneous remission rate appears to be drawn from Cappon's introductory description of his patients, in which he says that they 'had their presenting or main problems or dysfunction for an average of 15 years before the treatment'. Cappon was clearly dealing with a number of patients who had not shown spontaneous remission, and indeed if two-thirds of patients showed such remission, one-third did not; any figures must be based on some form of random sample, not on one which was clearly selected as having maintained neurotic symptoms for a number of years. There are other objections. Nearly half of Cappon's patients had disorders other than neurotic; there is no evidence that they had been untreated prior to attending Cappon; we cannot assume that the diagnosis at the beginning of treatment would correspond with their condition in the years prior to treatment; and so forth. Clearly this study is irrelevant to the question of frequency of spontaneous remission.

Another paper quoted by Bergin and cited as giving a spontaneous remission rate of 0 per cent is one by J. O'Connor, and again the title seems rather odd – 'The Effects of Psychotherapy on the Course of Ulcerative Colitis'. Ulcerative colitis is surely different from neurosis, and hence the relevance of the study to remission in neurosis is questionable. Diagnoses were made of the patients, but of the 57 patients with colitis who received psychotherapy, and the 57 patients who received no such treatment, only 3 in each group were psychoneurotic! Thus at best the numbers involved, even if the whole study were relevant to the problem of spontaneous remission, would be 3 versus 3, but in fact no percentage rate can be obtained from the reports as all the results are given as group means; hence the results for the 3 neurotics in the group which underwent treatment, and the 3 neurotics in the other which did not, cannot be identified!

Many other studies, quite bizarre in their relevance to the problem of spontaneous remission in neurosis, are quoted by Bergin, just as many far more relevant studies, with better methodology and much larger numbers, are omitted. It is safe to conclude that the widely cited figure of 30 per cent which Bergin reports is not based on adequate evidence, and should be disregarded. Any reader not convinced that Bergin's summary is entirely fallacious and indeed irresponsible should read the criticisms made by Rachman and Wilson in detail.

Another review of the evidence that has attracted much attention was published by L. Luborsky (B. Singer and L. Luborsky, 'Comparative studies in psychotherapies: is it true that everyone has won and all must have prizes?', in *Archives of General Psychiatry*, 1975, 32, 995–1008), who claimed to have found support for the view that 'everybody has won and all must have prizes' – the verdict of the Dodo in *Alice in Wonderland*. As he says, 'most comparative studies of different forms of psychotherapy found insignificant differences in proportions of patients who improved by the end of psychotherapy'. Alas, the methodology and execution of Luborsky's survey, like the quotation, come from *Alice in Wonderland*; he reached his conclusion by arbitrarily including or excluding studies in such a way that subjectivity is paramount. Again, detailed criticisms are made by Rachman and Wilson in their book already quoted, and it would be inappropriate to go into such detail here. Actually, Luborsky at the end of his paper appears to contradict all that he said before, and to conclude very much as I had done about the efficacy of therapy. He quotes at the end of his review a hypothetical 'sceptic about the efficacy of any form of psychotherapy' who says: 'See, you can't show that one kind of psychotherapy is any better than another, or at times even better than minimal or no psychotherapy groups. This is consistent with the lack of evidence that psychotherapy does any good.' His reply is that 'the non-significant differences between treatments do not relate to the question of their benefits – a high percentage of patients appear to benefit by any of the psychotherapies *or by the control procedures'*. This is a strangely ambiguous conclusion from one of the leading advocates of psychotherapy!

Last but not least, we must quote one further study, entitled *The Benefits of Psychotherapy*, by Mary Lee Smith, Gene V. Glass and Thomas I. Miller. This is a fascinating book, which comes to extremely positive conclusions as far as the effects of psychotherapy are concerned. This is what the authors have to say at the end of their book. *'Psychotherapy is beneficial, consistently so and in many different ways. Its benefits are on a par with other expensive and ambitious interventions, such as schooling and medicine. The benefits of psychotherapy are not permanent, but then little is.'* They go on to say:

The evidence overwhelmingly supports the efficacy of psychotherapy. Journalists may continue to make copy by casting aspersions on professional psychotherapy, but anyone who respects and understands how empirical research is performed and what it means must acknowledge that psychotherapy has more than proven its effectiveness. Indeed, its efficacy has been demonstrated with near monotonous regularity. The *post hoc* rationalizations from academic critics of the psychotherapy-outcome literature [who allege that the studies, all of them, are not adequately controlled or monitored] have nearly been exhausted. They can scarcely advance new excuses without feeling embarrassed, or without raising suspicions about their motives.

Their voices now rising in crescendo, they go on:

Psychotherapy benefits people of all ages as reliably as schooling educates them, or medicine cures them, or business turns a profit. It sometimes seeks the same goals sought by education and medicine; when it does, psychotherapy performs commendably well – so well, in fact, that it begins to threaten the artificial barriers that tradition has erected between the institutions of amelioration and cure. We are suggesting no less than that psychotherapists have a legitimate, though not exclusive, claim, substantiated by controlled research, on those roles in society, whether privately or publicly endowed, whose responsibility it is to restore to health the sick, the alienated, and the disaffected.

They continue for quite a while in this outburst of hopefulness to persuade the uninitiated of their cause, but a detailed examination of their work seems to lead to the opposite conclusion.

Smith and her colleagues criticize earlier summaries of the evidence, with their conflicting conclusions, for not making an exhaustive survey of the whole literature; they consider it inadvisable to concentrate on good research reports, and leave out bad ones, because that judgement is to some degree subjective. Accordingly, they collected all available research reports on the outcome of psychotherapy, given that the report included a control group as well as an experimental group. They then compared the outcome for these two groups in a quantified manner, and calculated an effect size score (ES) which was zero when there was no difference between the two groups. If the score was positive, then the experimental group had done better, and if it was negative, the experimental group had actually deteriorated when compared with the control group. They called this 'meta-analysis' and indicated that the data could also be broken down in various ways, e.g. by type of therapy, by length of treatment, by length of training of the therapist, etc. They finally presented their findings in a table which listed the average effect size for 18 different types of treatment, as well as the number of studies each of these 18 statistics was based on.

There is much that could be said about the method itself; it is very unusual in a review of scientific evidence to treat good and bad studies alike, giving them equal weight. Most scientists would regard this as anathema, and would exclude studies which were recognized as being poorly controlled, poorly carried out, and poorly analysed. However, let us disregard the many criticisms that can be made of the method itself, and concentrate on the actual findings. Psychodynamic therapy ends up with an ES of 0·69; this, the authors argue, is a very powerful effect, and fully substantiates their view that as compared with no treatment, psychodynamic therapy is extremely successful. They list many other treatments which are equally or more effective; thus systematic desensitization, an example of behaviour therapy to be discussed presently, has an ES of 1·05, i.e. almost 50 per cent higher than psychodynamic therapy!

The last entry in the table, Number 18, is labelled 'placebo treatment'. As explained earlier, 'placebo treatment' is a pseudo-treatment which has no rationale or meaning, and is not intended to benefit the patient; it is simply instituted to make him believe that he is being treated, while in actual fact he is receiving no kind of effective treatment whatsoever. A placebo treatment is a control for non-specific effects, such as a patient's going to see a therapist, believing that something is being done for him, and possibly talking to the psychiatrist or psychologist. It should therefore be a control, and it is interesting to see that its ES is 0·56, i.e. very close to that of psychodynamic therapy. In other words, when a proper control group is used, i.e. one receiving placebo treatment, then there is no effectiveness at all for psychodynamic therapy. There is evidence for systematic desensitization, and indeed in their assessment Smith and her colleagues find that the behaviour therapies are significantly superior to the talking therapies in general, but we will not insist on this point because there are other reasons for disregarding the conclusions of this survey altogether.

It is particularly interesting that Smith and her colleagues should have taken placebo treatment as an actual treatment, in view of the definition they adopt of psychotherapy. This definition, first advanced by J. Meltzoff and M. Kornreich, runs as follows:

Psychotherapy is taken to mean the informed and planful application of techniques derived from established psychological principles, by persons qualified through training and experience to understand these principles and to apply these techniques with the intention of assisting individuals to modify such personal characteristics as feelings, values, attitudes, and behaviours which are judged by the therapist to be maladaptive or maladjustive.

Whatever one may say of placebo treatment, it is certainly not a technique derived from established psychological principles, and it is not applied with the intention of assisting individuals to modify their personal characteristics! It is also interesting to note that others have carried out analyses of all studies in the literature using psychotherapy groups and placebo treatment groups, and found no difference in the outcome. Hence it is clear that when appropriate controls are used, the evidence still supports my original conclusion, and does not agree in any way with the conclusion erroneously drawn by Smith and her colleagues from their own data!

It is curious that the book by Smith, Glass and Miller is frequently cited by psychotherapists as conclusive evidence that their methods actually work, and that it has often been quite favourably reviewed in established journals of psychology, without any mention of this unorthodox view of placebo treatment. The reason is that the profession of psychotherapy employs more psychologists, psychoanalysts and psychiatrists than any other psychological discipline, and consequently there is an inherent professional interest in proving the value of their activities. Anyone looking at the literature has to bear this in mind; without doing so it is difficult to make sense of all the contradictory claims that have been advanced.

There are other interesting findings in the book which flatly contradict the conclusions drawn by the authors. Going back to the definition, we note that psychotherapy should be applied 'by persons qualified through training and experience', and consequently one would expect that the more prolonged the training of the therapist, the better the results. When this analysis was done by Smith and her colleagues, they found no evidence at all to support this conclusion – the most perfunctory training appeared as useful and effective in treating neurotic disorders as did the most extensive and lengthy type of psycho-analytic training. If this really were true, then obviously psychotherapy is not a skill that can be learned, but something that is acquired after a brief introduction to the field; this is apparently just as useful and productive of therapeutic success as is the most extensive and lengthy training available! Few psycho-therapists would agree with this conclusion, or accept its corollaries regarding the training of future psychotherapists. Yet on such an absurd basis Smith and her colleagues base their optimistic conclusions about the effectiveness of psychotherapy.

One would also imagine that the duration of psychotherapy

would play some part in its effectiveness, and that very short treatment would be less successful than very lengthy treatment. This is not the conclusion reached by Smith and her colleagues, who found that the time factor was not significant; the shortest type of therapy, lasting perhaps an hour or two, was just as successful as the longest, lasting for several years! This again would hardly find favour with psychoanalysts or other psychotherapists, who certainly believe that part of their theory demands lengthy investigation and treatment. Thus once again the very optimistic conclusions of Smith and her colleagues counter beliefs firmly held by psychotherapists themselves. Nor should it be thought that the most difficult cases receive the longest treatment, which would explain the comparative lack of success of long-term therapy. As we have already pointed out, psychoanalysis is the form of treatment particularly favouring very long-term application, yet psychoanalysts select as their patients those people least seriously ill, and most likely to recover quickly!

There are many other curious features about *The Benefits of Psychotherapy*, but enough has perhaps been said to convince the reader that the conclusions about the effectiveness of psychotherapy drawn by Smith, Glass and Miller are not supported by their own data, even though their book is often quoted as the best evidence for the notion that psychotherapy and psychoanalysis work. Even now, thirty years after the article in which I pointed out the lack of evidence for therapeutic effectiveness, and some five hundred extensive investigations later, the conclusion must still be that there is no substantial evidence that psychoanalysis or psychotherapy have any positive effect on the course of neurotic disorders, over and above what is contributed by meaningless placebo treatment. Treatment or no treatment, we get rid of our colds, and treatment or no treatment, we tend to get rid of our neuroses, although much less quickly and much less surely. Even if, after a period of two years, two-thirds of patients are cured, or very much improved, without treatment, this still leaves one-third unimproved, and hence the need for more effective and quicker-working therapies; if we could successfully treat those who would not otherwise recover through spontaneous remission, and reduce the two-year period of suffering for those who would secure

spontaneous remission, then clearly this would be of considerable social value. Are there, then, any alternative theories to the
Freudian, and do they give rise to types of therapy which can be
shown to be objectively more effective then Freudian psychoanalysis and psychotherapy?

The answer to this question is certainly yes. In my book *You
and Neurosis* I have already dealt with the promise held out by
behaviour therapy, and here will draw only a hasty outline of
the contents of the theory and the evidence about its effectiveness. There are, of course, many differences of detail within the
camp of behaviour therapists, and while it would be interesting
to go into these, this is not the place; this book is about Freud,
not about Pavlov who may be regarded as the father of behaviour
therapy! It was Pavlov who introduced the concept of conditioning and extinction, and it was J. B. Watson, the father of
American behaviourism, who showed that these concepts could
be introduced very successfully in accounting for the origins
and for the treatment of neurotic disorders.

A few words should perhaps be said about the principles of
conditioning. Most people are familiar with Pavlov's defining
experiment, in which he established first of all that dogs would
not salivate on hearing a bell ring in the laboratory but would
salivate when they saw food. What Pavlov succeeded in showing
was that if the bell (the so-called conditioned stimulus or CS)
was presented shortly before the food was shown or given to
the dogs (the unconditioned stimulus or US), then after several
repetitions of this pairing of CS and US, the dogs would salivate
to the CS alone. In other words, the experimenter would ring
the bell, and the dogs would salivate. This, in essence, is the
phenomenon of conditioning, and Pavlov's great contribution
was not only to have discovered and demonstrated it in the
laboratory, but also to have laid bare the laws according to which
conditioning proceeds. These are much too complex to be dealt
with here, but we must make reference to one law at least,
namely that of extinction.

Once we have established a conditioned response, it tends to
persist. If we wish to get rid of it, we must adopt a particular
method, namely that of extinction. This consists of presenting the
CS a large number of times without reinforcement, i.e. without

presenting any food. Gradually the salivation produced by the CS will diminish, and finally it will cease altogether. Thus the two fundamental properties of the conditioned stimulus are acquisition and extinction, and we know a great deal about the laws according to which acquisition and extinction proceed. Why is conditioning so important to the student of neurotic behaviour?

Before answering this question, let us briefly consider the nature of man. It is universally agreed that man is a biosocial animal. He is determined in his conduct partly by biological drives inherent in his make-up and derived from genetic causes; these biological determinants of his behaviour are firmly embodied in his morphology and have been shaped through millions of years of evolutionary progress. Equally, he is determined in his conduct partly by social factors – teaching, the shaping of attitudes and behaviour through intercourse with his fellow humans, and so forth. Some psychologists prefer to stress the biological, others the social, factors as determinants of conduct, but it is important to remember that man is a biosocial animal and that both groups of factors are vitally important if we are to account for man's behaviour.

All conduct, of course, is mediated very largely through the brain, and the brain bears unmistakable evidence of man's evolutionary history. As has often been pointed out, man has a triune or three-in-one brain. The oldest of the three, the so-called reptile brain, lies in the brainstem, which forms a bridge between the cortex itself and the many nerves entering and leaving the brain. Above it is the paleocortex, the so-called old brain, consisting largely of the limbic system and concerned with the expression of emotions. Surrounding it and arching above it is the neocortex, the so-called new brain; it is this that distinguishes man from most other animals by its huge development, and it is this that is responsible for thinking, language, problem-solving and all the cognitive processes that set man apart from beasts. Now, the neuroses are essentially disorders of the paleocortex or limbic system; it is characteristic of neurotic disorders that they can hardly be influenced by processes originating in the neocortex. A woman who has a cat phobia knows perfectly well in her neocortex that her actions are absurd, because there is no real danger involved; yet the feeling is there, and she cannot help it. The neocortex and the paleocortex are not completely incommunicado, but there is relatively little interaction between them.

Now, the language of the paleocortex is Pavlovian conditioning. Long before man developed his neocortex, his forebears had to learn to avoid dangerous places where they were likely to be attacked, to congregate in other places where food and drink would be found, and so forth. Animals acquire this experience through a process of Pavlovian conditioning, and in man, too, it has been found that emotions can be acquired in the same way. Ring a bell and then give a human subject an electric shock, and after a few repetitions you will observe him show the same physiological reactions to the bell as he showed originally to the shock! Anxieties and other fears, in particular, are easily acquired by man, and hence Pavlov, and later Watson, put forward the theory that *neurotic disorders are essentially conditioned emotional responses.*

A well-known experiment carried out by Watson illustrates the point. He conditioned an eleven-month-old boy called Albert, who liked playing with white rats, to develop a rat phobia, by making a frightening noise behind little Albert's head whenever the infant tried to touch the rats. After a few repetitions Albert showed considerable fear of the rats, which generalized to other furry animals, to Father Christmas masks, fur coats, etc. This fear persisted over a lengthy period of time, and Watson concluded that he had conditioned a neurotic phobia in the child. He also suggested that fears of this kind, and other types of anxiety, could be got rid of by processes of Pavlovian extinction. Mary Cover Jones, a student of his, demonstrated that this was indeed so by treating a number of children suffering from neurotic fears and phobias. All this happened in the early 1920s, and it is these theories and studies that form the basis of modern behaviour therapy.

There are several ways in which behaviour therapy can be used, the three major methods being desensitization, flooding, and modelling. I will briefly explain what these terms mean, beginning with desensitization. As an example, take a woman who has acquired a cat phobia through some kind of traumatic event in her past history. The behaviour therapist regards this as a conditioned response, and seeks a method of extinguishing it. In desensitization, the patient would first of all be taught methods of relaxation, i.e. the gradual slackening of tension in the various muscles of the body. Tension is one of the characteristics of high states of fear and anxiety, and this relaxation training lays the foundation for the process of extinction.

A hierarchy of fears is now constructed, in consultation with the patient, ranging from the least fear-producing aspect of the fear-inducing object or situation to the most fear-producing. Thus, in the case of the cat-phobic lady a low fear-producing stimulus might be a picture of a kitten shown to her at a great distance; a high fear-producing stimulus might be a large and fierce cat sitting on her lap. The patient is first instructed to relax completely, and when a state of relaxation is achieved, she is asked to imagine one of the low fear-producing stimuli, or is shown from a distance the picture of the kitten. The anxiety produced here is not strong enough to overcome the relaxation, and hence a small amount of extinction is achieved.

Gradually the therapist works through the hierarchy, going higher and higher, and when he has reached the highest rung, and extinguished the fear reactions completely, the patient is effectively cured; he or she will no longer show fear of the objects or situations which previously evoked this emotion. The method has been shown to work extremely well, and is applicable, of course, not only to simple phobias (which are relatively rare) but also to far more complex states of anxiety, depression and other neurotic symptoms. Here it has only been described in the simplest and most elementary outline; there are, of course, many complexities to the method which we have not discussed. Desensitization is probably the most widely used method of behaviour therapy, and undoubtedly one of the most successful.

The next method, flooding, is so called because it implies flooding the patient with the emotion related to particular anxieties, fears or phobias. In a sense it is the obverse to which desensitization is the reverse, for it starts at the top rather than at the bottom of the hierarchy of fears. This method, too, produces extinction, and as I will quote a lengthy example of its application presently, nothing more will be said about it now.

The third of the most widely used methods of behaviour

therapy is modelling. Here the patient is shown the therapist, or some other model, coping successfully with the situation or objects of which the patient is afraid. Thus if a child has a phobia for dogs, he may be shown a friend or relative approaching a dangerous-looking dog, stroking it and making friends with it. Gradually this produces extinction, and after a while the child is able to approach the dog himself, and overcome his phobia in this way.

Let us now consider a somewhat extended example of the application of behaviour therapy, and a comparison between it and psychoanalysis. From the large literature available we will have to choose one particular disorder, but it should not be assumed that because this disorder has been chosen as an example, it is the only one that can be treated with behaviour therapy. All the different disorders labelled as 'neurotic' can be, and have been, successfully treated by the methods of behaviour therapy. The reasons why obsessive-compulsive hand-washing has been selected as the example are as follows. In the first place, this particular disorder has a very clear-cut and measurable outcome, namely the length of time during the day that a person spends cleaning himself, avoiding contamination, and in other ways behaving in an irrational fashion as a result of the cleaning rituals he may have built up. Whether the removal of such rituals leaves behind any other, more complex, mental or physical symptoms we will have to decide presently.

The second reason for choosing this particular disorder is that it has been exceptionally resistant to spontaneous remission and equally resistant to all efforts to treat it by means of psychoanalysis, psychotherapy, electric shock, leucotomy, and many other methods that have been tried. For all practical purposes it may be said that nothing works, so that we start with a baseline of zero success. Dr D. Malan, one of the best-known British psychoanalysts, who is frequently cited in this field, admitted in a recent book (*Individual Psychotherapy and the Science of Psychodynamics*, 1979) that he had never seen a case of obsessive-compulsive hand-washing treated successfully by means of psychoanalysis, and that he thought behaviour therapy was the obvious method of treatment to use.

At first sight extensive hand-washing and other cleaning rituals may not seem a particularly serious form of disorder, but in actual fact they have a very destructive effect on a person's ability to cope with life, hold down a job, or bring up a family. A man suffering from this disorder is incapable of going out to work, because he spends so much time over his cleaning rituals, and has the greatest difficulties in leading any kind of family life, for the same reason. As a consequence of his rituals, and the enforced isolation from society, the patient often becomes anxious, depressed, and even suicidal. The disorder is then a very serious one, and one which has hitherto proved almost completely resistant to treatment, whether psychotherapeutic or physical.

There is one other reason why this disorder has been chosen here as an example of the application of behaviour-therapy principles. This reason is related to an objection often made to behaviour therapy, namely that it is based on conditioning principles derived mainly from animal experiments, and that human neuroses are much too complex to be encompassed by such a simple model. One reason for choosing obsessive-compulsive neurosis as an example, therefore, is that there is a good animal model from which the method of treatment is taken; this will illustrate that the objection is not realistic. We cannot decide *a priori* what level of complexity a treatment must reach in order to be successful; only empirical study can tell us this. If the treatment is clearly and unequivocally successful, then surely such theoretical objections must lose their potency.

The experimental paradigm from which the method of treatment is derived is as follows. A dog is put in a shuttle box, i.e. a room (or a large box) divided into two by a hurdle across the middle; each half of the room has a floor made up of metal bars which can be electrified to give a shock to the dog's feet. In addition the room contains a blinking light, the conditioned stimulus; the shock is the unconditioned stimulus. The experiment proceeds when the conditioned stimulus is lit up; ten seconds later the dog is given an electric shock, and he quickly jumps over the hurdle into the safe half of the room. The light goes off, and after a little while comes on again; ten seconds later the previously safe part of the room is electrified, and the dog again jumps over the hurdle, to the other part of the room. He soon learns to jump the moment the shock comes, and after a while jumps when the conditioned stimulus comes on, and before the shock is given. The dog is now conditioned, and the experimenter removes the electric connection so that the dog is never again subjected to an electric shock. Nevertheless, he will go on jumping to the conditioned stimulus a dozen times, a hundred times, even a thousand times; in other words, he has now acquired an obsessive-compulsive habit which is persistent and will not go away on its own. The similarity with the obsessive-compulsive hand-washing patient will be obvious. The patient washes his hands in order to relieve the anxiety relating to contamination; the dog jumps in order to relieve the anxiety relating to the possibility of receiving an electric shock. In actual fact contamination will not harm the patient, and the dog will not be given an electric shock; hence both habits are unrealistic and unadaptive. Nevertheless they are very strong, and difficult to eradicate. We have seen this already in connection with human patients; for dogs, too, it is difficult to eradicate this newly formed neurotic habit. One experiment, for instance, which has been tried, is to connect up the electricity again, and to electrify not the part of the room in which the dog happens to be, but the part into which he jumps for safety! This, however, does not work; it simply raises the dog's anxiety level, and makes him jump sooner, and more energetically.

How, then, can we cure the dog? The answer is by means of a method which behaviour therapists call 'flooding with response prevention'. This is what is done. The hurdle in the middle of the room is raised so high that the dog cannot jump over it. Then the conditioned stimulus is put on, and produces a considerable degree of anxiety in the dog. He yelps, runs round his part of the room, jumps up on the walls, urinates and defecates, showing signs of extreme fear. This is the 'flooding' part of the experiment; he is flooded with emotion resulting from the appearance of the conditioned stimulus. Under normal circumstances he could jump over the hurdle, or run away, or in some other way avoid the conditioned stimulus, but this has been made impossible through the method of response prevention, i.e. raising the hurdle so high that the dog cannot jump it.

This early demonstration of extreme fear soon gives way to less frightened behaviour; gradually the dog calms down, and after half an hour or so he seems quite relaxed; in other words, he has become desensitized to the situation, and a certain amount of extinction has taken place. Repeat the experiment a number of times, and the dog is completely cured. The hurdle may be lowered again, and, even though the conditioned stimulus is switched on, he will not bother to jump.

How can we adapt this method to the obsessive-compulsive hand-washing human patient? The answer is very simple. The therapist explains to the patient exactly what he is going to do, and the reasons for using this particular method of treatment. The patient then consents to undergo this treatment; he is, of course, given the right to choose any other form of treatment he may wish. He is then introduced into the treatment room, which is bare except for a table and two chairs, one for the therapist, one for the patient. On the table stands an urn filled with dirt, sand and other rubbish. The therapist digs his hands into this rubbish, and lifts bits of it out of the urn; he then asks the patient to do exactly the same. The patient complies, but immediately his anxiety rises to great heights, and he wants to go and wash his hands. The therapist tells him not to do this, but to remain seated, with his hands full of dirt. This produces the same kind of 'flooding' with emotion as the shuttle box experiment does for the dog, but equally, this fear gradually dies down, and after an hour or two the patient will sit on his chair, still looking somewhat unhappy, but nevertheless with his fear and anxiety greatly reduced. When he seems to show no more emotion at all, the experiment is terminated, and he is allowed to go and wash his hands. This procedure is repeated a number of times over a period of two or three months, with something like two repetitions each week, and according to the theory the patient ought to be cured at the end. Is this true?

S. Rachman and R. Hodgson, in their book *Obsessions and Compulsions*, give a detailed account of their experiments with this method of treatment, and the answer is that something like 85–90 per cent of all patients improve very much or are completely cured. Furthermore, follow-up discloses that they do not show any signs of relapse, and that there is no evidence of symptom substitution. Quite the opposite seems to be the case; their work life and their family life continue to improve after the treatment is over, and their general level of anxiety and depression is reduced. According to the accounts given by patients and their families, the treatment is eminently successful. This is not what Freud would have predicted, and in so far as it contradicts his confidently held assumptions about the consequences of 'purely symptomatic treatment', the experiment must be considered as providing strong evidence against psychoanalytic theories.

Obviously a single example is not sufficient to establish the superiority of behaviour therapy. Readers will find a lengthy discussion of the whole literature in a book by A. E. Kazdin and G. T. Wilson, *Evaluation of Behaviour Therapy: Issues, Evidence and Research Strategies*. By now the evidence is fairly conclusive that the methods of behaviour therapy are not only more successful than any other type of psychotherapy, but also that they work much more quickly; it is never a question of years, but of months, or even weeks, before success becomes apparent. The failure of relapses and symptom substitutions to occur after behaviour therapy, in spite of the clear-cut predictions made by Freud and the psychoanalysts, is one of the most telling arguments against psychoanalytic theory. We may consider it odd that those who cannot *even* cure symptoms accuse behaviour therapists of *only* curing symptoms!

The conditioning and extinction theory of neurosis enables us to explain many facts which would otherwise be very mysterious. It is apparently true that most types of psychotherapy (of which there are now hundreds) are reasonably successful, in the same way that using no treatment is successful, i.e. the patients get better. This happens regardless of the particular theory advocated by the founder of the type of therapy in question, and it occurs equally in cases of spontaneous remission. Perhaps what needs explanation more than anything else is the occurrence of spontaneous remission; once we can explain that, we should be able to explain the success of different methods of therapy along similar lines. Can this be done along the lines of the extinction theory?

Let us consider what really happens in cases of spontaneous remission. The patient takes his troubles to a priest, a teacher, a doctor, or friends and relatives; in any case, what he does is a relatively pale imitation of the process of desensitization already described. The person with whom he talks will usually be sympathetic, friendly and as helpful as possible; this lowers the general level of anxiety. The patient will thus be in a state of relaxation, and he will tend to discuss his troubles, starting with the ones which provoke least anxiety, and going on slowly to the more and more serious ones. Naturally the process is nothing like as successful as behaviour therapy, because it is not done systematically, but in as much as it resembles desensitization, it should be relatively successful. Along these lines, it seems, we can explain the relative success of 'spontaneous remission', which is thus seen not to be 'spontaneous' at all, but rather to be due to a process very much like that of behaviour therapy.

Exactly the same kind of thing happens when the patient visits a psychotherapist, of whatever persuasion; here too we have a friendly and sympathetic listener, helpful and congenial, and again we have the patient telling his story, complaining about his difficulties, and generally discussing his anxieties. Again, the process should be less successful than desensitization because it is not properly programmed, but it should be as successful as the spontaneous remission procedures. If we remember that Smith, Glass and Miller showed that the length of training of the therapist made no difference at all, we can readily extrapolate this finding to include among the therapists the priests, teachers, doctors, friends and relatives of the patient, who would not have had any systematic training, but whose very presence and willingness to listen should conduce to the process of desensitization. The training which psychotherapists of various persuasions have had will accord with the particular theory they follow, and this, as we have seen, is irrelevant to the success of the treatment. We would thus claim that the theory of extinction explains all the phenomena encountered, which is not the case with any alternative theory.

A question often raised is how is it possible that so many patients and so many therapists are convinced of the value of psychoanalysis as a curative technique, when objectively there is little evidence to support this? The answer probably lies in a well-known experiment, first carried out by B. F. Skinner, on the origins of superstition. He assembled a group of pigeons in a large cage, and left them there overnight. At irregular intervals an automatic mechanism threw some grains of corn into the arena. In the morning Skinner noticed that several of the pigeons were behaving in a very abnormal manner. One was walking about with its head high up in the air, another was circling round with one wing to the ground, and a third was constantly lifting its tail. What had happened? The answer, in terms of conditioning, is this. The pigeons were moving about in various ways when the corn was suddenly thrown into the arena; they immediately gobbled it up. According to conditioning theory, the corn should act as a reinforcement for whatever the pigeon was doing at the moment that the corn was thrown into the arena. In this instance, one pigeon had its head high up in the air, another had its wing down on the ground, and a third was lifting its tail. The pigeons probably repeated these modes of behaviour time and time again, and the next time corn was thrown into the arena these particular habits were again reinforced. When, on repeating the movements, the pigeons found that corn was thrown again, they became convinced that this was *because* of their movements. Thus a particular superstition grew up in these pigeons, and Skinner argues that the belief of patients and therapists alike about the efficacy of psychotherapy rests on a similar basis. Because patients get better anyway, as shown by the prevalence of spontaneous remission, they attribute this improvement to the treatment, as does the therapist, although there is no real connection between the two. When this state of satisfaction has been reached, the patient is dismissed as 'cured'; the fact that he often gets worse again afterwards does not concern the therapist any more, and does not disturb his convictions. Such superstitious beliefs are difficult to get rid of; their unfounded persistence and their imperviousness to reasoning or experiment indicate their irrational origin. It is one of the amusing paradoxes of psychology that psychoanalysts, who claimed to introduce scientific and rational ideas into the irrational and emotional field of mental disorder, should be subject to this conditioned superstition. That they should have been able to convince normal people of the truth of their theories and the efficacy of their methods of treatment is one of the miracles of the age.

CHAPTER FOUR

Freud and the Development of the Child

They reason theoretically, without demonstration experimentally,
and errors are the result.

MICHAEL FARADAY

Having dealt with the effectiveness of Freudian therapy, we
must now turn to his theories concerning the origins of neurotic
symptoms. According to Freud, 'only sexual wishful impulses
from infancy are able to furnish the motive force for the
formation of psychoneurotic symptoms'. Accordingly it is necessary to look in this chapter at Freud's theory of the development
of the child; this will also give us an opportunity to look at the
degree to which Freudian theories can be said to possess a
genuinely empirical character, and also to examine Karl Popper's
view that psychoanalysis is a pseudo-science because it does
not make falsifiable predictions. Last but not least, we will have
an opportunity to look at the case history of 'little Hans', which
is generally regarded as the beginning of child psychoanalysis,
and is rated as one of Freud's greatest successes. We will try to
see to what extent such an assessment is true, and whether
alternative theories might not be better able to explain the facts
of little Hans's neurotic symptoms.

It is interesting to begin by considering Popper's dictum
concerning the lack of falsifiability of Freudian doctrines. At
first sight it would appear that Popper must be wrong. There are
certainly deductions that can be made from Freud's theory, and
these can be empirically falsified. One such example is his
prediction that 'symptom-oriented' treatment should always be
followed either by a return of the symptom or by symptom

substitution. As we have seen, this is not so, and therefore constitutes a refutation of a fundamental aspect of Freudian theory. But to look only at falsifiability is to misunderstand Popper. Popper also characterizes as pseudo-scientific 'some genuinely testable theories [which] when found to be false are still upheld by their admirers'. What is characteristic of the Freudian opus is something altogether more original, more dangerous, and more difficult to refute than simple unfalsifiability. Frank Cioffi, in his essay on 'Freud and the Idea of Pseudo-Science', has made the point very well. He mentions that there is a host of peculiarities of psychoanalytic theory and practice which are apparently gratuitous and unrelated; he suggests that these can be understood as manifestations of one single impulse, namely the need to avoid refutation. He lists a number of these peculiarities concerning the apparent diversity of the ways in which the correctness of psychoanalytic claims may be assessed – observation of the behaviour of children, enquiry into the distinctive features of the current sexual or infantile sexual history of neurotics, awaiting the outcome of prophylactic measures based on Freud's aetiological claims – and points out that they all resolve themselves into one which itself ultimately proves illusory, namely *interpretation*. This process of interpretation has been formulated by Freud himself in a variety of ways, such as 'translating unconscious processes into conscious ones', 'filling in the gaps of conscious perception', 'constructing a series of conscious events complementary to the unconscious mental ones', and '[inferring] the unconscious fantasies from the symptoms and then [enabling] the patient to become conscious of them'.

As Cioffi points out, 'it is characteristic of a pseudo-science that the hypotheses which comprise it stand in asymmetrical relation to the expectations they generate, being permitted to guide them and be vindicated by their fulfilment but not to be discredited by their disappointment'. In other words, a pseudo-science tries to have its cake and eat it too; when observations and experiments are favourable, they are accepted as proof, but when they are unfavourable and seem to disprove the hypotheses in question, then they are rejected as being irrelevant. Cioffi uses Freud's theory of childhood development in order to illustrate Freud's overwhelming desire to avoid refutation. The ground is well chosen, and, as we shall see, there is much to support Cioffi's views.

It is interesting to note that according to Popper another famous pseudo-scientist, namely Karl Marx, also relied extensively on interpretation, rather than on direct verification through observable facts. In his case the hypothesis was that the proletariat was in the forefront of historical progress, but its wishes and plans had to be 'correctly' interpreted in order to be acceptable from the Marxist point of view; and who was better fitted to make these interpretations than the Marxist vanguard, as constituted in the Communist Party? The fact that these interpretations bore very little relation to the expressed wishes and views of the proletariat does not seem to have concerned Marx or his successors at all, just as Freud was not upset by the fact that his interpretations were often found unacceptable by his patients, and improbable by his critics. There is no ultimate criterion against which to check the truth-values of the interpretations if one relies on these rather than observable fact.

Freud's theory of childhood development is, of course, quite well known, but its details may be recounted in brief. The young boy has an innate desire to have sexual intercourse with his mother but feels threatened in the execution of these desires by the father, who seems to have prior rights to the mother. The child develops castration anxieties upon noticing that his sister is not possessed of a penis, the wonderful plaything which means so much to him, and his increased fear makes him give up and 'repress' all these unseemly desires, which live on as the famous Oedipus complex in the unconscious, promoting all sorts of terrible neurotic symptoms in later life. This Oedipus complex assumes the central role in Freudian speculations, and we shall see later whether there is any empirical and observational evidence to support it. There are other nuances in the Freudian account but enough has probably been said to give the reader an idea of the kind of theory Freud was developing.

These accounts are pretty startling and they certainly startled Freud's early readers. They are important because of their explanatory value as far as the origins of neurosis are concerned, and the evidence they afford of the validity of psychoanalytic methods. Freud obviously believed that these reconstructions were characteristic of childhood in general, and could thus be confirmed by the contemporary observation of children. As he himself said: 'I can point with satisfaction to the fact that direct observation has fully confirmed the conclusions drawn from psychoanalysis, and thus furnish good evidence for the reliability of the latter method of investigation.' He maintained on many occasions that his clinically derived theses regarding the infant's sexual life could be tested by the systematic observation of children's behaviour. Thus in the case history of little Hans, to which we will return presently, he refers to the observation of children as 'a more direct and less roundabout proof of these fundamental theories'. He also refers to the possibility of 'observing upon the child at first hand, in all the freshness of life, the sexual impulses and conative tendencies which we dig out so laboriously in the adult from among their own debris'. Elsewhere he maintains that 'one can easily observe' that little girls regard their clitoris as an inferior penis, and of the Oedipal phase he writes: 'At that period of life these impulses still continue uninhibited as straightforward sexual desires. This can be confirmed so easily that only the greatest efforts could make it possible to overlook it.'

The most clear-cut avowal that straightforward observation of ordinary children can give support to psychoanalytic theories comes in this statement by Freud:

In the beginning my formulations regarding infantile sexuality were founded almost exclusively upon the results of analysis in adults . . . it was, therefore, a very great triumph, when it became possible years later to confirm almost all my inferences by direct observation and analysis of children, a triumph that lost some of its magnitude as one gradually realised that the nature of the discovery was such that one should really be ashamed of failing to make it. The further one carried these observations on children, the more self-evident the facts became, and the more astonishing was it too that so much trouble was taken to overlook them.

In other words, straightforward observation is enough to verify Freudian theories, and one has actively to take trouble to look away in order to fail to note these facts.

What actually happens when a well-trained psychological observer, specially on the look-out for evidence in support of Freudian theories, studies the behaviour and 'all aspects of mental development in childhood up to the age of about 4 or 5', of his own five children? Professor C. W. Valentine, a well-known British psychologist and educationalist, published his observations in his book *The Psychology of Early Childhood*, in 1942. In addition to reports on his own children, he takes into account observations which a number of former students and colleagues made of their own children, in reference to special problems. He discusses all this evidence in relation to other published diary records made on the first three or four years of life by reliable observers; as he points out, some dozen or more of these valuable records were available to him. It cannot be said that Valentine started out as a critic of psychoanalysis, and hostile to Freud. On the contrary, as he reveals here, Valentine was initially sympathetic to Freud's speculations:

I may say that I was greatly attracted by the first of his [Freud's] writings to appear in English. I resented the prejudice that revolted against him merely because he wrote so frankly on matters of sex; and finally I published a brief book to expound some of his main ideas, and to link them with general psychology. I hope, then, I can be acquitted from prejudice against his views.

Let us now turn to what Valentine has to say about the relevance of his observations to Freudian theories. First he deals with Freud's views on the relations between infants of the same family, in particular the hypothesized rivalry between them. 'The foregoing observations of my own and of others are decidedly opposed to the views expressed by Freud as to the attitude of very little children towards younger brothers and sisters.' Freud had written: 'It is unquestionable that the little child sees and hates his rivals . . . Of course it often gives place to a more tender feeling or perhaps we should say it is overlaid by that, but the hostile seems very generally to be the earlier . . . we can most easily observe it in children of two and a half to four years old when a new baby arrives.' Valentine points out that his own observations show 'on the contrary in these children, the appearance *first* of an innate tenderness towards the little brother, considerably before anything in the nature of jealousy occurs: and the records given are typical of the reactions of all our children towards their little brothers and sisters. Indeed, rarely have I known greater delight experienced by any of them than the older ones experienced on hearing that they were to have another brother or sister . . . Further evidence . . . from other reliable reports suggests that by the majority of young children no jealousy at all is shown, though after the earliest years some may manage to conceal it.'

More decisive in regard to central theses of Freudian speculation are Valentine's observations on the 'supposed Oedipus complex'. As he points out:

Freud had asserted that after the age of about 2:0 boys begin to be passionately devoted to their mother and to be jealous and even to hate their father; thus revealing an 'Oedipus complex'. Girls, on the other hand, develop a new devotion to the father and regard the mother as a rival . . . I can find no evidence whatever in the observations on my own children for such an Oedipus complex. Indeed, it will be seen that most of the evidence is directly contrary to it, especially the fact that the girls preferred their mother more than the boys did after the age of about 2:0 when, according to Freud, the boys should begin to turn against the father and the girls should favour him. The relations of the children to parents are exactly as might be expected on general grounds. First, strong attachment shown by boys and girls for the mother – the nurse and comforter. Later, some attraction after the second year towards the father who can enter their play and, if the more severe at times, can provide the most exciting delights. But this increased attraction of the father after 2 or 3 showed much more in the boys than in the girls; the tastes and interests of the girls being even at this early age more in line with the mother's than with the father's.

Discussing the alleged sexual impulses of young children, Valentine states:

The fact that a number of neurotics (or of persons who, attracted by Freudian views or interested in their own abnormalities, undergo psychoanalysis) recall sex impulses in early childhood, is no proof that they are at all general: apart from the fact discovered later by Freud himself that in many or most of such cases the 'memory' is 'illusion' and the idea is really a 'retrogressive fantasy' . . . The evidence from direct observation of the existence, among normal children, of sex impulses directed towards a parent is of the flimsiest.

Valentine quotes many other direct observations by well-known psychologists, and describes the results of a questionnaire he issued to sixteen psychologists and scientists:

Summing up the results of this questionnaire we find that from every point of view – the preferences for M or F at different ages, by boys or girls, the reasons for changes in preferences, the influence of discipline, the occasions of jealousy – all these give ample reasonable explanations of the facts and supply no evidence for the supposed Oedipus complex.

Valentine finally concludes as follows:

As to the power of sex, experiences during adolescence and succeeding periods are surely sufficiently convincing; whether the ideas of infantile sexuality reported by patients are indeed (*a*) suggested by psychoanalysts – as Freud at one time suspected – or (*b*) are entirely or partly the patient's own interpretations of and exaggerations of relatively slight sensations and impulses, or (*c*) whether they are largely true but only in a few abnormal cases, this is not the place to discuss. But the fact that the reports of patients, which Freud himself took at first to be facts, proved to be mere fantasies is very significant.

His final general comment 'refers to the suggestion made by psychoanalysts that those who do not believe in the Oedipus complex and the supreme importance of sex in infancy are deliberately refusing to accept the truth', and he quotes Freud and Glover in this respect. Valentine then goes on to say:

The reply that I want to make at the moment to this accusation of prejudice and refusal to accept an unpalatable truth, is that the medical psychologist who believes in the influence of the unconscious should surely be chary of using such an argument against others. It might be replied, as indeed it has been, that once having surmised the truth of the Oedipus complex, Freud and his followers had to continue to assert that in the face of strongly conflicting evidence because of an unconscious desire to retain their own prestige. It might even be suggested that medical psychoanalysts who secure fee-paying patients for a hundred or two hundred visits not unnaturally wish to retain their own belief and the belief of others in the truth of their views and the value of their therapeutic measures. I am not suggesting that this is the cause of their beliefs. I do not myself believe that it is, at least usually or mainly. I wish to point out that for the believers in the Oedipus complex to accuse critics of blind prejudice and unconscious or unworthy motives is an example of people who live in very thin glasshouses providing their opponents with very large stones. They have also supplied a technical term for it – 'projection'. As Freud himself said: 'The polemical run of analysis obviously leads to no decision.' It is a pity that Freud and his followers have not accepted this sage remark.

Valentine's book was published originally in 1942; since then many other accounts have appeared which heavily support his conclusions. My own observations, less systematic than his but nevertheless sharpened by a desire to find out for myself how true Freud's assertion was that his hypotheses could be tested by straightforward observation of very young children, have also failed to find any evidence for either the Oedipus complex or early sexual desires in my own five children. I think we may take it that Freud was wrong when he asserted that these facts 'can be confirmed so easily that only the greatest efforts could make it possible to overlook it'. It is difficult to find evidence to support this view, even in people who, like Valentine, were from the beginning favourably disposed towards Freudian theories. How does Freud react to such a refutation of his most cherished beliefs? As Cioffi points out: 'On occasions when Freud is under the necessity of forestalling disconfirmatory reports he forgets the so-easily-confirmable character of his reconstructions of infantile life and insists on the esoteric only-observable-by-initiates status.' Thus Freud states: 'None, however, but physicians who practise psychoanalysis can have any access whatever to this fear of knowledge or any possibility of forming a judgement that is uninfluenced by their own dislikes and prejudices. If mankind had been able to learn from direct observation of children these three essays [*Three Essays on Sexuality*] could have remained unwritten.' As Cioffi replies, very reasonably: 'This retreat to the esoterically observable in the fact of disconfirmatory evidence is a general feature of psychoanalytic apologetics.' Indeed, Freud's apparent approval of direct investigation, along factual lines, of the behaviours he postulates is often curiously ambiguous. If the clinical reconstructions of early life experiences are genuine, and if the children had been threatened with castration, been seduced, or seen their parents engaged in intercourse, the accuracy of these recollections could surely be tested directly by suitable investigations. Freud does not agree. 'It may be tempting to take the easy course of filling up the gaps in a patient's memory by making enquiries from the older members of the family: but I cannot advise too strongly against such a technique. One invariably regrets having made oneself dependent upon such information. At the same time confidence in the analysis is shaken and a court of appeal is set up over it. Whatever can be remembered at all will anyhow come to light in the course of further analysis.' In other words, interpretation of doubtful symbolic meanings of dreams and everyday life behaviours is preferred as evidence to direct observational reports by actual witnesses, because these would constitute a 'court of appeal' which Freud is eager to avoid. There must be no external source of evidence against which his interpretations can be tested.

Even more curious is another statement by Freud where he suggests that the analysis of dreams is equivalent to remembering. 'It seems to me absolutely equivalent to recollection if the memories are replaced . . . by dreams, the analysis of which invariably leads back to the same scene, and which reproduce every portion of its content in an indefatigable variety of new shapes . . . dreaming is another kind of remembering.' This is a truly astonishing statement. The fanciful and quite subjective interpretation of the complex symbolism of a dream is surely very different from a firm recollection on the part of the patient; what we are looking for is some way of testing the veracity of the interpretation. Freud assumes that the interpretation of the dream is correct, but that, of course, is precisely the point to be proved. We will return to this question again in the chapter on the interpretation of dreams.

Freud makes one other intriguing point in his attempt to convince us of the authenticity of his reconstructions of infantile sexuality. He asserts that the truth of his theories is demonstrated by the fact that they lead to successful cures, thus immediately contradicting those of his followers who now wish to deny the argument that if the cure does not work, the theory is very likely to be wrong. What Freud says is this: 'Starting out from the mechanism of cure, it now becomes possible to construct quite definite ideas of the origin of the illness.' And elsewhere he writes that 'it is only experiences in childhood that explain susceptibility to later traumas' since 'it is only by uncovering these almost invariably forgotten memory traces and making them conscious that we acquire the power to get rid of the symptoms'. But, as we have seen in the preceding chapters, there is no evidence that psychoanalysis in fact gives us 'the power to get rid of the symptoms'; so if we take Freud's argument seriously, namely that the fact of a cure guarantees the correctness of his theories and reconstructions, then surely we must now argue that the fact that a cure does not take place invalidates his theories and reconstructions!

As many critics have pointed out, Freud's infantile theory of neurotic disorder is curiously ambivalent, expressing two contradictory points of view. On the one hand he appears to commit himself to a distinctive infantile sexual history for neurotics, which makes him vulnerable to refutation, while on the other he insists on the universality of the pathogenic features involved. Thus he says that 'at the root of the formation of every symptom are to be found traumatic experiences from early sexual life'. This seems to be clear enough: it declares that there is a causal relationship between the early traumatic experiences and the later development of neurotic symptoms. But Freud also says that 'investigation into the mental life of normal persons . . . yielded the unexpected discovery that their infantile history in regard to sexual matters was not necessarily different in essentials from that of the neurotic'. Surely, if this is so, the occurrence of traumas in the childhood of neurotics cannot give us grounds for belief in their causal relevance? There must be something in the child's reaction to these 'traumas' which distinguishes neurotic childhoods from normal, and Freud indeed states that 'the important thing . . . was how he had reacted to these experiences, whether he had responded to them with repression or not'. Is it then repression which differentiates between neurotic and non-neurotic childhood? The answer again must be no, for not only is 'no human being spared such traumatic experiences', but 'none escape the repression to which they give rise'. And, in another place, Freud says: 'Every individual has gone through this phase but has energetically repressed it and succeeded in forgetting it.' In fact, Freud never comes down to any definitive statement about what exactly distinguishes the early childhood of the neurotic from that of the normal adult.

Cioffi puts the matter very well when he says:

The explanation of these equivocations, evasions and inconsistencies is that Freud is simultaneously under the sway of two necessities: to seem to say and yet to refrain from saying which infantile events occasion the predisposition to neurosis. To seem to say, because his discovery of the pathogenic role of sexuality in the infantile life of neurotics is the ostensible grounds for his conviction that the neuroses are manifestations of the revival of infantile sexual struggles and thus for the validity of the method by which this aetiology was inferred; to refrain from saying, because if his aetiological claims were made too explicit and therefore ran the risk of refutation this might discredit not only his explanations of the neuroses but, more disastrously, the method by which they were arrived at. Only by making these prophylactic and pathogenic claims can his preoccupations and procedures be justified, but only by withdrawing them can they be safeguarded.

It will be seen that while Freud relies entirely on interpretations of dreams, errors of speech and action, and other nebulous data, these do not provide irrefutable evidence; their validity depends upon the assumption that the theory on which they are based has been proved beyond question. But clearly such independent proof is not forthcoming, and we may with advantage quote the well-known modern psychoanalyst, Judd Marmor:

Depending upon the point of view of the analyst, the patients of each school seem to bring up precisely the kinds of phenomenological data which confirm the theories and interpretations of their analyst! Thus each theory tends to be self-validating. Freudians elicit material about the Oedipus complex and castration anxiety, Jungians about archetypes, Rankians about separation anxiety, Adlerians about masculine strivings and feelings of inferiority, Horneyites about idealized images, Sullivanians about disturbed interpersonal relationships, etc. The fact is that in so complex a transaction as the psychoanalytic therapeutic process, the impact of patient and therapist upon each other, and particularly of the latter upon the former, is an unusually profound one. What the analyst shows interest in, the kinds of questions he asks, the kind of data he chooses to react to or ignore, and the interpretations he makes, all exert a subtle but significant suggestive impact upon the patient to bring forth certain kinds of data in preference to others.

When leading psychoanalysts themselves admit such fundamental faults in interpretation, does the critic really have to substantiate the point that other types of evidence are required if we are to believe in Freud's speculative theories, and conclude that it would be far better to rely on direct observational evidence, such as that provided by Valentine and many others, rather than to reject it in favour of the perennial uncertainties of interpretative manipulation? To quote Cioffi again:

Examination of Freud's interpretations will show that he typically proceeds by beginning with whatever content his theoretical preconceptions compel him to maintain underlies the symptoms, and then, by working back and forth between it and the explanandum, constructing persuasive but spurious links between them. It is this which enables him to find allusions to the father's coital breathing in attacks of dyspnoea, fellatio in a *tussis nervosa*, defloration in migraine, orgasm in an hysterical loss of consciousness, birth pangs in appendicitis, pregnancy wishes in hysterical vomiting, pregnancy fears in anorexia, an accouchement in a suicide leap, castration fears in an obsessive preoccupation with hat tipping, masturbation in the practice of squeezing blackheads, the anal theory of birth in an hysterical constipation, parturition in a falling cart-horse, nocturnal emissions in bed-wetting, unwed motherhood in a limp, guilt over the practice of seducing pubescent girls in the compulsion to sterilize banknotes before passing them on, etc.

A science cannot be based on subjective interpretations, and the Freudian account of childhood development, with its suggested basis for the development of neurotic symptoms, is quite unacceptable, and can be contradicted by solid facts. This conclusion will be strengthened by an examination of the case of little Hans, the corner-stone of Freudian theorizing, and the analysis which gave rise to childhood psychoanalysis.

Before turning to little Hans and his neurotic illness, it may be interesting to contrast Freud's accounts of two four-year-old children – little Hans, who was almost five, and little Herbert, some months younger. Herbert is described as a specimen of enlightened child-rearing, 'a splendid boy . . . whose intelligent parents abstained from forcibly suppressing one side of the child's development'. Apparently little Herbert shows 'the liveliest interest in that part of his body which he calls his wee-wee maker' because 'since he has never been frightened or oppressed with a sense of guilt he gives expression quite ingenuously to what he thinks'. Thus, according to Freud, little Herbert, brought up by psychoanalytically oriented parents, is likely to become one of the non-neurotic personalities of our time.

Contrast this with the unfortunate Hans who according to Freud was a 'paragon of all the vices'. Before he was four years old, his mother had threatened him with castration, and the birth of a younger sister had confronted him with the great riddle of where babies come from, as 'his father had told him the lie about the stork' which made it 'impossible for him to ask for enlightenment upon such things'. Thus, partly because of 'the perplexity in which his infantile sexual theories left him', he succumbed to an animal phobia shortly before his fifth birthday. Clearly, according to Freud's theory, little Hans was predestined by his upbringing to fall prey to neurotic disorders in the course of his life.

But wait! Jones, in his famous biography of Freud, tells us that Hans and Herbert are the same child, the account of Herbert being written *before* and that of Hans *after* the child had succumbed to his animal phobia (but not before the events which Freud was later to consider pathogenic). Indeed, Freud even suggested (as an afterthought) that Hans/Herbert suffered more strongly in the development of his phobia *because* of his 'enlightened' upbringing. 'Since he was brought up without being intimidated and with as much consideration and as little coercion as possible his anxiety dared to show itself more boldly. With him there was no place for such motives as a bad conscience or fear of punishment which with other children must no doubt contribute to making the anxiety less.' This ambiguity in Freud's argument makes testing his hypotheses completely impossible.

In turning to the case of little Hans, we are fortunate in having available the critical review and alternative interpretation by

Professors J. Wolpe and S. Rachman; I have followed their enlightening discussion in some detail because it illustrates beautifully the illogical elements in Freud's theorizing, and the importance and rationality of the alternative hypothesis they propose. Briefly, then, little Hans was the son of a psycho-analytically inclined father who was in close contact with Freud. In early January, 1908, the father wrote to Freud that Hans, then five years old, had developed 'a nervous disorder'. The symptoms he reported were fear of going out of doors, depression in the evening, and fear that a horse would bite him in the street. Hans's father suggested that 'the ground was prepared by sexual over-excitation due to his mother's tenderness' and that the fear of the horse 'seems somehow to be connected with his having been frightened by a large penis'. The first signs appeared on 7 January when Hans was being taken to the park, as usual, by his nursemaid. He started crying and said he wanted to 'coax' (caress) with his mother. At home, asked why he had refused to go any further, he 'had cried, but he would not say'. The following day, after hesitations and crying, he went out with his mother. Returning home Hans said, after much internal struggling, *'I was afraid a horse would bite me'* (original italics). As on the previous day, Hans showed fear in the evening and asked to be 'coaxed'. He is also reported as saying, 'I know I shall have to go for a walk again tomorrow,' and 'The horse'll come into the room.' On the same day he was asked by his mother if he put his hand to his widdler – the name he applied to his penis. He replied yes, and the following day his mother warned him to refrain from doing this.

Readers may be surprised at this point to find out that Freud's subsequent analysis was not based on any material he himself discovered; the material was collected by little Hans's father, who kept in touch with Freud by regularly writing reports. The father had several discussions with Freud concerning little Hans's phobia, but during the analysis Freud himself saw the little boy only once! This is a curious way of carrying out treatment, and of laying the foundations for child analysis, yet few analysts seem to have found the procedure peculiar.

At this point Freud provided an interpretation of Hans's behaviour and consequently arranged with the boy's father that he should tell him that his fear of horses was nonsense, and that the truth was that he was very fond of his mother and wanted to be taken into her bed. The reason he was afraid of horses now was that 'he had taken so much interest in their widdlers'. Freud also suggested giving Hans some sexual enlightenment and telling him that females 'had no widdler at all'.

After this, there were some ups and downs, but on the whole the phobia got worse, and the child's condition deteriorated after he had his tonsils taken out.

When he had recovered from the physical illness, Hans had many talks with his father about the phobia. The father suggested that there was a relationship between the phobia and little Hans's masturbatory habits, emphasizing the point that girls and women have no widdlers and generally trying to indoctrinate little Hans with psychosexual theories about the origins of his neurosis. It would take too long to go into all the details, but on 30 March the boy had a short consultation with Freud who found that Hans was still suffering from a fear of horses, despite all the enlightenment he had been given. Hans explained that he was specially bothered 'by what horses wear in front of their eyes and the black round their mouths'. Freud interpreted the latter as meaning a moustache. 'I asked him whether he meant a moustache,' he wrote; he then told Hans that he was 'afraid of his father' precisely because he was 'so fond of his mother'. He pointed out to Hans that his fear of his father was groundless.

A little later, Hans told his father that he was most scared of horses with 'a thing on their mouths', that he was afraid that the horses might fall, and that he was most frightened of horse-drawn buses. In answer to a question by his father, Hans then recounted an incident he had seen. The details were later confirmed by his mother. According to the father, the anxiety broke out immediately after little Hans had witnessed an accident involving a horse-drawn bus, in which one of the horses fell down. Apparently the 'black things round their mouths' referred to the fact that the horses were wearing muzzles.

All this time the father was trying to force psychoanalytic ideas on the little boy, making suggestions that little Hans usually rejected, although he did occasionally agree under duress.

Little Hans eventually recovered, as indeed one would have expected from the relatively mild degree of phobic fear he experienced. There is no evidence that psychoanalytic interpretations he received helped in any way, and indeed there is no relationship between the times when he improved and the times when he appeared to gain 'insight' into his condition.

What can we say on this case (which should be read in full, together with the Wolpe and Rachman critique, by anyone interested in the way that Freud conducted his enquiries)?

In the first place, the material has clearly been selected; the greatest attention is paid to items which can be related to psychoanalytic theory, while there is a tendency to ignore other facts. Freud himself pointed out that the father and mother were both 'among my closest adherents', and clearly Hans was constantly encouraged, directly and indirectly, to relate material of relevance to the psychoanalytic doctrine.

Secondly, it is clear that the father's account is highly unreliable, because his interpretations of what the child says are clearly not justified by the facts of the situation, or the words used by little Hans. There are many distortions in the father's reports, and they must be read with great care.

Similarly, Hans's testimony itself is unreliable. He told numerous lies in the last few weeks of his phobia, and gave many inconsistent and occasionally conflicting reports. Most important of all, however, is that many of the views and feelings attributed to Hans in fact belong to his father, who puts words into his mouth. Freud himself admits this, but attempts to gloss it over. He says:

It is true that during the analysis Hans had to be told many things which he could not say himself, that he had to be presented with thoughts which he had so far shown no signs of possessing, and that his attention had to be turned in the direction from which his father was expecting something to come. This detracts from the evidential value of the analysis, but the procedure is the same in every case, for the psychoanalysis is not an impartial scientific investigation, but a therapeutic measure.

Thus Freud would seem to agree with his many critics who say that 'psychoanalysis is not an impartial scientific investigation', and that suggestion enters into it to a large extent, possibly reducing its evidential value to nil.

Freud's interpretation of Hans's phobia is that the boy's Oedipal conflicts form the basis of the illness. He says:

> These were tendencies in Hans which had already been suppressed and for which, so far as we can tell, he had never been able to find uninhibited expression: hostile and jealous feelings against his father, and sadistic impulses (premonitions, as it were, of copulation) towards his mother. These early suppressions may perhaps have gone to form the predisposition for his subsequent illness. These aggressive propensities of Hans's found no outlet, and as soon as there came a time of privation and of intensified sexual excitement, they tried to break their way out with reinforced strength. It was then that the battle that we called his 'phobia' burst out.

This, of course, is the familiar Oedipus theory, according to which Hans wished to replace his father, whom he could not help hating as a rival, and then complete the sexual act by taking possession of his mother. As confirmation, Freud refers to 'another symptomatic act happening as if by accident' which involved 'the confession that he had wished his father dead'. 'Just at the moment that his father was talking of his death wish, Hans let a [toy] horse that he was playing with fall down – knocked it over in fact.' Freud thus claims: 'Hans was really a little Oedipus who wanted to have his father "out of the way", to get rid of him, so that he might be alone with his handsome mother and sleep with her.' The predisposition to illness provided by the Oedipal conflict is supposed to have formed the basis for 'the transformation of his libidinal longing into anxiety'.

What is the link between all this and the horses? At his sole interview with Hans, Freud told the child that he was afraid of his father because he himself felt jealousy and hostile wishes against him. Freud says: 'In telling him this I have partly interpreted his fear of horses falling; the horse must be his father – whom he had good, internal reasons for fearing.' Freud claimed that Hans's fear of the horses' muzzles, and of their blinkers, was based on moustaches and eyeglasses, and had been 'directly transposed from his father onto the horses'. The horses 'had been shown to represent his father'. Freud interpreted the agoraphobic element of Hans's phobia thus:

> The content of his phobia was such as to impose a very great measure of restriction upon his freedom of movement, and that was its purpose . . . after all, Hans's phobia of horses was an obstacle to his going into the street, and could serve as a means of allowing him to stay at home with his beloved mother. In this way therefore his affection for his mother triumphantly achieved its aim.

In their critique of the case, Wolpe and Rachman state categorically:

> It is our contention that Freud's view of this case is not supported by the data, either in its particulars or as a whole. The major points that he regards as demonstrated are these:
> (1) Hans had a sexual desire for his mother;
> (2) he hated and feared his father and wished to kill him;
> (3) his sexual excitement and desire for his mother were transformed into anxiety;
> (4) his fear of horses was symbolic of his fear of his father;
> (5) the purpose of the illness was to keep near his mother;
> (6) and finally, his phobia disappeared because he resolved his Oedipus complex.
> Let us examine each of these points.
> (1) That Hans derived satisfaction from his mother and enjoyed her presence we will not even attempt to dispute. But nowhere is there any evidence of his wish to copulate with her. The 'instinctive premonitions' are referred to as though a matter of fact, though no evidence of their existence is given . . .
> (2) Never having expressed fear or hatred of his father, Hans was told by Freud that he possessed these emotions. On subsequent occasions Hans denied the existence of these feelings when questioned by his father. Eventually he said 'yes' to a statement of this kind by his father. This simple affirmative obtained after considerable pressure on the part of the father and Freud is accepted as a true state of affairs and all Hans's denials are ignored. The 'symptomatic act' of knocking over the toy horse is taken as further evidence of Hans's aggression towards his father. There are three assumptions underlying this 'interpreted fact' – first, that the horse represents Hans's father, second, that the knocking over of the horse is not accidental, and

third, that this act indicates the wish for the removal of whatever the horse symbolized.

Hans consistently denied the relationship between the horse and his father. He was, he said, afraid of horses. The mysterious black around the horses' mouths and the things on their eyes were later discovered by the father to be the horses' muzzles and blinkers. This discovery undermines the suggestion, made by Freud, that they were transposed moustaches and eyeglasses. There is no other evidence that the horses represented Hans's father. The assumption that the knocking over of the toy horse was meaningful and that it was prompted by an unconscious motive is, like most similar examples, a moot point.

As there is nothing to sustain the first two assumptions made by Freud in interpreting this 'symptomatic act', the third assumption (that this act indicated a wish for his father's death) is untenable; and it must be reiterated that there is no independent evidence that the boy feared or hated his father.

(3) Freud's third claim is that Hans's sexual excitement and desire for his mother were transformed into anxiety. This claim is based on the assertion that 'theoretical considerations require that what is today the object of a phobia must at one time in the past have been the source of a high degree of pleasure'. Certainly such a transformation is not displayed by the facts presented. As stated above, there is no evidence that Hans sexually desired his mother. There is also no evidence of any change in his attitude to her before the onset of the phobia. Even though there is some evidence that horses were to some extent previously a source of pleasure, in general the view that phobic objects must have been the source of former pleasures is amply contradicted by experimental evidence.

(4) The assertion that Hans's horse-phobia symbolized a fear of his father has already been criticized. The assumed relationship between the father and the horse is unsupported and appears to have arisen as a result of the father's strange failure to believe that by the 'black around their mouths' Hans meant the horses' muzzles.

(5) The fifth claim is that the purpose of Hans's phobia was to keep him near his mother. Aside from the questionable view that neurotic disturbances occur for a purpose, this interpretation fails to account for the fact that Hans experienced anxiety even when he was out walking *with his mother*.

(6) Finally, we are told that the phobia disappeared as a result of Hans's resolution of his Oedipal conflicts. As we have attempted to show, there is no adequate evidence that Hans had an Oedipus complex. In addition, the claim that this assumed complex was resolved

was based on a single conversation between Hans and his father. This conversation is a blatant example of what Freud himself refers to as Hans having to 'be told many things which he could not say himself, that he had to be presented with thoughts which he had so far *shown* no sign of possessing, and that his attention had to be turned in the direction from which his father was expecting something to come'.

There is also no satisfactory evidence that the 'insights' that were incessantly brought to the boy's attention had any therapeutic value. Reference to the facts of the case shows only occasional coincidences between interpretations and changes in the child's phobic reactions . . . In fact, Freud bases his conclusions entirely on deductions from his theory. Hans's later improvement appears to have been smooth and gradual and unaffected by the interpretations. In general, Freud infers relationships in a scientifically inadmissible manner: if the enlightenments or interpretations given to Hans are followed by behavioural improvements, then they are automatically accepted as valid. If they are not followed by improvement we are told the patient has not accepted them, and not that they are invalid. Discussing the failure of these early enlightenments, Freud says that in any event therapeutic success is not the primary aim of the analysis (thus sidetracking the issue and contradicting his earlier statement that the psychoanalysis is a therapeutic measure not a scientific investigation!). Freud is not deflected from claiming an improvement to be due to an interpretation even when the latter is erroneous, e.g. the moustache interpretation.

How then would the modern psychologist interpret the origins of Hans's phobia? In the last chapter we mentioned Watson's experiments with little Albert, showing that phobic fears could be produced in young children through a simple process of conditioning, and would last for a long time. It might therefore be suggested that the incident to which Freud refers as merely the exciting cause of Hans's phobia was, in fact, the cause of the entire disorder, i.e. the moment when the street accident occurred and the horse fell down. Hans actually says: 'No. I only got it [the phobia] then. When the horse and the bus fell down, it gave me such a fright, really! That was when I got the nonsense.' The father says: 'All of this was confirmed by my wife, as well as the fact that the anxiety broke out immediately afterwards.' In addition, the father was able to report two other unpleasant incidents which Hans experienced with horses, prior to the onset of the phobia. It was likely that these experiences had sensitized Hans to horses or, in other words, he had already been partially conditioned to fear horses.

Wolpe and Rachman make the following points:

Just as the little boy, Albert, in Watson's classic demonstration, reacted with anxiety, not only to the original conditioned stimulus, a white rat, but to other similar stimuli, such as furry objects, cotton wool and so on, so Hans reacted anxiously to horses, horse-drawn buses, vans, and features of horses such as their blinkers and muzzles. In fact he showed fear of a wide range of generalized stimuli. The accident which provoked the phobia involved two horses drawing a bus and Hans stated that he was more afraid of large carts, vans, or buses than small carts. As one would expect, the less close a phobic stimulus was to that of the original incident, the less disturbing Hans found it. Furthermore, the last aspect of the phobia to disappear was Hans's fear of large vans and buses. There is ample experimental evidence that when responses to generalized stimuli undergo extinction, responses to other stimuli in the continuum are the less diminished the more clearly they resemble the original conditioned stimulus.

Hans's recovery from the phobia may be explained on conditioning principles in a number of possible ways, but the actual mechanism that operated cannot be identified, since the child's father was not concerned with the kind of information that would be of interest to us. It is well known that, especially in children, many phobias decline and disappear over a few weeks or months. The reason for this appears to be that in the ordinary course of life generalized phobic stimuli may evoke responses weak enough to be inhibited by other emotional responses simultaneously aroused in the individual. Perhaps this process was a true source of little Hans's recovery. The interpretations may have been irrelevant or may even have retarded recovery by adding new stress and new fears to those already present. But since Hans does not seem to have been greatly upset by the interpretation it appears more likely that the therapy was actually helpful, for phobic stimuli were again and again presented to the child in a variety of emotional contexts that may have inhibited the anxiety and in consequence diminished its habit strength. The *gradualness* of Hans's recovery is consonant with an explanation of this kind.

It may be rather rash to try to reinterpret a child's phobia that was treated seventy-five years ago. However, the facts fit in remarkably neatly, and at least we are provided here with an alternative theory which, to many people, will seem more plausible than the original one produced by Freud. However, what is clearly required is a method of proof which will decide between these alternative interpretations, not so much with regard to little Hans, but with regard to cases which may come up nowadays and which may be treated by methods derived either from Freud's type of theory, or from Wolpe's. We have already dealt with this topic in the last chapter, and therefore will only quote the conclusions to which Wolpe and Rachman come, on the basis of their examination of the case of little Hans, regarding the adequacy of support this case gives to Freudian theories:

> The chief conclusion to be derived from our survey of the case of little Hans is that it does not provide anything resembling direct proof of psychoanalytic theorems. We have combed Freud's account for evidence that would be acceptable in the court of science, and have found none ... Freud believed that he had obtained in little Hans a direct confirmation of his theories, for he speaks towards the end of 'the infantile complexes that were revealed behind Hans's phobia'. It seems clear that although he wanted to be scientific ... Freud was surprisingly naïve regarding the requirements of scientific evidence. Infantile complexes were not *revealed* (demonstrated) behind Hans's phobia: they were merely hypothesized.

It is remarkable that countless psychoanalysts have paid homage to the case of little Hans, without being offended by its glaring inadequacies. We shall not here attempt to explain this, except to point to one probable major influence – a tacit belief among analysts that Freud possessed a kind of unerring insight that absolved him from the obligation to obey rules applicable to ordinary men. For example, Glover, speaking of other analysts who arrogate to themselves the right Freud claimed to subject his material to 'a touch of revision', says: 'No doubt when someone of Freud's calibre appears in our midst he will be freely accorded ... this privilege.' And again: 'To accord such a privilege to anyone is to violate the spirit of science.'

We have now discussed in some detail the theory of child development favoured by Freud, the evidence relating to it, and the case of little Hans which he used to introduce the ideas of child psychoanalysis to the world. The outcome of this examination is a melancholy one. It portrays a complete lack of scientific attitude in Freud, a naïve reliance on interpretation of a highly speculative nature, a disregard and disrespect for observational and other facts, a failure to consider alternative theories, and a Messianic belief in his own infallibility, together with a contempt for his critics. This is not a mixture likely to generate scientific knowledge, and indeed even now, seventy-five years after the case of little Hans was analysed by Freud, we are no nearer to having any acceptable evidence for Freud's speculations about Oedipus complexes, castration fears, and early infantile sexuality. The terms have penetrated public consciousness, and are widely used to spice up the writings and the conversation of literary people and others without a scientific background, but among psychologists who demand some form of evidence for factual assertions, there is now little faith in the validity of these Freudian concepts. The reasons for this disbelief will have become clear in the course of this chapter, so let us merely state that it is remarkable that these unsupported speculations became so widely accepted by psychiatrists and psychoanalysts, that Freud managed to persuade highly intelligent people of the cogency of his arguments, and that his methods became so widely used and applied in the treatment of neurotic and other illnesses. It will be the task of historians of science to explain how all this came about. I have no suggestion to make on this truly miraculous development. It seems to me to partake more of a religious conversion than of a scientific persuasion, to be based on faith and belief rather than fact and experiment, and to rely on suggestion and propaganda rather than proof and verification. Is there, in fact, any experimental evidence in favour of the Freudian view? To this problem we must now turn in the next two chapters.

CHAPTER FIVE

The Interpretation of Dreams and the Psychopathology of Everyday Life

> History warns us that ... it is the customary fate of new truths
> to begin as heresies and to end as superstitions.
>
> T. H. HUXLEY

Second only to the use of psychoanalysis as a method of treatment, in the mind of the man in the street, are Freud's theory of dreams, and the closely related psychopathology of everyday life. Freud himself considered *The Interpretation of Dreams* his most important work, and he was emphatic in stating that 'the interpretation of dreams is the *via regia* to knowledge of the unconscious element in our psychic life'. The dream was the model on which Freud constructed the theory of the neuroses, using as an intermediary the method of free association he had borrowed from Sir Francis Galton, and starting from elements of the dream, or from the accidental errors, forgettings and misinterpretations that occur in the conscious state, and about which he wrote later in his *Psychopathology of Everyday Life*. He believed that these associations would lead back to the unconscious motivating forces which cause the dream or the *Fehlleistung* (literally 'faulty achievement', i.e. the faulty execution of perfectly ordinary and habitual activities; in English translations the usual term is 'parapraxia').

Freud makes a clear distinction between the apparent content of the dream and its *latent* content. As he says:

The dream-content ... is expressed as it were in a pictographic script, the characters of which have to be transposed individually into the language of the dream-thoughts. If we attempted to read these characters according to their pictorial value instead of according to their symbolic relation, we would clearly be led into error. Suppose I have a picture-puzzle, a rebus, in front of me. It depicts a house with a boat on its roof, a single letter of the alphabet, the figure of a running man whose head has been conjured away, and so on. Now I might be misled into raising objections and declaring that the picture as a whole and its component parts are nonsensical. A boat has no business to be on the roof of a house and a headless man cannot run. Moreover, the man is bigger than the house; and if the whole picture is intended to represent a landscape, letters of the alphabet are out of place in it since such objects do not occur in nature. But obviously we can only form a proper judgement of the rebus if we put aside criticisms such as these of the whole composition and its parts and if, instead, we try to replace each separate element by a syllable or word that can be represented by that element in some way or another. The words which are put together in this way are no longer nonsensical but may form a poetical phrase of the greatest beauty and significance. A dream is a picture-puzzle of this sort, and our predecessors in the field of dream-interpretation have made the mistake of treating the rebus as a pictorial composition: and as such it has seemed to them nonsensical and worthless.

The actual dream, as reported, is produced by the dream-work, which changes the latent meaning into the manifest dream. This produces the distortion which is so characteristic of dreams, and which Freud believed to be the work of a 'censor' who tries to protect the dreamer from facing the repressed infantile unconscious wishes which seek expression in the dream, and who renders them unintelligible through symbolic and other transformations.

As H. B. Gibson has pointed out in his book *Sleep, Dreaming and Mental Health*, Freud's theory of dreams can be stated in terms of four propositions. The first of these is that dreams serve the purpose of protecting sleep. Sleep itself was conceived as a state of unconsciousness which needed to be protected from stimuli likely to rouse the sleeper; these might come either from without, i.e. disturbing noises, flashing lights, the experience of heat or cold, etc., or from within, i.e. memories and unsatisfied psychological drives stored in the mind. In this, Freud was not proposing anything very novel; views such as these were current in the nineteenth century even before he wrote. And while these hypotheses (which he seemed to regard as axiomatic) may appear quite sensible to the man in the street, in fact it is very doubtful whether dreams really take place in a state of unconsciousness, and also, as we shall see, whether they really protect the sleep of the dreamer.

We now come to the second proposition. It is an essential part of Freud's general theory, as it was of the theories of many of his predecessors, that human culture imposes numerous restrictions on the expression of sexual and aggressive drives. Freud proposed that the control of these repressed wishes is somewhat weakened during sleep, but that because their emergence in an undisguised form would shock the dreamer awake, various protective mechanisms distort the shocking latent material to make the manifest dream sufficiently innocuous to get past the censor and allow the dreamer to go on sleeping. This self-same censor is, of course, also responsible for our parapraxias, and hence produces the psychopathology of everyday life, which we will examine in the later part of this chapter. According to Freud, 'the task of dream formation is above all to overcome the inhibition from the censorship; and it is precisely this task which is solved by the displacements of psychical energy within the material of the dream-thoughts'. Every dream, and every element in every dream, represents to Freud a wish, but not an ordinary, conscious, everyday kind of wish. He says that a dream 'is a [disguised] end of fulfilment of a [suppressed or repressed] wish', and holds, furthermore, that this repression dates back to the earliest infantile years of the dreamer's life.

The third proposition states that the material of which dreams are constructed consists largely of remembered events from the day before – 'day residues', as Freud calls them. As he expresses it, the so-called 'residues from the previous day' can act as disturbers of sleep and dream-producers; they are thought processes from the previous day which have retained effective cathexis and to some extent withstood the general lowering of energy through sleep. These residues are discovered by tracing back the manifest dream to the latent dream-thoughts . . . These residues from the previous day, however, are not a dream itself: they even lack the most essential constituent of the dream. They could not themselves form a dream. They are strictly speaking only the psychical material which the dream-work employs, just as sensory and somatic stimuli, either incidental or produced under experimental conditions, constitute the somatic material for the dream-work. To attribute to them the main part in dream formation is simply to repeat in a new guise the pre-analytical error by which dreams were explained on the hypothesis of stomach trouble or skin pressure.

Day-residues for Freud are simply the building blocks used to form dreams, the dreams themselves being concerned with very different matters. These various harmless and trivial events which happened during the day, or which have been recalled from the past by a chain of associations, appear in the manifest content of the dream, not because we have recently been preoccupied with them, but because they serve as a convenient screen for matters that *really* concern us, which Freud interprets as sexual materials and erotic wishes. Indeed, he says that 'dreams that are conspicuously innocent invariably embody coarse erotic wishes'. He does concede that repressed wishes may be concerned with hatred, envy and aggression, but he considers the sexual drive far the most important.

The fourth proposition is that the dream as told eventually to the analyst, or as eventually remembered after a lapse of time by the dreamer, has undergone 'secondary elaboration'. This is undoubtedly true; the records of dreams which are recalled immediately upon waking are strikingly different from records of the same dreams recalled a day or a week later. Modern research on learning and memory has shown conclusively that memory is an active process, not a passive one; it changes, distorts and adapts the remembered materials so that they will fit better into preconceived schemata. Hence modern (and even pre-Freudian!) researchers in this field insist on dreams being recorded immediately upon waking: only in this way can we minimize the importance of secondary elaboration. According to Freud, secondary elaboration is most liable to occur when the censor 'which has never been quite asleep, feels that it has been surprised by the already admitted dream'. In other words, if the dream we remember still appears shocking to the censor, it is carefully altered by the memory process so as to be less shocking and more readily accessible to our super-ego.

Freud, it should be noted, never got his patients to recall their dreams immediately upon waking; neither did he himself follow this sage advice. Hence in Freud's writings we never deal with dreams as such, but rather with constructs elaborated by memory from whatever the dream-content may have been, and changed from the true dream beyond recognition. One of the oddities of *The Interpretation of Dreams* is that Freud realized this, but nevertheless failed to heed his own insight. Another, which we have already noted in the first chapter, is the fact that all the dreams quoted by Freud in his book as illustrating and proving his theories, in fact do the opposite; none of them is based on wishes arising from infantile repression, and hence his chosen examples serve to disprove his own theory!

The dream-work makes use of four major methods of disguise. These are condensation, displacement, dramatization and symbolization. *Condensation* is a process based on the discovery that the manifest content of the dream is an abbreviation of the latent content. 'The dream is meagre, paltry, and laconic, in comparison with the copiousness of the dream-thoughts.' As an example, consider a dream published and interpreted by E. Frink, an American psychoanalyst. A young woman dreamt that she was walking along Fifth Avenue with a lady who was a friend of hers. She stopped for some time in front of a milliner's shop-window to look at hats. She seemed to remember going in at last and buying a hat.

Analysis provided the following data. The presence of the friend in the dream reminded the dreamer that on the previous day she had actually been walking on Fifth Avenue with the lady in question, although she had not bought a hat. Her husband had been ill in bed that day, and although she knew that it was nothing serious, she had been very uneasy, and could not get rid of the notion that her husband might die. In the midst of all this her friend called, and her husband suggested that a walk might do her good. The young woman further remembered that during the walk she had talked of a man whom she had known before her marriage; she thought that she had been in love with him. When asked why she had not married him the young woman laughed and said that the marriage had never been arranged, adding that his financial and social position was so far above her own that it would have been fantastic to dream of it.

The young woman was asked for associations about the buying of the hat in the dream. She said that she had much admired a hat in the milliner's shop-window, and that she would have very much liked to buy it, but this was impossible because of her husband's poverty. Clearly the dream was satisfying her wish by allowing her to buy a hat. But in addition, the dreamer suddenly remembered that in her dream the hat which she bought had been a black hat, a *mourning hat* in fact.

The analyst's interpretation is as follows. The day before the dream, the patient was afraid her husband would die. She dreamt that she was buying a mourning hat, and therefore fulfilled the death-fantasy. In real life she was prevented from buying a hat by her husband's poverty, but in her dream she was able to buy one, which implied that she had a rich husband. These associations lead us to the rich man with whom she was admittedly in love, and to the assumption that if she were his wife, she would be able to buy herself as many hats as she pleased. The analyst safely concluded that the young woman was tired of her husband; that her fear of seeing her husband die was only a compensation-process, a defence-reaction against her real wish for his death; that she would like to marry the man with whom she was in love, and to have enough money to satisfy all her whims. It is interesting to note that when the analyst acquainted the patient with the interpretation of her dream, she admitted that it was justified, and told him several facts which confirmed it. The most important of these facts was that after her marriage she had learnt that the man with whom she had been in love had also been in love with her. This revelation had naturally revived her feeling and she had regretted her hasty marriage, believing that if she had waited a little longer, she would have done much better for herself.

This dream illustrates the process of condensation. A large number of different ideas is condensed into a very short and rather uninteresting dream. In the psychoanalytic literature this dream has been quoted several times in support of Freud's position, but it is difficult to see how that can be. It contains no repressed infantile wishes; indeed, most of the wishes are apparently quite conscious as far as the woman is concerned. She is perfectly conscious of the fact that she is still in love with the man she would like to have married; she is conscious of the fact that she is regretting her marriage, and also of the fact that she is poor and would like to be rich. Word association can indeed help us to interpret dreams, but the meaning of this dream is entirely different to the kind of latent content which Freud postulates in the theory. Consequently the only conclusion we can come to from the psychoanalytic interpretation of this dream is that Freud's theory is wrong. It is interesting that this is not the conclusion drawn by professional psychoanalysts.

Displacement is a process whereby the affective charge is detached from its proper object and is directed towards an accessory object – in other words, the emotion properly belonging to one object of the dream is not shown in relation to that object, but to a different one. Here is an example of a dream manifesting displacement. A girl dreamt that she was in the presence of someone whose identity was very vague, but to whom she was under some sort of obligation; wishing to thank him, she made him a present of her comb. This is the total content of her dream. To understand it, something must be known about the background of the patient. She was a Jewess whose hand had been sought in marriage a year earlier by a Protestant. Although she fully returned his feelings for her, the difference of religion had prevented the engagement. The day before the dream she had had a violent quarrel with her mother, and as she was going to bed she thought it would be better for herself as well for her family if she were to leave home. She went to sleep thinking about ways and means whereby she could support herself without having to rely on her parents.

Asked about the associations of the word 'comb', she answered that sometimes, when someone was about to use a brush or comb belonging to somebody else, people said: 'Don't do that, you will mix the breed.' This suggests that the person in the dream whose identity remains vague is the ex-suitor; by offering him a comb, the patient shows her wish to 'mix the breed', i.e. to marry him and bear his children. In her dream, the comb has displaced the ex-suitor, in an otherwise quite unintelligible manner; it becomes the central emotional object through the process of displacement.

We may note again that this dream interpretation, while perfectly sensible, does not support Freud's hypothesis, but directly counters it. There are no repressed wishes here, let alone infantile wishes; the patient is perfectly aware of her feelings for the ex-suitor, and the reasons for this. Why the censor should object to a direct dream stating these perfectly conscious facts is difficult to understand. Again we see that Galton's method of free association is valuable in leading to a meaningful interpretation of an apparently senseless dream, but that is all; any peculiarly Freudian theory is clearly contradicted by the interpretation of the dream.

Dramatization is a term used by Freud to refer to the fact that in dreams the major part is played by visual images. Conceptual thought is replaced by movie-like visual representation. This process is so obvious and so well known to the dreamer that we will not waste time on recounting a dream and its analysis. However, we will come back to this point later on in dealing with Hall's theory of dreaming, as this is a crucial element in it. Dramatization is in many ways similar to symbolization, the mechanism to which we will now turn.

Of all the dream-mechanisms that of *symbolization* is probably the best-known, and the one most closely related by many readers to the name of Freud. We often talk about 'Freudian symbolism', meaning the use of symbols to denote sexual objects and activities. This may be the best-known of Freud's hypotheses, but it can hardly be said to be a very original one! Symbolism has been the standby of interpreters of dreams for thousands of years; we may recall Joseph's interpretation of the Pharaoh's dream of the seven fat kine and the seven lean kine, in terms of their symbolizing years of affluence and years of famine. Nowhere is the absurdity of linking Freud's name with alleged new discoveries more obvious than in relation to the sexual interpretation in symbolic terms.

Many people thus talk about Freudian symbolism as if Freud had in fact discovered the idea that sharp and pointed objects may symbolize the male genitals, and curved objects and containers the female genitals. Followers of Freud often encourage this impression, but of course this type of symbolism has been well known to writers and philosophers, poets and psychologists, and even the man in the street, for many thousands of years. In Latin, for instance, the male sex organ was vulgarly known as *mentula* or *verpa*, but these terms were regarded as obscene, and hence many different metaphors were used – indeed, these are very similar to those found in Ancient Greek. As J. N. Adams has pointed out in his book *The Latin Sexual Vocabulary*, 'no objects are more readily likened to the penis than sharp instruments, and it is likely that metaphors from this romantic field abound in all languages'. In Latin, symbolic terms to denote the penis are, for instance *virga* (rod), *vectis* (stake), *hasta* (lance), *rutabulum* (rake, poker), *terminus* (boundary marker), *temo* (pole), *vomer* (plough), *clavus* (tiller, as a nautical metaphor). Many other examples are given by Adams, and he also points out that 'the snake was felt to have phallic significance by Latin-speakers', so even here Freud did not add anything new.

The vulgar term for the female genitals, *cunnus*, is on a par with *mentula* and is hardly used outside graffiti and epigrams. However, metaphors abound. Adams says: 'The frequency (in Latin and other languages) of the metaphor of the field, garden, meadow, etc., applied to the female pudenda reflects in part the external appearance of the organ, and in part the association felt between the fertility of the field and that of females. The metaphor complements the verbal metaphors of sowing and ploughing used as the male role in sexual intercourse.'

No one familiar with Ancient Greek and Roman literature, or medieval plays and texts, can have any doubt about the prevalence of sexual symbolism, or the fact that it was known to practically everyone. To imagine for a moment that such symbolism was discovered by Freud is as absurd as to imagine that its use in dreams was discovered by him; the use of symbolism in dreams also has a long history, going back to the beginning of written language. It is not the use of symbols in dreams that is novel in Freud's account, but the *particular* use he makes of them, and the interpretation he gives of the purpose of symbolism. Here, as elsewhere, what is new in his theories is not true, and what is true in his theories is not new. Symbols are certainly used in dreams, but they are not 'Freudian' in any sense of the term.

So, in brief, we have an account of Freud's interpretation of dreams. The theory underlying it is certainly not as original as he claims; historical accounts have been given by many writers of the large numbers of philosophers and psychologists who antedated Freud and expressed views remarkably like those he held. The index of *The Interpretation of Dreams* contains a list of some 80 books, but most of these are not referred to in the text itself, and even when they *are* referred to, Freud does no more than mention them briefly, doing scant justice to their importance. There are, in all, 134 books and articles on dreams published before *The Interpretation of Dreams* which Freud did not mention in the text of any edition of his book, but which nevertheless were listed in the bibliographies of various editions.

There are many other oddities and inconsistencies in Freud's account; eminently reasonable criticisms of these have been made in Gibson's book on sleep already referred to. Here we will give an account of only some of them. The first has already been mentioned, namely the failure of Freud to consider the importance of secondary elaboration, and to get his patients to write down their dreams immediately after waking up. Such precautions were taken by some of his predecessors, but Freud did not regard this as a matter of scientific integrity, and summarized his position as follows:

In the 'scientific' works about dreams, which in spite of their repudiation of dream-interpretation have received a new stimulus from psychoanalysis, one repeatedly finds very superfluous care exercised about the accurate preservation of the text of the dream. This is thought necessary in order to guard it against the distortions and accretions supervening in the hours immediately after waking. Even many psychoanalysts, in giving the patient instructions to write down the dream immediately upon waking, seem not to rely consistently enough upon the knowledge of the conditions of dream-making. This direction is superfluous in the treatment; and the patients are glad enough to make use of it to disturb their slumbers and to display eager obedience where it cannot serve any useful purpose.

Clearly Freud not only did not care about the distortions

which memory inflicted on the dream as told to the analysts, but he rather liked it that way. A patient coming to his consulting-room hours, or even days, after having had a particular dream, would give an account much changed from the original due to the secondary elaboration that occurred during the waking hours. But even more important, the patient, having learnt the principles of Freud's methods of interpretation, would consciously or unconsciously remodel his dream to fit in with Freudian theory. It is now admitted by most psychoanalysts that the patients' dreams are powerfully influenced by the analyst's theories; thus Freudian patients dream in Freudian symbols, Jungian patients in Jungian symbols, and so forth. The patient is trained and learns what kind of dreams and symbols are pleasing to the analyst, and consciously or unconsciously, aided by secondary elaboration, is only too pleased to accede!

This can hardly be disputed as psychoanalysts themselves have frequently admitted that the facts are very much as stated. Here, for instance, is a passage from a well-known American psychoanalyst, Judd Marmor; it has already been quoted in another connection, but it is so relevant here also that it is repeated again. Writing in 1962, this is what he had to say:

Depending upon the point of view of the analyst, the patients of each [rival psychoanalytic] school seem to bring up precisely the kind of phenomenological data which confirm the theories and interpretations of their analyst! Thus each theory tends to be self-validating. Freudians elicit material about the Oedipus complex and castration anxiety, Jungians about archetypes, Rankians about separation anxiety, Adlerians about masculine strivings and feelings of inferiority, Horneyites about idealized images, Sullivanians about disturbed interpersonal relationships, etc.

This is a remarkable admission by a convinced and prominent psychoanalyst, which really indicates the extreme subjectivity of interpretation, and the influence of suggestibility on the dreams and free associations of the patients.

As Gibson points out, experimenters have tested the degree to which dreams remembered at the moment of waking might be significantly altered when later told to psychoanalysts. The patients were wakened during the night when electrophysiological measures of REM (Rapid Eye Movement) indicated that they were dreaming, and they were made to recall their dreams immediately. Records of these dreams were then compared with the accounts that patients gave to the psychoanalyst later on, during the day. It was found that certain dreams were told to the experimenters during the night, but not to the psychoanalyst; conversely, certain dreams were 'recalled' for the psychoanalyst, but had little relation to what was actually remembered in awakening! The differences were not random; those dreams which the patients expected to provoke a negative response from the analyst were not reported to him. It is therefore clear that whatever Freud may have been interpreting, it was not the *dreams* of his patients, but elaborations, partly conscious, partly unconscious, of those elements of their dreams which the patients thought would be likely to find favour with him.

Freud held the view that 'the fact that dreams are distorted and mutilated by memory is accepted by us but in our opinion constitutes no obstacle; for it is no more than the last and manifest portion of the distorting activity which has been in operation from the very start of the dream formation'. This point is important because it relates directly to the Freudian theory. The censor is supposed to disguise a latent dream in order to keep the patient from waking, and to spare his blushes, as it were; but the memory activity that distorts the dream is not subject to the same censorship since it occurs during the waking life. Hence any information the dream might give about the activities of the censor must be considerably distorted by secondary elaboration, so that we simply do not know how to test Freud's theory!

The fact of secondary elaboration makes plain one interesting feature of the dreams analysed and recounted by Freud, which sets them apart from dreams recorded both before and after he wrote *The Interpretation of Dreams*. The philosopher Wittgenstein once remarked that 'Freud very commonly gives what we might call a sexual interpretation. But it is interesting that among all the reports of dreams which he gives, there is not a single example of a straightforward sexual dream. Yet these are as common as rain.' Gibson quotes many authors, both early and recent, to show that this is perfectly true; and most readers will be able to testify to it. One of the best-known of recent collectors of dreams, Calvin Hall, writes: 'There is no lack of dreams in our collection in which the most distasteful and shameful things happen. Fathers and mothers are murdered by the dreamer. The dreamer has sex with members of his family. He rapes, pillages, tortures, and destroys. He performs all kinds of obscenities and perversions. He often does these things without remorse and even with considerable glee.' This contrasts very much with the dreams recorded by Freud, which are, as Gibson points out, rather humdrum and indeed prim. Clearly some process of selection has taken place, and this was not due to Freud's 'censor', but much more likely to the conscious refusal of his middle-class Viennese patients to speak out about such obscene and pornographic things. But if we dream directly about all these things, which according to Freud would be objected to by the censor, what then is his true function? And is there any reason to suppose that he really exists?

As Gibson points out:

It is obvious . . . why Freud had to intimate to his patients one way and another that the accounts of dreams that they told him should be rather humdrum and prim . . . if they were not, it would be apparent that they had not been censored in the process of the dream-work, and the theory would be invalidated. It is not suggested that Freud deliberately coached his patients in what they could and could not tell him; the process is more subtle than that . . . To suggest that the censor is part of the *unconscious* as Freud does, and operates while the brain is fast asleep is contrary to all known fact . . .

It is important to appreciate why patients would be reluctant to tell Freud the unvarnished facts about their dreams, but instead to subject them to considerable secondary elaboration before the telling. Earlier we have pointed out that dreams that involved crude scenes of sexual behaviour, undisguised hatred and coarse language would need some bowdlerization for decency's sake, and if patients had told them to Freud in the original form they would be, in effect, challenging the whole legitimacy of his theory of dreams and thereby questioning his competence. It would be much easier to retain good relations with the analyst by wrapping the dreams up, so to speak, and letting him unwrap them. Thus if a patient had a crude dream about 'poking a tart', by the time secondary elaboration had got to work on it during the day, it might be told in terms of prodding a fruit pie with a stick when related in the consulting room . . . It is a serious matter that neither Freud nor his followers have properly answered. Patients would soon learn the rules of the game and behave accordingly, *consciously* censoring dreams that had been quite uncensored when they were dreamt.

One other point may be worth mentioning. D. Foulkes, in his book on children's dreams, quotes a number of research studies to the effect that:

Clinical dreams have still another bias over and above that introduced by their method of sampling. It has been demonstrated both for adults . . . and for adolescents . . . that more disturbed persons have more disturbing dreams. That is, one cannot generalize from the dreams – however collected – of clinic patients to those of unselected ('normal') populations.

As Gibson comments:

If indeed there is a censor watching over the material that is permitted to be displayed in the manifest content of dreams, just as the TV Viewers Association of Mrs Whitehouse attempts to monitor the content of television programmes, then it must be a very inconsistent and indeed crazy censor. It permits some material that would be more appropriate to the worst of videotape 'nasties' to be mixed in with material suitable for the children's hour and much that is just boring and inconsequential.

Furthermore, the censor allows the 'nasties' to appear in the dreams of those least capable of tolerating such material, namely neurotics and other mentally ill patients!

Is there really any evidence that we *need* a censor to protect our sleep? It appears from large-scale studies of dreams that people do not wake up when they have the most vivid, erotic, obscene and pornographic dreams, or when the dream is filled with uncontrolled and overwhelming violence. If we can dream that we are raping our mothers and murdering our fathers, without waking up, then surely the usefulness of the censor must be called into question! As Jocasta says to Oedipus: 'Many young men dream of sleeping with their mothers!' Why prepare an elaborate disguise in one dream when it is disregarded in another?

We have so far looked at internal contradictions in Freud's

theory, and at fairly obvious errors and misinterpretations. We may now ask the simple question, how would one try to prove such a theory? One obvious way would be to link it with psychoanalytic treatment, so that the interpretations of the dreams give an answer to the problem presented by the patient's neurosis, while at the same time the insights thus gained would relieve the patient of his symptoms. This indeed was Freud's original notion, and if it had worked in that way we might say there was some evidence, although falling far short of scientific 'proof', in his favour. However, this is not what happened, and Freud and his followers had to admit that not only were patients frequently not cured by being acquainted with the interpretations of their dreams, but that even if 'cures' occurred, there was no relationship in time to the 'insights' gained by interpreting their dreams. Thus the results must be regarded as disproof of Freudian theories.

Could we regard the patient's acceptance of Freudian interpretations of his dreams as support? The answer surely must be no. In the first place, the patient is in a poor position to argue with the analyst; he has spent much time and money on the treatment, and if he disagrees with the analyst he is indicating dissatisfaction, or even disloyalty, and is implicitly suggesting that he has wasted his time and money. In the second place, Freud had a very clever ploy for dealing with disagreement. If the patient agreed with his interpretation, then Freud claimed that the interpretation was obviously correct. If the patient disagreed, however, Freud claimed that this was because of psychoanalytic 'resistance', which makes interpretation unacceptable precisely *because* it is correct; hence disagreement also indicates the correctness of the theory. Clearly there is no way in which the theory could be disproved – a very fortunate state for a scientific theory to be in, one might have thought. In actual fact, of course, the opposite is true: if a theory cannot be disproved by any observable fact, then as Karl Popper has pointed out so many times, it is not a scientific theory at all.

Of course, there are experimental methods for investigating dreams which are much more likely to lead us to acceptable theories. Consider as an example the work done by Alexander Luria in the USSR in the early 1920s. He was concerned, as the title of his book proclaims, with *The Nature of Human Conflicts*, and used the method of word association in an experimental context. He also applied his method to the study of dreams. He argued, reasonably enough, that the usual method of dream analysis put the cart before the horse. Accepting for the moment the distinction between the latent and the manifest dream, Freud and other interpreters would start from the manifest dream and try to arrive at the meaning of the latent dream. However, by definition that meaning is unknown, and consequently it is impossible to prove or disprove the correctness of the interpretation. If we want to do a proper scientific analysis, then we must start with a known latent dream, and discover how this is altered to become the manifest dream.

Luria proceeded to do this by clever use of hypnosis. He would hypnotize his subjects, make them live in their imagination through a very traumatic event, and then instruct them to dream about this event, but to forget all about the hypnosis as far as their conscious mind was concerned. Readily hypnotized subjects are quite capable of following these instructions, and Luria was able to collect a number of dreams in their manifest form, while knowing (through his instructions) the nature of the latent dreams, i.e. the content remodelled by the dream-work.

As a young student I was very impressed with Luria's work, which was unfortunately brought to an end by the strict scientific censorship of the Stalin era. Luria went on to work in the field of neuropsychology and never returned to his very promising early experiments in psychology. I tried to reproduce some of his experiments, and found exactly the same results as he had presented in his book. One example from this work must suffice. The instructions given to the subject, a young female student, were as follows: 'You are going to have a very unpleasant experience. I will describe the experience to you now, and you will experience it as if it were real, with the appropriate emotions. When I wake you up at the end of this experience you will forget all about it, but when you go to sleep you will have a vivid dream about this experience. You are going home late at night, after a party with fellow students, and you are walking through a graveyard. You hear some footsteps behind you, and on turning around you see that a man is following you. You break into a run, but he overtakes you, throws you to the ground and rapes you. Then he runs off. You are terribly distressed, and go home and tell your parents all about it.'

The dream consequently recounted usually follows the general outlines of the story fairly closely, but the rape is nearly always changed through the use of symbolism. Thus the man raping the girl may be displaced in the dream by a man carrying a knife with which he threatens the girl, or which he uses to stab her; alternatively, he may be described as violently snatching the girl's handbag. These symbolic mechanisms, already used by the Ancient Greeks and Romans, emerge very clearly in the dreams, but of course they do not present any evidence for Freudian mechanisms of repressed infantile wishes, or indeed wish-fulfilment of any kind; it would be going too far to imagine that the dreamer actually wished to be raped! It is very unfortunate that Luria was prevented from continuing this work, and that few other psychologists seem to have taken it up; much would have been learnt about the nature of dreaming if this line of study had been followed.

We have seen that the Freudian theory is neither new nor true, but is there anything better to replace it? Much recent work has been concerned with experimental studies, such as those involving REM (Rapid Eye-Movement) sleep, and the tendency for dreaming to occur in conjunction with this type of sleep. Interesting though these experimental studies are, they do not tell us much about the meaning of the dream. In my view the best alternative to the Freudian theory, and much superior to it, is the work of Calvin S. Hall, whose work is described in his book *The Meaning of Dreams*. He collected more accounts of dreams than any other student of the subject has ever done, and his theories based on this work are practical and convincing. It cannot, of course, be claimed that they are necessarily correct; in the absence of strict experimental work, which is very difficult in this field, it is impossible to make any such claims. But the theory does explain most, if not all, of the major features of dreams, and it does so without having recourse to miraculous and mythological entities like censors.

Hall made a useful addition to the methodology of dream

interpretation when he suggested the analysis of a *series* of a person's dreams, rather than the analysis of single dreams. As he puts it: 'One tries various combinations, fitting this dream with that dream, until all of the dreams are joined together and a meaningful picture of the dreamer emerges. In this method, which we call the dream series method, the interpretation of any one dream is a hunt until it has been verified by falling in place with interpretation made of other dreams.' Hall gives many examples of how the interpretaion is facilitated by having several dreams to consider, but it would take us too far afield to follow him in this.

The major innovation in Hall's theory is his view of symbolism. He believes that there are symbols in dreams, and these symbols have a necessary function, but it is not the function of *disguise*, as in Freud's theory; the symbols of dreams are there to *express* something, not to hide it. Dreaming, as he points out, is a form of thinking, and thinking consists of formulating conceptions or ideas. During dreaming these conceptions are turned into pictures, which are the concrete embodiments of the dreamer's thoughts; they give visible expression to what is invisible, namely concepts, ideas and thoughts.

He goes on to argue that the true reference of any dream symbol is not an object or activity, but always an *idea* in the mind of the dreamer. He gives as an example the possible ways in which the male penis can be symbolized. It may be by way of a gun or a knife; this would symbolize *aggressive* sexual thoughts. Or the image may be a screwdriver, or a petrol dispenser being inserted in the petrol tank of the car; this would symbolize a *mechanical* view of intercourse ('screwing'). Or the penis might be represented by a limp flower, or a broken poker; this would illustrate ideas of sexual *impotence*.

Another example he gives is the many ways in which one can dream about one's mother. If the dreamer wants to express a feeling that his mother is a *nurturant* person, he might dream about a cow; if he sees his mother as being rather *remote* and *authoritative*, he might dream of her as a queen. In other words, the dream does not only symbolize the given person or activity (the noun in the sentence), but also adds a description (the adjective) – aggressive, nurturant, etc. The symbolisms are used to convey, in terse and concise language, complex and abstruse conceptions.

Let us quote one example from Hall's book. He tells of a young woman who dreamed that it was her first wedding anniversary, and she and her husband were going to re-enact the ceremony. She could not at first find her wedding gown, in spite of a frantic search. Finally, when she found the gown, it was dirty and torn. Tears of disappointment in her eyes, she snatched the gown and hurried to the church, where her husband enquired why she had brought the gown with her. She was confused and bewildered, and felt strange and alone.

Hall suggests that in her dream the state of her wedding dress symbolized her conception of her marriage. Other dreams supported this interpretation. She dreamed about a recently married girl who was getting a divorce, which suggested that the idea of divorce was in her own mind. In another dream she had a difficult time trying to get home to her husband, losing her way, falling on the sidewalk, being delayed by a train and never reaching her destination. This dream suggested that she was trying to find reasons for not returning home to her husband. In another dream the diamond in her engagement ring was missing, suggesting the hope that perhaps this would nullify her unhappy marriage. Finally, she dreamed that a girlfriend who was getting married received a lot of useless wedding presents. This suggested that in her mind the state of marriage was like so much useless rubbish. 'For truly these dreams indicate that the dreamer conceives of her marriage as an unhappy one and corroborates the hypothesis that a torn and dirty wedding dress is a concrete embodiment of this idea.'

The function of dreaming, as Hall maintains, is to reveal what is in the person's mind, not to conceal it. 'Dreams may appear enigmatic because they contain symbols, but these symbols are nothing more than pictorial metaphors, and like the verbal metaphors of waking life their intention is to clarify rather than to obscure thought.' The mind is constantly active, thinking about problems, trying to discover solutions, full of anxieties about one thing and another, and generally concerned with the past, present and future. Dreaming is simply the continuation of thinking by other means, i.e. by means of pictorial representations and symbolism. Our thoughts, our worries, our anxieties, our attempts to solve problems, are all translated into pictorial language, and continue the conscious work of thinking during certain periods of sleep. Dreams may represent wish-fulfilments, but these would usually be quite conscious wishes, not repressed infantile ones. But dreams may also represent fears, problem solutions, or anything that might occur in waking thought. This theory accounts for the facts far better than Freud's does, without running into all the difficulties that beset Freud's theory. For the time being there is no better theory, and provisionally I think it ought to be accepted and used as a basis for further experimentation and observation.

There is a close link between the interpretation of dreams, with which we have been concerned so far in this chapter, and the interpretation of *Fehlleistungen* or parapraxias, i.e. errors in linguistic performance, lapses in everyday behaviour, etc. These, too, are interpreted by Freud along the lines of Galton's free-association technique, and as a dream is traced back to some hypothetical repressed wish, so is the linguistic or behavioral lapse. Temporary forgetfulness of proper names is included in this general category, as is false recollection, i.e. the substitution of the wrong name for the one which is sought.

Freud asserts confidently that errors in linguistic performance are *always* caused by repression. He gives many examples through which he attempts to convince readers that this is indeed so, and that repressed material can have motivational effects of the kind mentioned. Two examples may illustrate Freud's method. The first refers to a Professor who stated, in front of his class: 'In the case of the female genitals, in spite of many *Versuchungen* [temptations] – I beg your pardon, *Versuche* [experiments] . . .' The second example concerns a President of the Lower House of Parliament who wanted to open a sitting and said: 'Gentlemen, I take notice that the full quorum of members is present and herewith declare the sitting closed.' The interpretation of the disturbing intention in the first example is self-evident, while in the second example Freud states: 'It is clear that he wanted to open the sitting (i.e. the conscious intention), but it is equally clear that he also wanted to close it (i.e., disturbing intention). That is so obvious that it leaves us nothing to interpret.' Nothing, except to prove that this was indeed the intention of the President! Freud assumes, without any grounds whatsoever, that the error represents the actual intention of the President, but might it not have been simply an unmotivated slip of the tongue?

As a young student I was interested in Freud's book *The Psychopathology of Everyday Life*, and particularly in his interpretation of a lapse in everyday behaviour, where he gives as his example a man choosing the wrong key to open the front door of his house. Freud interprets this as showing that the man really wishes to be at the house whose door the key will actually unlock. It seemed to me that one could advance a psychological explanation not making use of intentions, whether repressed or conscious, in this connection. I kept my keys in a leather case, where they lay parallel to each other, suspended by metal hoops from a bar at the top of the case. Experimental psychology would suggest two major causes for choosing the wrong key on occasion. The first of these would be *similarity* of appearance between the keys in question; if both were Yale keys, then confusion could easily occur. If one was a Yale key and the other a very large, old-fashioned metal key, then confusion should be almost impossible. The second principle would be *position* (nearness). Keys close to each other would be much more readily interchanged than keys lying far from each other.

Even before becoming an absent-minded Professor, I was an absent-minded student, and often found myself in the position of using the wrong key. I made a record of the occasions, carefully noting the key that should have been used, and the key that was in fact used, on these occasions. It was, of course, easy to construct the gradient of proximity between two keys simply by counting the number of keys intervening; i.e. two keys were next to each other, there was no key intervening; one, two, three or more keys intervening would indicate how far apart the keys in question actually were. As regards similarity, I had this rated by colleagues who knew nothing about the purpose of the experiment.

I continued this experiment over many years, and there are literally thousands of occasions when errors of this kind occurred. There was a very clear-cut linear relationship between number of errors committed, on the one hand, and similarity of keys; the more similar the keys, the greater the number of errors. Similarly, there was a linear relationship between the distance between the keys in the case, and the number of errors; the closer together the keys, the greater the number of errors. Taking both causes together it was possible to account for practically all the errors that were committed. Two Yale keys next to each other accounted for much the greatest number of errors, while a Yale key at one end of the case and a large old-fashioned metal key at the other were never mistaken for each other.

I am not offering this as an experiment disproving Freud's theory; obviously more subjects would be needed, more controls, and more sophisticated statistical treatment. Furthermore, I was not in the happy position enjoyed by his patients, who seem to have had various mistresses living in different parts of Vienna, so that the keys to their apartments could be mistaken for those of the patient's own home, expressing his wish to be with one of his mistresses rather than with his wife! What I am trying to indicate is simply that this is an obvious alternative explanation for certain types of parapraxia, and that any attempt to deal with the matter scientifically would have to take such alternatives into account. Freud never did so, although the principles involved were well known in his time.

Much the same kind of argument has been put forward in relation to linguistic errors, but with far more experimental support. Thus in a book edited by V. Fromkin, entitled *Errors in Linguistic Performance: Slips of the Tongue, Ear, Pen, and Hand,* it is shown that the bulk of linguistic errors fall into two broad classes. The first class comprises errors in which the substitute word is similar in phonological *form* to the intended word, as in the following examples: 'signal' instead of 'single', 'confession' instead of 'convention', 'suburbs' instead of 'subways'. The second class consists of errors in which the substitute word is related in *meaning* (semantically or associatively) to the word it replaces, as in the following lapses: 'Don't burn your finger' instead of ' . . . your toes'; 'I know his father-in-law' instead of '. . . brother-in-law'; 'a small Japanese restaurant' instead of '. . . Chinese restaurant'. All but two of Freud's lexical substitution errors can be classified as similar to the intended word either in form or meaning. Details are given in Fromkin's book, but it would take us too far to go into these here. These two classes of errors are similar to the two classes of errors I used in analysing my own slips in choosing the wrong key; they make perfectly good sense in ordinary psychological terms, without requiring elaborate psychoanalytic interpretations in terms of repression.

When it is a question of accessing memory, the notion of 'habit' is certainly as prominent as that of 'motivation', and has received much better experimental support. In selecting the proper key, I made more errors with newly acquired keys than with others which I had had for a long time; in the latter case, countless repetition had resulted in a habit of finding the right place, whereas the locale of the newer keys had not been as firmly established by the habit mechanism. Similarly, it has been shown that words that have been frequently used by a person are much more readily accessed than words that are relatively new or have only been used rarely. Habit, as well as the other factors mentioned above, would certainly have to be ruled out before we could accept an interpretation of slips in terms of motivation only.

It is actually quite erroneous to think of Freud as the first man to be interested in these slips of tongue and pen, or to write extensively about them. The first major psycholinguistic analysis of such errors, together with a collection of over 8,000 illustrated errors, was published in Vienna by Meringer and Mayer, under the title *Versprechen und Verlesen*; this preceded Freud's book by six years. Still others had preceded Meringer and Mayer, some works appearing up to nine years before theirs, which demonstrates that there was a lively interest in the matter at that time.

In the debate between Meringer and Freud, both took up an extreme position. Freud argued that all speech errors, except perhaps for some of the simplest cases of anticipation and perseveration, could be accounted for by this theory of the unconscious and explained as being caused by repressive mechanisms. Meringer took an equally extreme position by totally discounting any such causes! The evidence certainly does not support Freud, but in view of the difficulty of complete disproof of the possibility of motivational errors, Meringer's position too cannot be supported in its entirety.

In a chapter by Ellis and Motley in Fromkin's book, 51 lexical substitution errors from the total of 94 slip errors listed in Freud's *Psychopathology of Everyday Life* are analysed. They conclude that 'the lexical substitution errors which Freud had used in support of this theory of conflicting intention do not deviate on formal or structural grounds from the errors analysed by psycholinguists'. It is thus not necessary to infer non-linguistic mechanisms to account for them.

Some interesting attempts have been made to compare the influence of motivational and linguistic factors. One of these experiments was concerned with spoonerisms, i.e. the legendary linguistic lapses by the Reverend Dr William Archibald Spooner (1844–1930), who was Warden of New College, Oxford, from 1903 to 1924. Spoonerisms are, of course, the accidental transpositions of initial letters of two or more words, such that both the original and transposed words have a meaning in English; an example would be 'You have hissed the mystery lectures' instead of 'You have missed the history lectures'. Spooner was reputed to make such errors in speaking (and also apparently in writing) but most of the famous spoonerisms are probably inventions by others.

Michael T. Motley made use of linguistic and motivational factors in inducing students to produce spoonerisms involuntarily in an experimental situation. In one of these experiments he showed his subjects two words, requiring the students to pronounce these words. The students were divided into three groups, each receiving a different kind of treatment. One condition was designed to create a situational cognitive set towards an electric shock. Subjects were attached to false electrodes ostentatiously connected to an electric timer, and were told that the timer was capable of emitting random, moderately painful, electric shocks, and that during the course of their task they might or might not receive such a shock (no shocks were administered, of course!) This treatment was administered by a male experimenter. The second treatment condition was created to establish a situational cognitive set towards sex. For this purpose the task was administered by a female confederate experimenter who was attractive, person-able, very provocatively dressed, and seductive in behaviour. (Psychology students get all the fun!) The sex set treatment was administered in the absence of electrical apparatus. Finally, a neutral set control treatment was administered by a male experimenter in the absence of electrical apparatus. These sets were designed to produce motivational factors relating to electric shocks or to sex, or to produce no motivational sets at all.

Subjects were presented with words which would be non-sensical, but could by means of spoonerism be translated into meaningful words, related either to the electricity set or to the sex set. Examples of the former would be *shad bock*, which could be spoonerized into 'bad shock', or *vany molts*, which could be spoonerized into 'many volts'. For the sex set the nonsense words might be *goxi furl* which could be spoonerized into 'foxy girl', or *lood gegs* which could be spoonerized into 'good legs'.

Each target set of words was preceded by three interference words designed to create phonological bias towards the expected spoonerism error. For instance, the target *bine foddy*, expected to be spoonerized into 'fine body', was preceded by the interference words 'fire bobby', 'five bogies', etc., suggesting that the first word should begin with an f, the second with a b. The results were that spoonerism occurred more frequently for the targets whose errors matched the treatment cognitive set than for targets whose errors were unrelated for the treatment. In other words, the sex set yielded more sex errors than electricity errors, the electricity set more electricity errors than sex errors, with the neutral set giving equal numbers of errors of both types. Motley considered this to be evidence for Freud's theory, but of course it is nothing of the kind. It is doubtful if the sets are motivational; they may merely call up different habits and associative connections. But worst of all, Freud's theory implies that the motivational factors are *unconscious repressed infantile wishes*; not even Motley would argue that the emotions produced by being told that you would receive random electric shocks, or by the sight of a provocatively dressed pretty girl, would be unconscious! The experiment is an interesting one, but it is irrelevant to Freudian theories. Much the same must be said about all other similar experiments that have been reported in the psychological literature. They are interesting in themselves, but they do not test Freud's theory in one way or another.

Let us now turn to a typical Freudian example of linguistic slips. The one used here has often been praised, not only by Freud himself but also by his followers and critics, as supremely impressive and an outstanding example of 'the Freudian slip'. It has also been analysed in very great detail by Sebastiano Timpanaro, a well-known Italian linguistic expert, in his very important book, *The Freudian Slip*. Interested readers ought to consult Timpanaro's full account, which is brilliantly written and full of insight; here we can do little but give an idea of the way his argument goes.

Let us begin with the Freudian story itself. Freud strikes up a conversation in a train with a young Austrian Jew who laments the position of inferiority in which Jews are held in Austria–Hungary. In his passionate discussion the young man wishes to quote a line from Virgil, spoken by Dido who has been abandoned by Aeneas and is on the point of suicide: *Exoriare aliquis nostris ex ossibus Ultor*. For reasons to be discussed presently this is difficult to translate, but means something like 'Let someone arise from my bones as an Avenger' or 'Arise from my bones, O Avenger, whoever you may be'. However, the young Jew quotes the line incorrectly, as *Exoriare ex nostris ossibus Ultor*, i.e. he omits *aliquis* and inverts the words *nostris ex*.

Challenged by the young man, who knows him by name and has heard of the psychoanalytic method, Freud attempts to 'explain' this error in psychoanalytic terms. Using Galton's method of free association, Freud says: 'I must ask you to tell me *candidly* and *uncritically*, whatever comes to your mind if you direct your attention to the forgotten word without any definite aim.' Freud then recounts the young Jew's sequence of association to the word *aliquis*, which begins as follows: Requiem – Liquidation – Fluid. Next comes St Simon of Trent, a child martyred in the fifteenth century, whose murder was attributed to the Jews, and whose relics in Trent the young Jew had visited not long before. This is followed by a succession of saints, including San Gennaro (St Januarius) whose clotted blood, kept in a phial in the cathedral at Naples, miraculously liquefies several times a year; the excitement that grips the superstitious people of Naples if this liquifying process is retarded, is expressed in picturesque invective and threats hurled at the saint. Finally we come to the young Jew's anxiety and worry which according to Freud caused the original slip, namely the fact that he is himself obsessed with thoughts about an 'absent flow of liquid', since he is afraid he has made an Italian woman pregnant, when he was with her in Naples; he is expecting to receive confirmation of his worst fears any day. In addition, one of the other saints in the sequence of associations following St Simon is St Augustine, and Augustine and Januarius are both associated with the calendar (August and January), i.e. their names must have a ring of dread for a young man afraid of becoming a father (it is unimportant to Freud that the two months are so far separated, and not even separated by the fatal nine months for that matter). Freud connects the murder of the child saint, Simon of Trent, with the temptation of infanticide: abortion as equivalent to infanticide. He concludes with considerable satisfaction: 'I must leave it to your own judgement to decide whether you can explain all these connections on the assumption that they are matters of chance. I can, however, tell you that every case like this you care to analyse would lead you to "matters of chance" that are just as striking.'

What Freud is suggesting is this. The young Jew is worried that he has got his Italian girlfriend with child, and this repressed worry emerges in the form of the verbal slip when he quotes Virgil. The chain of associations starting with the words involved in the slip leads to ideas involving babies, fluids, months of the calendar, infanticide and other notions which, according to Freud, are clearly associated with the failure of the young man's girlfriend to have her periods. One may wonder why anyone should regard these worries as in any sense 'repressed'; they are certainly not unconscious but very much to the forefront of the young Jew's consciousness, but the hypothesis that free associations from the slip lead to complex or worrying thoughts in his mind can hardly be rejected. But does all this prove, or even support, Freud's general theory?

Before looking critically at Freud's analysis, let us consider how Timpanaro, the linguistic expert, would explain the slip. 'What is the explanation of this double error?' he asks. The explanation lies in the well-known fact of *banalization*, i.e. the fact that words and expressions which are more archaic, high-flown, and unusual stylistically, and therefore further removed from the speaker's cultural-linguistic tradition, are replaced by simpler, more usual ones. The person who is transcribing or reciting tends to replace words or phrases from the literary heritage by forms of expression in more common use. In the line from Virgil quoted by Freud's young travelling companion, the construction is dramatically anomalous. The anomaly consists in the *coexistence* of the second person singular (*Exoriare*) with the indefinite pronoun (*aliquis*): Dido uses the familiar form of address, equivalent to the French *tu*, to the future Avenger, as if she already saw him standing in front of her, while at the same time she expresses with *aliquis* his indeterminate identity. Thus Dido's expression is at one and the same time an augury, as vague as such auguries tend to be ('Come, sooner or later, someone to avenge me'), and an implicit prophecy of the coming of Hannibal, the Avenger whom Virgil certainly had in mind when writing this passage.

Now in German, the language spoken by Freud's young friend, as well as in English, such a construction is virtually untranslatable in the literal sense. Timpanaro points out the difficulty: 'Something has to be sacrificed: either one wishes to bring out the character of the mysteriously indeterminate augury, which means rendering *Exoriare* by the third person singular rather than the second person (" . . . let some avenger arise"); or one prefers to conserve the immediacy and directly evocative power of the second person singular, which means modifying somewhat, if not suppressing outright, the *aliquis* ("Arise, O Avenger, whoever you may be . . .").' Translators of Virgil into German have, as Timpanaro points out, tended to choose one or the other alternative, and it is likely that the young Austrian, for whom Dido's words were no doubt little more than a distant memory from grammar school, was led unconsciously to banalize the text, i.e. to assimilate it with his linguistic knowledge. The unconscious elimination of *aliquis* corresponds to this tendency; the rest of the sentence can easily be translated into German without any need to strain the order of words. This tendency is furthered by the fact that Virgil's original reading is unusual not only from the point of view of German, but also within the context of Latin; this would easily lead a young man who had been moderately well taught to 'restore' the kind of grammatical order which he had learned at school. Timpanaro goes into much greater detail than is possible here, but puts forward a very good case for the phenomenon of banalization as an explanation of this 'Freudian slip'. But what about the chain of associations?

Here Timpanaro makes a very good suggestion. He points out an assumption made by Freud for which there exists no evidence at all. Freud assumes that it is the worry about the mistress's failure to have a period which caused the slip, and that the chain of association proves this. But it is equally possible that *any* chain of associations, starting from any arbitrarily chosen word, would lead to whatever was uppermost in the mind of the 'patient', because his thoughts would always tend to go back to this dominant theme. Timpanaro gives a number of examples to show how easily chains of association to the young Jew's worry and anxiety could be constructed, starting with any word from Virgil's quotation; he points out that these chains of association would be no more grotesque and tortured than those which Freud used as evidence. He also points out that Freud in fact did not allow the patient to freely associate; he subtly guided the chain of associations by comments which led in the direction which the young man finally took. Thus the so-called 'free associations' are in part determined by Freud's suggestive comments, in part by the young Jew's knowledge of Freud and his theories, and above all by his interest in sexual matters. This must to some extent have determined the direction his associations would have taken, starting from any point whatever.

But let us return to the crucial question. If we could have started with any word and by a chain of association arrived at the same conclusion, then clearly the Freudian theory is completely erroneous. This would be a necessary control experiment, and a very obvious one; yet Freud and his followers have never attempted to put the matter to the test. When I was psychologist at the Mill Hill Emergency Hospital during the war, I tried out the experiment on a number of the patients who came to the hospital with neurotic or mild psychotic complaints. I would ask them to recount their dreams, and then get them to freely associate to the various elements of the dream. I found, as Galton and Freud had done, that indeed, following this method, we would soon arrive at certain deep worries and anxieties which troubled the patients, although these would normally be quite conscious, and not indicative of repressed infantile wishes.

However, I then tried the control experiment. Having thus analysed along Freudian lines the dreams of Mr Jones and Mr Smith, I would then ask Mr Jones to freely associate to the elements of the dream recounted by Mr Smith, and vice versa. The result was very straightforward; the chains of association ended in precisely the same 'complexes' when the associations were to the other person's dreams, as they had when the person was associating to his own dreams! In other words, the chain of associations is determined by the 'complex', not by the starting point. This completely invalidates the Freudian theory, and one can only wonder why psychoanalysts have not tried out these very simple experimental methods of checking on alternative hypotheses.

I am not stating here that this alternative hypothesis is necessarily true. I am merely saying that, in conjunction with banalization, it provides a very strong and important alternative hypothesis to the Freudian, and that in science it is absolutely vital for alternative hypotheses to be submitted to an experimental test. Psychoanalysts have no right to claim the correctness of their view as long as no such empirical test has been conducted, in sufficient detail and on a sufficient scale, to give convincing results one way or the other. The existing evidence is certainly not sufficient to 'prove' Freud's theory, and indeed in many ways it would seem to contradict it. Not only are there alternative hypotheses, which have good experimental backing, but in addition it can be seen that in most cases cited by Freud the 'complex' is not at all unconscious or repressed. The young Jew in the story was very much aware of what he was afraid of, and was indeed constantly thinking about it. Thus motivational factors may have been active (if we wish to reject banalization as the simple explanation of the slip), but these are not the Freudian kind. Attentive readers of Freud's book will notice that this is true in almost every case. Therefore, as in the case of

Freud's book on dream interpretation, the examples given by him to strengthen his case in actual fact weaken it.

We can only conclude that the widespread acceptance of Freudian theories of dreaming and slips of tongue and pen is not based on a rational and critical reading of his works; he gives no real evidence for the correctness of his theories, but rather quotes impressive and interesting but irrelevant interpretations which, if we accept his own explanations, contradict his specific theories. The theories are testable, and it is to be hoped that proper large-scale tests will be carried out in due course, comparing Freudian with alternative theories. Until this is done, however, it is impossible to accept Freudian theories as proven, or even likely; the alternative theories have much more support, and are more in line with common sense. To talk about 'Freudian slips' and 'Freudian symbols' is an absurdity; both symbolism and interpretation of slips were current long before Freud formulated his theories, and so was the method of association which he used to support his case. Whatever dreams and slips of tongue and pen may be, they are certainly not the royal road to the unconscious; at best they may at times be motivated by conscious ongoing thoughts which may or may not be charged with strong emotion. For this there is some evidence; for the 'unconscious' and 'repressed' wishes in the Freudian equation there is no evidence at all, not even in Freud's own examples.

In recent years a new view about the *aliquis* slip has been put forward, which throws an entirely fresh light on it. The story begins with the 'revelation' that Freud had a secret affair with his wife's sister, Minna. As is well known, Freud's sexual history was in large part a history of frustration, beginning with his abstinence during his four-year courtship of Martha Bernays, and continuing with the restrictions imposed during the first nine years of their marriage, during which she was usually pregnant, often ill, and thus sexually not available to Freud; all this was followed by years of further abstinence after her sixth and final pregnancy when the couple, while not completely ending their marital sexuality, came very close to it, having decided that abstinence was the only way to avoid having more children.

It has been suggested that Freud's growing interest in sexual sublimation, Oedipal rivalry, and penis envy was largely caused by personal concern; in his dreams at the time he certainly seems to have raged that he was being emasculated, that he had been deprived of sexual rights by his wife, and that his children had turned his sexual organs into relics. It was at this point that Freud took up with his sister-in-law Minna, according to Carl Jung, Freud's one-time friend and later rival. The story was published by an American disciple of Jung's, named John Billinsky, who revealed that when Jung had first visited the Freuds in Vienna, Minna had approached him, saying that she felt guilty about her relationship with Freud. Billinsky quotes Jung as saying: 'From her I learnt that Freud was in love with her and that their relationship was indeed very intimate. It was a shocking discovery to me, and even now I can recall the agony I felt at the time.' Jung's reaction is surprising since he himself, as is well known, was not averse to extra-marital relations.

The story would be of little interest to anyone except prurient gossips, were it not for the fact that in recent years two writers, Oliver Gillie and Peter Swales, argued that the young Jew in the *aliquis* story was not an acquaintance of Freud's, but Freud himself! They suggest that when Freud and Minna travelled together in Italy, in the August of 1900, Minna finally gave in to Freud and became pregnant. The main evidence for their suggestion is in the *aliquis* interpretation. According to Gillie and Swales, it was Freud who was worried that Minna might supply him with a piece of very awkward news; it was no Italian lady whose periods had stopped, but Freud's sister-in-law herself!

What other reasons are given by Swales for this suggestion? First of all, there are the personal similarities between the young man in the anecdote and Freud himself – both were Jewish, both were concerned about the frustration of Jewish needs by anti-Semitism, and both were ambitious. Furthermore, the young man was familiar with some of Freud's psychological publications, even the rather obscure one on unconsciously motivated forgetting. He could quote from the *Aeneid*, very much like Freud, and he also seemed to be familiar with other authors whom we know Freud appreciated. The young man had visited the church at Trent where St Simon's relics were kept, which Freud had recently visited with Minna; and in conversation he even used the metaphor for reincarnation, 'new editions', which Freud himself had already used several times in writing.

If this story were true, then the interpretation of the linguistic slip would assume an altogether different aspect, and the apparently miraculous discovery of the 'hidden' complex in another person would become much more readily intelligible as referring to Freud's own conscious worries. But is the interpretation a likely one? Allan C. Elms has looked at the evidence carefully, and raises many queries which would seem to make Swales's story unlikely. At the end of his account Swales challenged 'those who may still choose to argue what I consider should henceforth be regarded as the *eccentric* point of view, namely that Freud's claim is to be believed. Let them find real evidence that the "young man" existed anywhere other than in Freud's imagination!' Elms took up this challenge and suggested that 'the young man did exist at the right place and at the right time. Swales even mentions his name, without seriously considering that he could have been *the young man*. His name was Alexander Freud, and he was Sigmund's younger brother.' Elms presented much evidence for this point of view, starting with the fact that Alexander was a well-known womanizer, was familiar with Freud's publications (even obscure ones), had recently travelled abroad, had encountered Freud at the right time, and in many other ways fitted the description. Obviously any conclusion reached now, so long after the event, can be based only on speculation. Freud's possible extra-marital affairs cannot be of any great interest in themselves, except in the light they might throw on his theories. Gillie and Swales argue, for instance, that major components of Freud's sexual theories can be understood only with reference to this alleged affair with Minna; Gillie states that 'it is clear that Freud's view of incest was coloured, if not inspired, by sexual relationship with his wife's sister, Minna Bernays', and Swales attributes the entire Oedipus theory to Freud's 'incestuous' affair.

Even if the young man in question was Alexander Freud, and not Sigmund Freud himself, we would still look upon the whole story in rather a different light. Freud would be well acquainted with all the circumstances of Alexander's life, much more so than he would be with a casual acquaintance met in a train, and consequently his thoughts would almost inevitably start from the well-known fact of Alexander's being a womanizer and reach a natural interpretation, namely the possibility of his inamorata being pregnant and missing her periods!

To end this rather odd story, I will quote Elms's final comment, which I think sums up in a very reasonable fashion the whole storm in a tea-cup:

Freud proposed that *unconscious* incestual longings are blocked by unconscious taboos, so that Oedipal feelings are commonly expressed not in real incestuous relationship with a family member but in fantasy, neurosis, and sublimated behaviour. By 1900, Freud was far more interested in incestual fantasies than in the real thing. He may have fantasized about Minna, but no reliable evidence that he ever carried such fantasies into action has yet appeared. Anyway, he didn't need Minna to make him particularly sensitive to issues of incestual desire. He had always had his mother!

Perhaps this episode ought to have been inserted in the first chapter, on 'Freud the Man', but because it is so relevant to the *aliquis* story it seemed appropriate to insert it here. It does illustrate, however, the point made in the first chapter, namely that the events of Freud's personal life are very relevant to his theories, whether these were inspired by an affair with Minna or by his fantasies about his mother.

CHAPTER SIX

The Experimental Study of Freudian Concepts

Sit before fact as a little child, be prepared to give up every
preconceived notion, follow humbly whenever and to whatever
abysses nature leads, or you shall learn nothing.

T. H. HUXLEY

We have seen in preceding chapters that Freud effectively
refused to use two of the major, well-established, scientific
methods for supporting his theoretical contentions. He opposed
the use of clinical trials, with experimental and control groups,
to evaluate the effectiveness of the therapy on which he had
based his claims for the scientific value of his theories. Equally,
he refused to recognize the relevance of detailed, factual observation of children in order to demonstrate his psychosexual
theories of development. What was his attitude to the third
major method which scientists use to support their theories,
namely the experimental approach? Here the experimenter
varies one condition thought to be relevant to the phenomenon
in question, and observes the effect of this on the phenomenon
itself; that is, he manipulates the independent variable and
studies its influence on the dependent variable.

Freud's attitude to this, probably the most decisive and
convincing scientific method, is revealed in his famous postcard
to Rosenzweig, dated 1934, which is a reply to the account
Rosenzweig sent him of his attempts to study repression
experimentally. Freud stated: 'I cannot put much value on these
confirmations because the wealth of reliable observations on

which these assertions rest make them independent of experimental verification.' He added graciously: 'Still, it can do no harm.' Nothing could demonstrate more clearly the non-scientific character of Freud's thinking; in his view, experiments were not needed to confirm his hypotheses, nor could they influence them. No other discipline claiming attention has so clearly and decisively cut itself off from experimental testing of its theories – even astrology and phrenology make claims which are empirically testable, and have been tested, albeit unsuccessfully.

Clearly there are difficulties in performing experiments where human subjects are concerned, and where the theories deal with rather intangible phenomena. Ethical considerations play a prominent part; we cannot produce strong emotions in our laboratory subjects, because to do so would clearly not be permissible. Altogether, Freudian theories deal largely with emotions, and these are difficult to produce artificially. The laboratory setting makes most subjects uneasy, and this often interferes with what the experimenter hopes would be normal reactions to experimental stimuli. Experiments on humans are not impossible, but they are difficult, and require a deal of ingenuity and persistence. A good deal of work has been done along such lines, despite Freud's disclaimer, and an admirable account of these studies is given in Paul Kline's book, *Fact and Fantasy in Freudian Theory*. H. J. Eysenck and G. D. Wilson, in their book *The Experimental Study of Freudian Theories*, have concentrated on what are supposed to be the experiments most supportive of Freudian theories, pointing out the methodological and statistical fallacies involved, and the neglect of alternative theories to explain the results, a failure which is characteristic of much of this literature. In this chapter we can only glance at some of the more interesting and memorable research that has been done, mainly to indicate the ways in which psychologists have tried to get round the difficulties inherent in the experimental approach.

Some of the procedures used by psychologists and psychoanalysts are very curious indeed, and in fact might not be regarded as experimental in a meaningful sense at all. Consider, for instance, the 'experiments' done by G. S. Blum using the so-called 'Blacky pictures'. These pictures are a set of twelve cartoons portraying a family of dogs in situations which are peculiarly relevant to psychoanalytic theory. The family consists of four dogs: the parents, Blacky (who can be male or female, depending on the sex of the subject taking the test), and Tippy, a sibling of Blacky. The subjects are required to tell a little story about what they think is going on in each picture, and how each of the characters is feeling. The experimenter then scores this spontaneous story for the presence or absence of disturbances in the areas concerned. In addition, the subject is asked several questions about the cartoons, and is required to sort the pictures into those liked and those disliked, and from these groups to choose the one most liked and the one most disliked. These two choices are supposed to be symptomatic of disturbances in the relevant areas. As an example of this kind of interpretation, one of the cartoons shows a male Blacky watching his parents making love; this is supposed to be indicative of Oedipal intensity. Blacky licking his genitals is supposed to be indicative of masturbation guilt; Blacky watching the parents fondle Tippy, sibling rivalry; and so on. Another picture shows Blacky watching Tippy, who is apparently about to have her tail cut off; this is supposed to be indicative of castration anxiety in males or penis envy in females!

Kline has reviewed a large number of studies done with these pictures, and concludes that 'most of the studies were found not to relate with any decision to the theory. Only two studies seem to be truly relevant . . . one of these supported the theory (the anal character), the other failed to do so (the oral character).' In these two studies, the hypothesis tested was Freud's notion that children pass through a variety of stages (anal, oral, genital) and may become fixed at any of these stages, developing an appropriate temperament. The anal character is supposed to be constituted of the traits of parsimony, orderliness and obstinacy, being derived from repressed anal eroticism. The oral character, on the other hand, is characterized by impatience, hostility, talkativeness and generosity. It appears that persons having the so-called anal character show the appropriate reaction to the relevant Blacky pictures, but those having the so-called oral character fail to show the correct reaction to the pictures relevant to the oral character. At best, then, we would seem to have an outcome that is quite indecisive, but are there not alternative explanations of the apparently positive result? As has been remarked, rather coarsely, the 'anal' Blacky pictures are a rough index of attitudes to shitting dogs, and one would have expected the reaction of the rather introverted type of person (who behaviourally resembles the so-called anal type) to differ from that of the extraverted type. Thus there is a clear-cut alternative explanation, not considered by those who carry out these tests.

In any case, the sum of positive outcomes is hardly large enough to justify any great confidence in the value of the technique, or the alleged verification of Freudian hypotheses. Other so-called 'projective' techniques, i.e. studies in which pictures or ink-blots are shown to the subject, and he has to make up stories about them, thus allegedly 'projecting' his ideas on to the figures, have also been used to study the Oedipus and castration complexes. Kline has reviewed them all, and finds them quite inconclusive, with the possible exception of one study in which kibbutz and non-kibbutz Israeli boys were compared, using the Blacky pictures. The hypotheses were that when kibbutz-reared children were compared with family-reared children, fewer kibbutz children would exhibit Oedipal intensity, and family children would show greater identification with the father. These hypotheses were supported, on quite small samples, but do the results really support Freudian theory? In the kibbutz, children are reared by a nurse, live communally, and see their parents for only a short time during the day (usually in the evening). Such a regime would seem to give rise to the observed differences – the less you see your parents, the smaller will be the emotional attachment to them. This does not seem to have much to do with the Oedipus complex; there is a perfectly natural interpretation on common-sense grounds. Thus work with the Blacky pictures, perhaps the most widely cited example of empirical studies supporting Freudian theories, will be seen to have very little veridical value as far as these theories are concerned. The deductions made are of doubtful value, the interpretations are frequently found to be unreliable, and responses are known to vary from one occasion to another. Worst of all, such allegedly positive results as are found can usually be interpreted more readily in common-sense terms which do not have recourse to Freudian hypotheses at all. Kline devotes many pages to a discussion of the various findings of authors using the Blacky pictures, and comes, on the whole, to a similarly pessimistic conclusion.

Freud's psychosexual theory, which is of central importance in his work, implies three basic empirical propositions. The first is that certain adult personality syndromes exist and can be measured and demonstrated, and the second, that these syndromes are related to infant-rearing procedures. The third implication, namely that pregenital eroticism may be observed in infants, has already been discussed and will not be dealt with here. Freud essentially postulates three phases leading to a fourth and final phase. As he says: 'Sexual life does not begin only at puberty but starts with clear manifestations soon after birth . . . sexual life comprises the function of obtaining pleasure from zones of the body – a function which is subsequently brought into the service of that of reproduction.' This sexual drive is manifested through the mouth during the first year of the infant's life; this is the so-called *oral phase*. This is followed by the *anal phase*, when around the third year of life the erotogenic zone of the anus becomes central. Third, at around the age of four, comes the *phallic phase*. The final phase of sexual organization is the *genital phase*, which is established after puberty, when all the previous phases are organized and subordinated to the adult sexual aim of pleasure in the reproductive function.

Freud maintains that this infantile sexuality is critical in the personality development of the individual, and its repression produces certain adult personality traits, such as the triad of parsimony, orderliness and obstinacy, which is supposed to be derived from repressed anal eroticism. As Freud says: 'The permanent character traits are either unchanging perpetuations of the original impulse, sublimations of them or reaction-formations against them.' Thus he regards kissing as the perpetuation of oral eroticism, orderliness as a reaction-formation against anal eroticism, and parsimony as a sublimation of anal eroticism. Differential upbringing of the child, such as duration and nature of the feeding and weaning process, is responsible for producing the final effect seen as personality traits in the adult. What of the evidence? It may be said that there is some observational evidence that the traits Freud believed went together to form these various constellations do in fact go together. This is a necessary but not a sufficient condition for accepting his scheme. As an example, let us take oral pessimism as opposed to oral optimism. This was investigated by Frieda Goldman-Eisler who selected 19 traits which had been mentioned by psychoanalytic writers as having an oral connotation; namely, optimism, pessimism, exocathexis (i.e. emotional relations to external things and events), endocathexis (similar relations to internal events), nurturance, passivity, sociability, aloofness, oral aggression, autonomy, aggression, guilt, dependence, ambition, impulsion, deliberation, change, conservatism, and unattainability. These traits were rated on 115 adult subjects, and their interrelations established. What emerged was a clear-cut dimension, ranging from the oral optimistic pole (exocathexis, optimism, nurturance, ambition, change) to the oral pessimistic pole (aloofness, endocathexis, pessimism, dependence, passivity). Apparently, then, the Freudian hypothesis has been upheld.

However, a closer inspection of the detailed results and the actual items used for the rating makes it quite clear that the dimension labelled by Goldman-Eisler 'oral optimism versus oral pessimism' is in fact very similar, or even identical, to a well-known dimension of personality, namely extraversion–introversion. Exocathexis and endocathexis are simply Greek translations of the terms 'extraversion' and 'introversion'; extraverts are known to be optimistic, introverts pessimistic; it has been well established that extraverts seek for change, while introverts are passive and aloof; and so on. Indeed, these observations go back to Hippocrates and the Ancient Greeks, so it is hardly surprising that Freud noted the same trait relationships which had been pointed out frequently, by philosophers and by psychologists, for hundreds of years. Consequently it may be said that this relationship is quite irrelevant as an assessment of the veridical nature of Freudian theory.

What is important, of course, is Freud's causal hypothesis,

relating these trait constellations to early events in the child's history. On *a priori* grounds this is an unlikely postulate, because in the first place there is now sound evidence that personality traits of this type are very strongly based on genetic foundations; in other words, they are largely inherited rather than acquired. This immediately reduces to a considerable extent the importance of environmental manipulation.

Possibly even more important, however, is the distinction made by modern behavioural geneticists who speak of within-family and between-family environmental determinants. When we talk about between-family environmental determinants, we refer to such things as different socio-economic status, different educational facilities, different intellectual quality of the home, different paternal and maternal values, habits and upbringing practices, etc.; in other words, we are looking at those environmental features which distinguish one family from another.

Within-family environmental determinants would relate to factors which differentially affect children within the same family. An example would be one child's encountering a particularly good teacher, while his or her siblings were rather less lucky. Or a child might contract a serious disease, while the other children in the family escaped. Now, it has been clearly demonstrated in several large-scale studies in the United States, the United Kingdom and Scandinavia, that the environmental determinants of personality which are left over when the genetic determinants have been taken care of are within-family, and not between-family, factors – in other words, there is no evidence for the type of environmental determinant that Freud posits! For these reasons alone we would not expect to find any positive evidence for the determination of the observed personality clusters by the early history of the feeding, weaning, toilet-training, etc., of the child.

On the whole, the evidence fails to provide any valid proof on this point. Quite small relationships are occasionally found (not always in the expected direction), but where these occur there is usually an alternative explanation much more securely supported than the Freudian. Thus Frieda Goldman-Eisler obtained slight correlations between early weaning and oral pessimism, and interpreted this in Freudian terms. But considering the frequently demonstrated importance of genetic factors, is it not equally likely that introverted, passive and aloof mothers would have introverted, passive and aloof children, and that such mothers would wean their children earlier than optimistic, extraverted mothers? Once again, therefore, we have a case in which an environmental explanation of the correlation between parent and child is preferred when there is no evidence that enables us to discount the genetic alternative.

It should also be noted that there are many features in the Goldman-Eisler study which go directly counter to Freudian prediction. Thus, as she notes, 'the data do not confirm the psychoanalytic contention that all frustration, impatience and oral aggression are inseparable *or even related*!' In her statistical analysis, she found it necessary to postulate two factors to explain all the interrelations between the traits, rather than the one that Freudian theory would postulate. Kline, in the first edition of his book, summarizing findings relating to psycho-sexual personality syndromes, was forced to the following conclusion: 'From the considerable number of studies attempt-ing to relate infant-rearing procedures to personality develop-ment only two studies give even slight support to the Freudian theory.' Here he refers to the Goldman-Eisler study just dis-cussed, and to one of his own, in which he used the Blacky pictures. Kline is considerably more sophisticated than most authors in this field, and in particular he is at pains to show that psychoanalytic theory in this area is more complex than many researchers have supposed. He points out that 'in addition to the environmental variable (pot-training) there is the *constitu-tional* variable (the anal stamp) . . . only when severe training is applied to a child of the anal stamp will the anal character develop'. In other words, he realizes that genetic factors play an important part, and interact with environmental variables, such as potty-training, to produce (if indeed they do produce!) the anal character. What Kline found was that high scores on his scale of obsessionality and other similar questionnaires corre-lated significantly with the degree of disturbance shown by students confronted with the cartoon of a small black dog defecating between the kennels of its parents (relative to their response to a variety of other Blacky cartoons). The correlation with obsessionality held positive for responses to the critical Blacky picture whether they were classified as 'anal expulsive' (revenge or aggression expressed against the parents) or 'anal retentive' (mention of concealment from parents of the need for cleanliness).

It is difficult to see how these correlations enable him to claim that 'the study supports the Freudian hypotheses concerning the aetiology of obsessional traits and symptoms'. In the paper he admits that since psychoanalytic theory specifically hypothesizes that the anal character results from fixation at the *retentive* phase, 'strictly, perhaps, there should be a *negative* correlation with the expulsive score'; the fact that the correlation is positive does not seem to worry him too much, although normally in science one would feel that to get results which were exactly the opposite of what one had predicted would not enable one to claim that the results supported the hypothesis!

Kline also claimed that his results must support Freud's theories because 'there is no logical reason to link responses to a picture of a defecating dog with obsessional traits'. But looking at his questionnaires we find that they contain items relating to concern with cleanliness, e.g. 'When eating out, do you wonder what the kitchens are like?' and 'Do you regard the keeping of household dogs as unhygienic?' Is it really unreasonable to expect answers to these questions to relate to responses to a picture of a defecating dog? Concern with hygiene, cleanliness, tidiness and self-control (aptitudes to these qualities are inevitably tapped by this particular Blacky picture) are clearly central to the obsessional personality syndrome as defined by Kline's questionnaire, and because of this content overlap no Freudian explanation is necessary to account for his results.

Last but not least, Kline throughout assumes that the picture of Blacky defecating is a measure of 'anal eroticism', but while we might agree that the picture is somehow related to the 'anal' part of the phrase, it is difficult to see any justification for assuming that it is also 'erotic'. In English, this word refers to love (particularly of a sexual kind); exactly what it means to Freud is not made clear in Kline's paper, and he does not appear to feel any responsibility for specifying in what way the Blacky picture should be regarded as an 'objective measure of anal eroticism'. Thus, neither the Goldman-Eisler nor the Kline study give us any reason to suspect that there is any aetiological significance to the factors supposed by Freud critically to determine personality.

There are other sources of evidence which apparently support the view that early environmental events in the history of the child determine later character development, in line with Freudian hypotheses. Some of the most prominent of these will be looked at later when we deal with the influence of Freud on anthropology, and the evidence found in cultures other than our own. We will see there that the evidence is equally tenuous, and entirely fails to support the psychoanalytic view.

Consider now what are more properly called experimental studies, being directed to the problem of repression. According to Freud, 'the essence of repression lies simply in the function of rejecting and keeping something out of consciousness'. Repression is a kind of defence mechanism, to protect the individual from unwelcome emotional experiences. There are several studies illustrating the experimental approach to this concept. In one of these, two stories of a dream theme were used, one an Oedipal dream sequence, the other a similar but non-Oedipal sequence. Subjects were read either one story or the other, and afterwards were required to recall the stories. Recall for the Oedipal theme was significantly worse, as was predicted on the basis of Freud's theory.

In another study, subjects were given a word association test using 100 words, in which they were required to say a word in response to the stimulus word presented by the experimenter; during this test various physiological measures and reaction time measures were taken. The experimenter then showed each subject 10 words with association disturbances, such as long reaction times, physiological indices of emotion, etc., and 10 without. Each subject then had to learn to say a particular word in response to a picture. Following this, different groups of subjects were brought back after various time intervals (15 minutes, 2 days, 4 days, 7 days) and required to remember as many of the learned words as possible in 5 minutes; they then had to relearn the paired associate task.

There were two findings. Emotive words took significantly

more trials to learn than neutral words, and there was no difference in retention of disturbing and neutral words. The first of these conclusions was thought to support the Freudian theory, but the second failed to do so. However, there was a far greater variety of associations to disturbing words, and since this factor of the number of associations to neutral and disturbing words was not controlled, the allegedly positive results of the study cannot be used to support the Freudian concept of repression.

There are other studies which demonstrate, using better experimental techniques, that the forgetting of associations is related to the emotionality of the stimuli, and Kline concludes that 'this, therefore, is a clear example of Freudian repression'. Unfortunately there are alternative hypotheses to account for such facts. It has been demonstrated experimentally that learning passes through two stages. The first of these, short-term memory, consists of reverberating circuits in the cortex which can hold information only for a short period of time. To become readily available later on, information has to be transferred to the long-term memory, which consists of chemical engrams in the cells. This transfer process is called consolidation, and is facilitated by cortical arousal, i.e. by the degree to which the brain is energized. There is evidence to show that not only does this process of consolidation take time, but that while the material is being consolidated, it is not available for retrieval, i.e. the person cannot recollect it. This is the so-called theory of 'action decrement', and it causes considerable difficulties in interpreting such findings as those mentioned above. Emotion-producing words are known to increase cortical arousal, and hence produce the action decrement during consolidation. This is an alternative theory to the Freudian, not considered by the authors who wrote up the experiments discussed above; it has a much firmer experimental background than the Freudian, and unless it can be ruled out experimentally, we must conclude that the experiments on repression do not give us any kind of clear-cut answer to the question. A much more careful design of the experiment would be needed to rule out an interpretation in terms of the action decrement.

Indeed, what emerges again and again from examination of

the empirical and experimental literature is that authors practically always fail to look at their studies and results from the point of view of psychological theory, to see whether they could have been predicted as well, or better, in terms well known to academic psychologists, rather than in Freudian terms. We have already observed this attitude in the case of little Hans, where even though the facts of the situation can be very easily explained in terms of conditioning theory, psychoanalysts have never made any attempt to do this, or to design empirical tests which would differentiate between these two types of theory. The design of experiments to decide between two such theories is regarded as an exceptionally useful and valuable occupation for the scientist, and although clear-cut answers and crucial experiments are difficult to come by, to interpret results in terms of one theory alone, completely disregarding possible alternatives is certainly not in the best tradition of scientific research.

Let us now look at some studies* recognized as being especially well designed and decisive in their conclusions, with particular reference to possible alternative explanations. The first study to be considered is one on thumb-sucking. A study was made of the relationship between early-feeding experiences in infancy and thumb-sucking in children, testing various Freudian hypotheses relating thumb-sucking to orality. The first thing to note is that two of the central hypotheses failed to obtain confirmation. The amount of breast-feeding that a child had been given did not predict either the duration or severity of thumb-sucking in later childhood, nor was there any significant relationship between the age of weaning to the cup and the duration or intensity of thumb-sucking. These findings are decisively anti-Freudian. Two findings which might be interpreted in Freudian terms were the following: late-weaned children showed a more severe reaction to weaning than early-weaned children, and children who had short average feeding times, whether on bottle or breast, showed greater severity and persistence of thumb-sucking. Can these findings really be used to support Freudian theories?

Note first of all that the children were not assigned at random

* Details are given in the books by Eysenck and Wilson and by Kline (see Bibliography).

to an early-weaning group, as opposed to a late-weaning one. Consequently we are not able to rule out the possibility of genetic links between the behaviour of the parents and the behaviour of their children. Insufficient or over-indulgent feeding on the mother's part might reflect a personality characteristic in her which is manifested in the child as severe or prolonged thumb-sucking (e.g. general emotionality and neuroticism). Another possibility is that the behaviour of the infants might have influenced the way in which they were treated by their parents. For example, the finding that late-weaned children showed a more severe reaction to weaning might have arisen because certain children were allowed to remain on the bottle or the breast longer than they would otherwise have been *because they reacted strongly against weaning*. Similarly, one might well question whether a short feeding time necessarily implies 'inadequate gratification' as the author supposes. Are we to believe that the short-feed mother actually snatched the bottle away from the child before it was finished? It is more likely that she withdrew it following cues from the child indicating that it had had enough (e.g. vomiting). Most mothers are aware that infants vary enormously, both in the rate at which they extract milk from the bottle or breast, and in the amount they require before reaching satiation. It seems probable, then, that feeding time was determined as much by the child as by the mother.

Concerning the relationship between shortness of feeding time and amount of thumb-sucking in later childhood, which is really the only positive finding with any bearing on the Freudian theory of oral eroticism, we might again have recourse to the genetic connection between the mother's behaviour and that of the child, or we might once more suggest that the short feeding times have been determined by the child rather than the mother. If we were to postulate a generalized 'sucking drive' which varies from one child to another independently of the amount of food required for appetite satisfaction, then the infant who sucks very hard on the breast or bottle (thus showing a short feeding time because gratification point is reached more quickly) would also tend to be the child who shows more persistent and severe thumb-sucking. This would be an alternative genetic theory which fits in with the actual findings.

There is another possible explanation. All the data in question were obtained from retrospective reports by the mothers, and even though a limit of six months was placed on the time that was permitted to elapse between the events concerned and the interview in which they were recorded, we must nevertheless allow for some distortion due to the effects of motivation on memory. If we are to assume a 'social desirability' factor which leads some mothers to want to impress the doctor more than others, then the mother who reports that her child does little thumb-sucking is also likely to be the mother who reports that she spent a great deal of time patiently feeding her infant! Thus we have a plethora of alternative hypotheses, none of which are considered by the author of the report, but all of which are probably more likely than the Freudian theory which he did consider.

One of the areas in which psychoanalysis has been particularly important has been that of psychosomatic disorders, i.e. certain diseases which are supposed to be precipitated by mental events, related to infant sexuality, Oedipus and other complexes, etc. Asthma is one such disease, and much of the recent emphasis on the psychological genesis of asthma has been concerned with the view that the significant psychodynamic process in the asthmatic patient is the unconscious fear of the loss of the mother, and that the asthmatic attack is equivalent to a repressed cry. Another aetiological approach to asthma has been the consideration of the role of odours, and one pair of investigators tried to test the hypothesis that asthmatic attacks represent 'a means of physiologically defending against the activation by odours of unresolved childhood conflicts'. The authors used two approaches: first, they gathered information about the types of odours that provoked attacks in asthmatics, and were able to classify 74 per cent of these as 'anal derivative'; second, they recorded free associations of asthmatics and healthy controls to a variety of odours, and found that the asthmatics showed more 'blocking of associations' than the controls did. All this is supposed to support a psychodynamic theory postulating some form of anal aetiology of asthma. It is difficult to see how the facts bear this out. The smells said by asthmatics to be implicated in their attacks were classified three ways: those connected with *food* (bacon, onion and garlic), those connected with *romance* (perfume, spring, flowers) and those concerned with *cleanliness–uncleanliness* (including dirty and nasty smells, disinfectant, sulphur, smoke, paint, horses, etc.). Having offered this classification, the authors suddenly make a 'logical' leap that ensures support for psychoanalytic theory: these three groups of odours are called 'oral', 'genital' and 'anal' respectively, and since 74 per cent of them fall into the latter category the entire Freudian theory about the significance of toilet-training experiences in childhood, etc., is held to be supported! It does not seem to have occurred to the authors that their 'anal' category was considerably broader than the other two categories combined, in terms of the odours encompassed, or that the 74 per cent of smells falling into this category have dirty associations and are much more *unpleasant* than food odours and perfumes to the vast majority of non-asthmatic people. Only 2 out of 45 in this category were anal in the literal sense (i.e. the smell of faeces); the connection of the anus with smells of smoke, bleach, paint, camphor, etc., seems rather tenuous.

All that seems to have been demonstrated, in fact, is that the odours which evoke asthmatic attacks tend to be those which most healthy people would regard as unpleasant! On evolutionary grounds alone we might have expected that these smells would produce a biological aversion reaction, and since the symptoms of asthma involve a constriction of air passages it is not unreasonable to interpret them as representing an attempt to avoid taking in smells that are particularly offensive to the individual. It is difficult to see what this finding has to do with either the anus or 'unresolved childhood conflicts'; it seems to fit the physiological theory of asthmatic hypersensitivity quite well, but is quite irrelevant to the Freudian theory.

The greater number of 'blocked associations' should, according to Freudian theory, have occurred only to anal odours, but actually the difference between the asthmatic and control groups was found in all three categories of smells. And even if we are willing to accept the blocking of associations as a valid measure of emotionality, it is not self-evident that odours, in so far as they are implicated in the onset of asthmatic attacks, will tend to be more threatening to asthmatics than to controls, and hence to arouse greater emotion? After all, the symptoms of asthma are quite unpleasant; why should we be surprised that patients show signs of emotionality when exposed to stimuli that are likely to precipitate an attack?

In another study the hypothesis was tested that oral passive wishes play an important role in causing peptic ulcers. The differentiation here is between food characteristics which afford differential opportunity for oral passive (sucking), as opposed to oral aggressive (biting), gratification. According to the theory, we might expect oral passive persons to prefer the former of each of the following food characteristics, and oral aggressive persons to prefer the latter: soft versus hard, liquid versus solid, sweet versus bitter, sour versus salty, wet versus dry, bland versus seasoned, thick versus thin, rich versus light. According to psychoanalytic theory, the frustration of intense cravings for oral passive gratification plays a significant aetiological role in the formation of peptic ulcers. The authors of the study compared 38 peptic ulcer patients with 62 non-ulcer gastro-intestinal patients on a food preference questionnaire, and found that the former group obtained a higher 'oral passive' score, i.e. they chose soft, liquid, sweet, sour, wet, bland, thick and rich food rather than their opposites. Do these results support the psychoanalytic hypothesis? The most obvious possibility seems to be that ulcer patients prefer the 'passive' foods because they are easier to digest and irritate the stomach less than the 'aggressive' foods. No such consideration would seem to play a part in the control group, where the diagnoses included suggest that the disorders suffered by many of the subjects could be classified as acute or traumatic, compared to ulcers which are characteristically chronic and constitutional. Disorders such as hiatus hernia, cancer, and car accident injuries are unlikely to have troubled patients over such long periods of time that they would have led to a modification of food preferences, whereas ulcers tend to develop slowly over long periods of time before necessitating surgery – time enough, perhaps, for adaptive changes in food selection to occur either spontaneously or on medical advice.

What this study has actually demonstrated is a relationship

between ulcers and food preferences. This tells us little about the direction of cause and effect. Perhaps the food preferences are directly implicated in the aetiology of ulcers, and our biochemical constitution is partly influenced by the chemicals that we take into our body in the form of food. There are many other alternative hypotheses, such as that both ulcers and food preferences reflect some third variable, perhaps emotional instability, or anxiety. The study clearly leaves the door wide open to alternative interpretations.

As the last example of the empirical study of psychosomatic disease processes of a psychodynamic kind, consider the following. In 1905, Freud had described the case of Dora, and in doing so related appendicitis to birth fantasies. At the age of seventeen this patient suffered a sudden attack of appendicitis; she was analysed by Freud a year later. He discovered then that the earlier illness occurred nine months after an episode in which she received improper proposals from a married man. She had been caring for this man's children (by his real wife) and had secret hopes that he would marry her. Freud's conclusion was that 'her supposed attack of appendicitis had thus enabled the patient . . . to realize the fantasy of childbirth'. Other psychoanalysts, such as Stoddart and Groddeck, generalized this idea, and several other investigators have taken it up. Yizhar Eylon carried out a detailed investigation to test the hypothesis that 'some events in real life give rise to birth fantasies which initiate acute pain in the right iliac fossa, leading to the diagnosis of acute appendicitis and appendectomy'. He compared a group of appendectomy patients with a matched group of other surgical cases, and found a significantly greater number of 'birth events' in the recent histories of the experimental group. These 'birth events' included actual births, the pregnancies of close relatives, and weddings attended by the patient herself. Can this be counted as evidence for the Freudian hypothesis? The answer is no.

Implicit in the Freudian hypothesis is the expectation that 'the proportion of normal appendices will be higher in appendectomies following birth events than in appendectomies not following birth events'; i.e. post-operative pathological examination of the appendices after removal should reveal a connection between birth events and *pseudo-appendicitis* rather than genuine appendicitis. Eylon's results do not support this hypothesis.

Another hypothesis tested by Eylon which could be regarded as fairly critical to Freudian theory is that the association between birth events and appendicitis should be particularly strong for *young* females since they are presumably more susceptible to birth fantasies than older females. In this case the results were in the opposite direction to the prediction. All that is left, therefore, is a rather peripheral positive result, namely a general association between appendectomies and birth events. Even here, it is worth noting that with the criteria that Eylon initially set for defining birth events, no significant connection with appendectomy was detected. It was only by restricting the 'five psychologically closest people' to relatives of the patient, and resetting the time limit from one month to six months before or after the operation, that it was possible to obtain a significant difference in the direction created by the hypothesis. Such manipulation of data is very much frowned upon by scientists, because it gives undue latitude to the unearthing of accidental relations that have no statistical significance, and are not replicable. These and many other reasons make it impossible to accept Eylon's results as in any real sense supporting the psychodynamic hypothesis.

It will be clear to any experimental psychologist, and indeed to any scientist, that the tenuous chain of deduction used in the majority of these studies, the curious and clearly unreliable means of measurement employed (such as the Blacky pictures), and the failure to look at alternative hypotheses, would disqualify most of these studies right from the beginning as having any evidential value in this field. It would be difficult, for instance, to find a single study that paid the slightest attention to the influence of genetic factors, in spite of their recognized importance in the field of personality, mental abnormality and neurosis. Such a complete disregard of scientific propriety, both in the setting up of the experiment and in the interpretation of the results, does not suggest a serious effort to find the truth. In almost every case where a positive relationship has been claimed by the investigator, a genetic hypothesis is as likely to explain the observed events as is a psychodynamic one, and in view of the fact that we know far more about the genetics of personality development than we do about any other cause, such a neglect of an obvious causal factor is inexplicable and inexcusable.

Clearly genetic factors are not the only ones disregarded in explaining the outcome of such experiments as those detailed in Kline's book, or that by Eysenck and Wilson. A great deal is known, for instance, about the relationship between memory and learning, on the one hand, and emotion and cortical arousal, on the other. These facts have been securely established in thousands of laboratory studies, and provide sufficient explanation of most of the findings interpreted by their authors as supportive of Freudian ideas. Yet it is rare to find any of the authors in question even alluding to these well-established facts and theories in experimental psychology as alternative explanations; they interpret their results in Freudian terms, completely disregarding much better established alternative principles. This, again, is not the way science should be practised, and it does not make it any easier to take seriously the efforts of experimentalists who study Freudian concepts.

Critics might grumble that we talk about these studies as being 'experimental', when in fact most of the reported investigations of Freudian theories are at best empirical, with very little manipulation of the independent variable. Technically, such an objection would probably be correct in most cases, but is, of course, purely semantic. Astronomers talk about an 'experiment' when they observe the bending of light rays from a distant star by the gravitational field of the sun during an eclipse; obviously the astronomer has not manipulated the moon and placed it in front of the sun! From the point of view of a popular exposition, these studies resemble the true experiment more closely than do the very simple observational notes made by Freud and his followers during sessions on the couch. Perhaps 'empirical' would be a better term than 'experimental', but for the sake of convenience I have used the latter term.

My interpretation of the evidence presented, for example, in Kline's book is that there is no support for any specifically Freudian hypotheses. This would seem to contradict Kline's own conclusion, to the effect that 'any blanket rejection' of

Freudian theory as a whole 'simply flies in the face of the evidence'. There are two points to be made here. The first of these is that Kline fails to look for alternative explanations of the findings he discusses; this point has been made above, and we will not go into it again. The second point, however, may require more detailed discussion. It is simply that, as pointed out before, what is true in Freud is not new, and what is new is not true. There is indeed much that is true in what Freud has to say, but it is not new, and therefore not essentially Freudian. As we have seen in the last chapter, it is, of course, true that dreams are related to the waking concerns of the dreamer, and that they are expressed in symbolic form; but it would not be correct to say that these are Freudian notions – they have been held quite widely for some two thousand years. We have already seen that the notion of 'the unconscious' is one which has been held by philosophers and psychologists for many centuries, and to credit Freud with the discovery of the unconscious is absurd. We must be very careful, when labelling a particular concept or notion 'Freudian', to consider historical developments and to note that similar ideas may have been expressed by others before Freud; he should be credited only with what is truly new.

As an example of the mixture of new and true in Freud, consider his concepts of the id, the ego and the super-ego, the three parts into which, according to him, the mental apparatus is divided. Freud says: 'To the oldest of these mental provinces or agencies we give the name of id. It contains everything that is inherited, that is present at birth, that is fixed in the constitution – above all therefore the instincts.' The id obeys what Freud calls the pleasure principle, and its mental processes are subject to no laws of logic, and are unconscious.

'The ego was developed out of the cortical layer of the id, which, being adapted for the reception and exclusion of stimuli, is in direct contact with the external world.' Its function is to calculate the consequences of any proposed behaviour, and to decide whether actions leading to the satisfaction of the id should be carried out or postponed, or whether the demands of the pleasure principle should be suppressed altogether. The ego is the representative of the reality principle, and some of its activities are conscious, some preconscious and others unconscious.

The super-ego, regarded by Freud as the heir of the Oedipus complex, internalizes the teachings and punishments of the parents, and continues to carry on their functions. 'It observes the ego, gives it orders, corrects it and threatens it with punishment exactly like the parents whose place it has taken.' The notion of the super-ego is very similar to that of the conscience in Christian thinking. As Freud puts it: 'The long period of childhood . . . leaves behind it a precipitate which forms within the ego a special agency in which the parental influence is prolonged. It has received the name of super-ego.'

Clearly the ego has a difficult role, having to satisfy the instinctual demands of the id, and the moral dictates of the super-ego. This general theory has received much acclaim, and is, in part, in line with common sense, and with psychological thinking since the days of Plato. Indeed, a very similar distinction is made by Plato in his famous fable of two horses pulling a chariot, with the driver trying to control them. The driver is the ego; the bad, wilful and impulsive horse is the id, and the good horse is the super-ego. Both Plato and Freud are clearly using the mechanism of a fable to illustrate a perfectly sensible and well-known feature of human behaviour. We are biosocial animals, with biology dictating certain instinctual needs for food, drink, sex and so forth, but our actions are also controlled by social demands incorporated in rules and laws, and transmitted by parents, teachers and others. The individual person is driven and guided by these two sets of directive impulses, and has to mediate between them. All this is true, and being true might seem to give credence to the Freudian theory. But note that nothing in this is new; the specifically Freudian notions, such as that the super-ego is the heir of the Oedipus complex, are not only unlikely but completely unproven. It is much more likely that Pavlovian conditioning mediates the demands of the outer world (parents, teachers, peers, magistrates, priests), through rewards and punishments, i.e. through the formation of conditioned responses. Again, there is never any mention in the psychoanalytic literature of such alternative theories, but as I have tried to show in my book on *Crime and*

Personality, they have been developed through laboratory studies and have found much support.

Freud had an enviable gift of language, and the terms he uses, such as pleasure principle and reality principle, make his version of an old story seem new and appealing to the uninitiated. It is when we look at the novelty of his teaching that we begin to have doubts; the general view is probably true, but that which is specifically Freudian in it is almost certainly false. In this it resembles much of the Freudian opus.

Much empirical work done in relation to Freudian hypotheses has not been examined in this chapter, such as the formation of dreams and their interpretation, psychophysiology of everyday life, etc. Some of these are dealt with in separate chapters, where I reach the same conclusions as are drawn here. Perhaps I may end this chapter with a quotation from T. H. Huxley, who bemoaned 'the great tragedy of science – the slaying of a beautiful theory by an ugly fact'. Whether Freud's theory is a beautiful one may be doubted; he certainly tried to protect it from being slain by ugly facts by phrasing it in such a way that critical experiments are very difficult to carry out. Nevertheless, over eighty years after the original publication of Freudian theories, there still is no sign that they can be supported by adequate experimental evidence, or by clinical studies, statistical investigations or observational methods. This does not prove them to be wrong – it is equally difficult to prove a theory wrong as it is to prove it right – but it should make us at least doubtful about their evidential value, and their meaningfulness as scientific theory. As another great scientist, Michael Faraday, once said: 'They reason theoretically, without demonstration experimentally, and errors are the result.' These words might well be carved on the grave of psychoanalysis as a scientific doctrine.

CHAPTER SEVEN

Psycho-Babble and Pseudo-History

> It takes a great deal of history
> to produce a little literature.
> HENRY JAMES

Freud applied the so-called 'insights' of his theory to many problems which previously had not been thought to lie within the province of psychiatry, such as the explanation of wit and humour, the causes of war, anthropology and, in particular, the investigation of historical figures and events in terms of motivational factors. The field is too vast for us to discuss all these different types of application of psychoanalysis; so we will concentrate on what has become known as 'psycho-history', i.e. the notion that we can gain an insight into the lives of historical figures by using the methods and tenets of psychoanalysis, and on the application of psychoanalytic methods to anthropology. The field of psycho-history has been well discussed by David E. Stannard, in his book *Shrinking History: On Freud and the Failure of Psycho-History*, a 'must' for all those interested in this topic, and that of psychoanalysis and anthropology has been well surveyed by Edwin R. Wallace, in his book *Freud and Anthropology: A History and Reappraisal*. Here only a brief account can be given of these vast fields.

What is the difference between history and anthropology? As Claude Lévi-Strauss commented in 1958, the principal difference between the two lies 'in their choice of complementary perspectives: history organizes its data in relation to conscious expressions of social life, while anthropology proceeds by examining its unconscious foundations'. In the same year, William L. Langer, the President of the American Historical Association, followed

Freud in attempting to obliterate this distinction, and invited the membership of that organization to examine and analyse the unconscious foundations of the social life of the past. Many historians have followed this siren call, some even advocating individual psychoanalysis as part of the professional training of the budding academic historian. There are now two specialist journals of 'psycho-history', and the movement is gaining more and more adherents. The real question that needs to be answered, of course, is whether there is any substance to this new movement. Stannard ironically precedes his account by a quotation from Shakespeare's *Henry IV*, where Glendower claims: 'I can call spirits from the vasty deep,' and Hotspur replies: 'Why, so can I, or so can any man; but will they come when you do call for them?' This, indeed, is the question.

There are two ways open to the investigator in this field. He can look at many examples cursorily, or examine one in considerable detail. For reasons of space alone, I have chosen to study in detail Freud's book on Leonardo da Vinci, which was published in 1910 and is regarded as the first true example of psycho-historical analysis. Stannard comments:

> Within its brief compass this work contains some of the brightest examples of what makes the best psycho-history so stimulating: insight, learning, sensitivity, and, most of all, imagination. It also contains some of the clearest illustrations of the pitfalls of works of this sort: it is dazzlingly dismissive of the most elementary canons of evidence, logic, and, most of all, imaginative restraint.

Freud begins his account by stating that Leonardo possessed certain traits which may contain the clue to his greatness. The first of these is what Freud calls a 'feminine delicacy of feeling'; he derived this notion from Leonardo's vegetarianism, and his habit of buying caged birds in the market, in order to set them free. He was also capable of apparently cruel and insensitive behaviour, as exhibited in his studying and sketching the faces of condemned criminals prior to their execution, and designing 'the cruellest offensive weapons' of war. Freud comments also on Leonardo's seeming inactivity, his indifference to competition and controversy, his habit of leaving work unfinished, and of working very slowly. But what is of most interest to Freud, as one might have imagined, is Leonardo's apparent combination of 'rigidity', a 'cruel repudiation of sexuality', and a 'stunted' sexual life, linked with 'an insatiable and indefatigable thirst for knowledge'.

Freud regards this combination of traits as being in line with the theory of psychosexual development, and he attributes it to the process of sublimation. 'When the period of infantile sexual researches has been terminated by a wave of energetic sexual repression, the instinct for research has three distinct possible vicissitudes open to it owing to its early connection with sexual interests.' The first is an inhibition of curiosity, and the second a return of curiosity in the form of 'compulsive brooding', but it is the third which Freud suggests is evident in Leonardo's life. 'In virtue of a special disposition . . . the instinct can operate freely in the service of intellectual interest . . . [while] it avoids any concern with sexual themes', by virtue of sublimating the repressed sexuality into investigative impulses.

Here, it seems, Freud comes to an impenetrable barrier. As he has often pointed out, to reach back into the childhood development of the sexual impulse we need to use the patient's dreams and other materials, to which he can freely associate and by means of which he can be led back to these early stages of development. But Leonardo was not available for this purpose; nor is much information available about his childhood. All we know is that he was born in 1452, the illegitimate child of Piero da Vinci, a notary by profession, and 'a certain Caterina, probably a peasant girl'. How does Freud set about making bricks without any straw?

He does so by a typically Freudian side-step. There appears in Leonardo's writings on the flight of birds, in which he took a scientific interest, a curious passage:

It seems that I was always destined to be so deeply concerned with vultures; for I recall as one of my very earliest memories, that while I was in my cradle a vulture came down to me, and opened my mouth with its tail, and struck me many times with its tail against my lips.

It is this passage which Freud proceeded to use, by means of 'the techniques of psychoanalysis', to 'fill the gap in Leonardo's life history by analysing his childhood fantasy'. In doing so, he interprets the tail of the vulture as a 'substitutive expression' for a penis, and the whole scene as an instance of fellatio, i.e. a 'passive' homosexual experience. He also suggests that the fantasy may have another side, i.e. that the desire to suck on a penis 'may be traced to an origin of the most innocent kind . . . merely a reminiscence of sucking – or being suckled – at his mother's breast'.

Freud then analyses the reasons for choosing a vulture in this context. He points out, among other things, that in ancient Egyptian hieroglyphics 'the mother is represented by a picture of the vulture' (phonetically, the words for 'mother' and 'vulture' sounded the same – rather similar to the German *Mutter*, 'mother'); and again, that Mut was the name of an Egyptian female deity resembling a vulture. Freud goes on to list several other possible sources, including an old belief that male vultures did not exist; there were only females, and they were impregnated by the wind – a belief used by certain churchmen to explain virgin birth. Freud ends by stating that the importance of the vulture fantasy to Leonardo lay in his recognition 'that he had also been such a vulture-child – he had had a mother, but no father . . . [and] in this way he was able to identify himself with the child Christ, the comforter and saviour not of this one woman alone'. This notion also explains the lack of information on Leonardo's childhood since 'the replacement of his mother by the vulture indicated the child was aware of his father's absence and found himself alone with his mother'. The vulture fantasy may serve as a replacement for the missing historical data as it seems to tell us that Leonardo spent 'the first critical years of his life not by the side of his father and stepmother, but with his poor, forsaken, real mother, so that he had time to feel the absence of his father'.

These wild notions were accepted as fact by Freud, and he believed that spending 'the first years of his life alone with his mother' had a 'decisive influence' on the formation of Leonardo's inner life. According to Freud, Leonardo not only missed his father, but must have brooded on the problem with special intensity, and was 'tormented . . . by the great question of where babies came from and what the father has to do with their origin'. This explains, as 'an inevitable effect of the state of affairs', why Leonardo 'at a tender age became a researcher'.

Freud goes on to try to explain, in terms of his theory of infantile sexual development, Leonardo's alleged homosexuality. He starts with the clinical observation that in early life homosexuals have 'a very intense erotic attachment to a female person, as a rule their mother', which is 'evoked or encouraged by too much tenderness on the part of the mother herself, and further reinforced by the small part played by the father during their childhood . . . The presence of a strong father [which] would ensure that the son made the correct decision in his choice of object, namely someone of the opposite sex' can avoid the development of sexual attachments, but if, as Freud believed, Leonardo was brought up by his mother in the absence of the father, then the homosexual tendencies would seem to follow.

Is there any evidence of Leonardo's homosexuality? There is very little indeed. At the age of twenty-four Leonardo was anonymously accused of homosexuality, together with three other youths, but the accusation was investigated and the charges dismissed; this is hardly good evidence for such an important item in Freud's reconstruction! He goes on to say that Leonardo often chose handsome young men as his pupils, and that he showed them kindness and consideration. Leonardo's diary contained mention of small financial expenditures on his pupils – according to Freud, 'the fact that he left these pieces of evidence [of kindness] called for explanation'.

Also to be found among Leonardo's papers is mention of the money paid for the funeral of a woman identified only as Caterina; Freud, in the absence of any evidence on the point, suggested that this Caterina was Leonardo's mother. Stannard summarizes Freud's rather convoluted arguments, bringing all these facts and surmises together in the following way:

When set side by side with the entries regarding expenditures on his pupils this note for funeral expenditures tells a dramatic and hitherto unknown story: although constrained and inhibited from conscious expression, Leonardo's repressed feelings of erotic attraction for his mother and his pupils take on the character of an 'obsessional neurosis' made evident by his 'compulsion to note in laborious detail the sums he spent on them'. The artist's hidden life now becomes apparent as this wealth of accumulated evidence allows us to see Leonardo's unconscious mind betraying what his conscious mind never could: 'It was through this erotic relation with my mother that I became a homosexual.'

Last but not least, Freud attempts to indicate the relevance of his analysis to an understanding of Leonardo's artistic genius. According to Freud, 'the key to all his achievements and misfortunes lay hidden in the childhood fantasy of the vulture'. This fantasy 'is compounded from the memory of being suckled and being kissed by his mother . . . this may be translated: my mother placed innumerable passionate kisses on my mouth'. Armed with this notion, Freud tries to interpret one of the obvious characteristics of Leonardo's later paintings, 'the remarkable smile, at once fascinating and puzzling, which he conjured up on the lips of his female subjects'. This 'smile of bliss and rapture', portrayed in Leonardo's *Mona Lisa*, according to Freud awakened something 'which had for long lain dormant in his mind – probably an old memory' – the memory, of course, of his mother and the smile that had once found expression on her mouth. 'He had long been under the dominance of inhibition which forbade him ever again to desire such caresses from the lips of women', but 'he was under no inhibition to try to reproduce the smile with his brush, giving it to all his pictures'.

So much for a brief and somewhat truncated account of Freud's theory, which even on first reading will seem remarkably speculative, with very little factual support. There would appear to be a few rather striking coincidences but, as Stannard in his account makes clear, these vanish immediately one begins to look seriously at the evidence.

The whole analysis is based on the vulture episode, and Freud's extraordinary ability to weave long and detailed tales around a single element is nowhere better illustrated than in his elaboration on this fantasy. Leonardo in fact mentions vultures only once in his writings, under the heading 'Gluttony', and this is what he says: 'The vulture is so given up to gluttony that it would go a thousand miles in order to feed on carrion, and this is why it follows armies.' As Stannard comments: 'Now this statement, I think it fair to say, does not lend much support to Freud's thesis that Leonardo unconsciously associated the image of the vulture with his beloved mother, thus recognized "that he had also been such a vulture-child", and by extension was led to identify himself with the child Christ.' On the contrary, the entry suggests that Leonardo had a rather different image of the vulture than the virgin-mother of the Church Fathers – the image of which Freud had asserted 'it can hardly be doubted' Leonardo was aware.

The recollection of an early memory on which Freud based his interpretation certainly exists; it is written on the back of a page containing various notations on the flight of birds, but it refers, not to a vulture, but a kite, a small hawk-like bird! The 'vulture' turns out to have been a simple mistranslation of 'kite', and thus all Freud's speculation is based essentially on a misconception! All the rich allusions to vultures in Egyptian writings, and in the theological speculations of the Church Fathers, turn out to be quite irrelevant to Leonardo's fantasy. What in fact were Leonardo's views about the kite? It is mentioned under the heading 'Envy', and the entry says: 'Of the kite one reads that when it sees that its children in the nest are too fat it pecks their sides out of envy and keeps them without food.' This is hardly sufficient to support Freud's thesis!

Freud's followers were aware of this crucial error, but attempted to argue it away. James Strachey, who edited *The Standard Edition of the Complete Psychological Works of Sigmund Freud*, called it 'an awkward fact' in a letter to Ernest Jones, but elsewhere dismisses the error as but 'one piece of corroborative support' for the 'psychological analysis of the fantasy', claiming that the 'main body of Freud's studies is unaffected by his mistake'. Others, such as Ernest Jones, have called the error 'this unessential part of Freud's argument' and Kurt Eissler maintains that the resulting problem affects not 'the kind of conclusion that Freud drew but only . . . the particular premise on which the conclusion rested', and thus 'in so far as Freud's interpretation does not refer specifically to the kind of bird, it may be expected to be correct'. Stannard comments that 'these are words that deserve careful re-reading' and goes on:

These are brave, but misguided, rescue efforts. To put it simply: Freud built most of his analysis in the manner of an inverted pyramid, the whole structure balancing on the keystone of a single questionable fact and its interpretation; once that fact is shown to be wrong, and removed as support, the entire edifice begins to crumble. And no amount of rhetorical waffling or smoke-screening can conceal that process of natural disintegration.

Stannard then goes on to dismantle this 'entire edifice'. The elimination of the vulture fantasy means that we no longer have any reason to believe that Leonardo was concerned about his father's alleged absence during his childhood, an idea solely generated by this vulture symbolism. Again, Freud had relied entirely on his analysis of the vulture fantasy to re-create Leonardo's childhood history; its dismissal means that we have no reason at all to believe that Leonardo did spend those years alone with his mother, and indeed recent evidence suggests that Leonardo was in fact a member of his father's household from the time of his birth! Stannard discusses the problem of Leonardo's homosexuality, and goes into great detail to show that the alleged 'evidence' Freud produces is completely worthless and irrelevant. As he concludes:

> Thus far, then, after discarding those of Freud's notions that are flatly incorrect, unsupportable, and/or irrelevant, we are left with the following: Leonardo left no record of sexual activity of any sort; he kept a record of small expenditures, some of which concerned his pupils; he was also very curious about things. That is all.

What about Freud's extension of his analysis to Leonardo's artistic creations? It is crucial for Freud's hypothesis that the famed 'Mona Lisa' smile first appeared in that particular picture, and was observed only in this and later works. This is because it was the woman depicted in the painting who reawakened Leonardo's 'old memory' of his mother's smile which had 'long lain dormant in his mind', according to Freud. But, as Stannard points out in a fascinating discussion of the historical evidence, there is one bit of actual evidence that makes Freud's case simply wrong. It is the fact that there exists a preliminary cartoon of the *Anna Metterza* picture that predates the *Mona Lisa* by several years. And in that cartoon the faces of Anne and the Virgin Mary possess the very same smiles as in the later full painting, the same painting that Freud incorrectly assumed *followed* the inspiration induced by 'Mona Lisa'. 'In short, mere chronology is sufficient to show Freud's thesis to be incorrect.'

Freud's book on Leonardo da Vinci exemplifies in curious form the four great sets of problems of psycho-history. As Stannard lists them, there are problems of fact, problems of logic, problems of theory, and problems of culture. He illustrates his discussion of these problems by reference to a number of writings published by followers of Freud; some of these will be quoted in what follows.

Problems of fact, of course, constitute a fairly obvious set, being related to what many might consider the main business of the historian, namely finding out exactly what happened in the past. Psychoanalysts in the 'psycho-history' business have a tendency to invent and by interpretation suggest what might have happened, and then proceed as if what they have reconstructed actually *did happen*. Freud's reconstruction of Leonardo's childhood is an outstanding example of this; his reconstruction is based, as we have seen, on erroneous interpretations of non-existent facts, and his suggestions, such as the absence of paternal influence on Leonardo, have been disproved by modern research. As another example, consider the work of Erik Erikson, who is generally regarded as a leading light among psycho-historians. In his book on *Young Man Luther*, Erikson singles out a key event in the life of his subject, very much as Freud concentrated on the alleged 'vulture' fantasy. As Erikson's story runs, Luther was seated in the choir of the monastery at Erfurt when he heard the reading from the gospel of the exorcism of a deaf and dumb demoniac. He fell to the floor 'and roared with the voice of a bull – "I am not! I am not!" Erikson interprets this in terms of Luther's making, in effect, the 'child-like protestation of somebody who has been called a name or who has been characterized with loathsome adjectives: here, dumb, mute, possessed'.

Erikson goes on to consider that it would be 'interesting to know whether at this moment Martin roared in Latin or German'. As Stannard comments dryly:

It would, in fact, be more interesting to know whether he roared at all. It is probable, considering the quality of the evidence, that he did not. The evidence for the 'fit in the choir' incident is a bit of gossip filtered through several levels of hearsay and promoted entirely by outspoken enemies of Luther. For Erikson to repeat the incident and to use it as a key event in the first analytic chapter in his book is, as one theologian notes, rather like citing seriously and discussing extensively a report about Freud whose only source is a succession of Nazi anti-Semites, and which was published by one of them only in its fourth retelling.

Erikson's psychoanalytic description of Luther's childhood

development requires that young Martin have a malicious and tyrannical father, in order that the young man's harsh image of the 'father in heaven' could be regarded as a projection of his earthly father. Now, there are practically no facts in existence regarding Luther's childhood, so Erikson's picture has to be manufactured practically out of thin air, using misinterpretations of two accounts which state that he was beaten once by his mother, once by his father! The first of these accounts indicates, however, that the mother meant well, and the second that the father subsequently made great efforts to win back the boy's affection. Indeed, even these references are very doubtful, since they were recorded by his students when he was fifty years old, appear in different versions, and were never seen by Luther himself. In addition, as Stannard notes:

> This flimsy and anecdotal evidence runs directly contrary to a comparative wealth of material indicating that a great deal of love and respect obtained within the household of Luther's childhood. It is this sort of loose overstatement in the face of patently contradictory evidence that has led even the most open-minded of authorities on Luther . . . to refer to Erikson's 'violent distortions', his 'heap of exaggerations and groundless speculations'. In both cases his critics were not at all unfriendly to the idea of psycho-history, but were simply insistent that 'a pyramid of conjectures' was insufficient grounding for such an effort – as [one of them] put it, one must first simply 'get the facts straight'.

This is, of course, the problem with Freud's contribution in all fields; facts are never stated as facts, but are always imbricated with speculations, interpretations, suggestions, and other types of non-factual material.

The way in which Freud and his followers proceed is subsumed by Stannard under *problems of logic*. As he points out, they commit the elementary error which is known in logic as *post hoc ergo propter hoc*, i.e. the notion that because *B* follows *A*, *B* must have been caused by *A*. (It will be remembered that the identical logical error arose also in our discussion of Freud's curative efforts!) Historical writing in general is not free from this false assumption, but Freud has elevated it to a major art form. It is no longer necessary in psychoanalytic writings for Event *A* to have existed at all; if *B* is found to exist, it can safely be assumed that *A* must have happened, since psychoanalysis posits that *B* is a consequence of *A*! In other words, Freudian theory is regarded as being an absolute, and a safe guide even for retroactive arguments going from consequences to antecedents, where nothing is known about these antecedents. The writings on Leonardo da Vinci and on Martin Luther both illustrate this point extensively.

This problem of logic leads inexorably to *problems of theory*. As Stannard points out:

> This problem involves the *method* that the psycho-historian uses to invent the facts of a subject's childhood before showing those facts to be the causes of adult behaviour. One can read through stacks of psycho-historical writings without ever encountering evidence that the author did anything but take psychoanalytic theory as a scientific given – as Freud put it, 'the key' to understanding action. If psychoanalytic theory is such a key, then at least some of the weakness inherent in the problems of facts and logic might be dissipated. But it is not.

We need hardly document this point; this whole book is an attempt to show that psychoanalytic theory is in large measure, if not in its entirety, mistaken, and cannot therefore be used as the key to understanding action. Thus psycho-history inverts the usual procedure of science; it interprets facts in terms of a theory prior to demonstrating the applicability or indeed the truth-value of that theory, even disregarding the mounting evidence that such truth-value is almost completely lacking. We are told that an event must have happened because psychoanalysis says so, but without demonstration that it actually did happen. Such reliance on theory is quite unacceptable, not only in *Naturwissenschaft*, but even in *Geisteswissenschaft*.

The last group of problems encountered by psycho-history is *problems of culture*. Freud usually argues, as do his followers, from his own perception of the meanings of actions which, in fact, might have had quite different meanings at different times and in different cultures. I have already mentioned the fact that Freud regards Leonardo's habit of buying and freeing caged birds as evidence of his gentleness. He seems to be ignorant of the fact that this was a popular practice which was believed to bring good luck. Leonardo did have a gentle and kind side, but this particular behaviour could in fact be explained much more readily in other terms by anyone sufficiently knowledgeable about the popular culture of his time.

An interesting example of this tendency is given by Stannard, who takes it from Fawn Brodie's book, *Thomas Jefferson: An Intimate History*. Brodie is very much taken up with Jefferson's involvement with Sally Hemings, a young mulatto slave, and she posits certain psychoanalytic reasons for this involvement. As evidence of his preoccupation with the 'forbidden woman', and her importance for his 'inner needs', she quotes the fact that descriptions of the landscape in the journal of his trips through Holland include eight references to the colour of the land as 'mulatto'. Brodie does not seem to be aware that the word 'mulatto' was commonly used by eighteenth-century Americans to describe the colour of the soil! Nowadays the term seems unusual in reference to colour, and we tend to give it an interpretation quite different from that it would have been given two hundred years ago. Historians are supposed to know such facts, but 'psycho-historians', ignorant of the time and culture of which they write, may well misinterpret the facts they unearth.

Stannard concludes his discussion by stating:

> Traditional criticisms concerning vulgarity, reductionism, trivialization, and the like, all remain valid observations on the psycho-historical enterprise. But the most important and fundamental reason for the rejection of that enterprise is now clear: psycho-history does not work and cannot work. The time has come to face the fact that, behind all its rhetorical posturing, the psychoanalytic approach to history is – irremediably – one of logical perversity, scientific unsoundness, and cultural naïveté. The time has come, in short, to move on.

Readers not convinced of the soundness of Stannard's conclusion are invited to study his book, which contains all the detail that has inevitably been omitted here.

What has been said about Freudian 'psycho-history' may also be said, in even stronger terms, of the Freudian contribution to anthropology. Freud's theory here, as outlined in his *Totem and Taboo*, is too well known to need any lengthy introduction. As portrayed by Freud, man began his cultural career under a form of social organization in which a single patriarch governed the whole tribe in a dictatorial fashion, holding exclusive sexual sway over his sisters and daughters. As the patriarch grew weaker and his sons stronger, these sexually deprived youngsters plotted their father's murder, killed him, and ate him. However, the brothers were then overcome with guilt, and repressed their desire to have sexual relations with their mothers, sisters, or daughters. At the same time they tried to expiate the murderous deed and cannibalistic orgy by creating the myth of the Totem, the animal symbol of their father, which henceforth was tabooed as food except on ritual occasions. Along these lines the primal parricide, helped along by hereditary memory traces in the 'racial unconscious', gave rise to the Oedipus complex, nuclear family incest taboo, group exogamy, totemism and many other features of primitive civilization.

Freud used this anachronistic framework in an attempt to handle the problem of the diversity of cultures. Rather like his theory of childhood development with its series of stages, he equated savage personality with infantile personality, each modern individual, as it were, recapitulating the evolution of the culture by passing through the various stages of progress towards maturity. Certain cultures, like some individuals, suffer an arrest in their development at various points short of 'civilization' (maturity). This is a breath-taking picture, but one completely lacking in evidence, resemblance to historical fact, logic, or acceptable methodology. Boas, perhaps the outstanding anthropologist of his time, had this to say about Freud's speculations:

> While, therefore, we may welcome the application of every advance in the method of psychological investigation, we cannot accept as an advance in ethnological method the transfer of a novel, one-sided method of psychological investigation of the individual through social phenomena the origin of which can be shown to be historically determined and to be subject to influences that are not at all comparable to those that control the psychology of the individual.

This critique was followed by the important empirical work of Malinowski, which appeared to disprove the universality of the Oedipus complex. As he showed, the Trobriand islanders lived in a culture where it was the mother's brother, not the father of the child, who was the figure of authority. This meant that repressive discipline did not originate in the man who sexually monopolized the child's mother, thereby depriving the father–son relationship of the ambivalent love–hatred features which Freud had (allegedly) observed in his European patients.

Another nail in the coffin of Freud's theories in so far as they relate to anthropology, was supposed to be the work of Margaret Mead, who carried out her field studies in Samoa. Boas set her the task of defeating the notion of a narrowly fixed racial or panhuman hereditary human nature. In order to follow this mandate she stressed in her writings that amongst Samoans adolescence is not a time of stress, that the child is not necessarily more imaginative than adults, that women are not necessarily more passive than men, etc. Unfortunately her work was of such low quality and so contrary to fact, that Derek Freeman was recently able to show in his book *Margaret Mead and Samoa* that in practically every detail her account contradicts that of all the other numerous anthropologists who have studied the Samoan culture.

Oddly enough, many readers have felt that the idealistic picture Mead paints of Samoa as a tropical paradise in which boys and girls grow up in an atmosphere of no tension, no sexual problems, and idyllic love affairs undertaken without any serious thoughts of consequences, as a society in which there is co-operation but no competition, no crime, and above all a beautiful sense of happiness and satisfaction, is somehow close to a Freudian ideal world in which there are no inhibitions, and where neurotic complexes have ceased to exist. Many people have indeed taken Margaret Mead's Samoa as a kind of sexual Utopia towards which to work, in the hope of establishing something similar in the western world. The reality, as firmly demonstrated by Freeman, is, of course, the opposite – Samoans have the highest incidence of rape of any documented culture, the men are hostile and belligerent, they jealously guard the virginity of their women, and are fiercely competitive and aggressive! Of all the criticisms of Freud's anthropology, those based on Margaret Mead's findings may safely be dismissed as irrelevant.

In general, of course, the objections by Boas and his colleagues to the Freudian notions are well taken; there are simply no grounds for the evidence which Freud puts at the centre of his anthropology. The Freudians, of course, hit back, and they use, as always, not a rational argument, but an *argumentum ad hominem*. A typical example is what Géza Roheim had to say about the criticisms from the Boas school, which insisted on the fundamental importance for anthropology of the diversity of different human groups:

> But the point we are now making is that this impression of complete diversity of various human groups is largely created by the Oedipus Complex, that is to say, the Oedipus Complex of the anthropologist or psychiatrist or psychologist. He does not know what to do with his own Oedipus Complex – he therefore *scotomizes* clear evidence for the Oedipus Complex, even when his training ought to enable him to see it . . . This repression of the Oedipus Complex is paralleled by another *pre-conscious* tendency, that of *nationalism*. The idea that all nations are completely different from each other and that the goal of anthropology is simply to find how different they are is a thinly veiled manifestation of nationalism, the democratic counterpart of the Nazi racial doctrine or the Communist class doctrine. Now, of course, I am quite aware of the fact that all those who advocate the study of differences are well-meaning people and that consciously they are in favour of the brotherhood of mankind. The slogan of 'cultural relativity' is supposed to mean just this. But I am a psychoanalyst. I know that all human attitudes result from a compromise formation of two opposite trends and I know the meaning of reaction formation: 'You are completely different, but I forgive you' is what it amounts to. Anthropology is in danger of being led down a blind alley by being subjected to one of the most ancient tendencies of mankind, that of in-group versus out-group.

In other words, when you disagree with me, you are wrong because what you say is a product of a repressed Oedipus complex; consequently I do not have to answer your factual objections. This, it may be said, is not a good attitude for the promotion of scientific agreement.

The psycho-cultural analysis made by Freudians uses essentially the same methods of analysis as 'psycho-history', and is essentially subject to the same criticisms. I shall give two examples of this tendency to interpret alleged facts based on hypothetical causes which in actual fact are irrelevant or non-existent. The first of these is 'The Case of the Japanese Sphincter'. The Freudian notion that adult personality is closely related to infant-training institutions was used during the war to establish a relationship between toilet-training and the allegedly compulsive personality of the Japanese, as shown both in their national character and in their cultural institutions. Geoffrey Gorer, a British psycho-analyst, invoked a toilet-training hypothesis to account for the 'contrast between the all-pervasive gentleness of Japanese life in Japan, which has charmed nearly every visitor, and the over-whelming brutality and sadism of the Japanese at war'. Gorer's account associated this brutality with 'severe early cleanliness training' which created a repressed rage in Japanese infants because they were obliged to control their sphincters before the appropriate muscular and intellectual development had been acquired. A similar suggestion is made in Ruth Benedict's *The Chrysanthemum and the Sword*, where there is a similar affirmation of the strictness of Japanese toilet-training, and the pattern is regarded as one of the facets of the Japanese concern for neatness and orderliness (an important aspect of Freud's anal character).

Attractive as these speculations may seem, they were made without benefit of field research, or intimate knowledge of the toilet-training habits of Japanese mothers. When such research was undertaken after the war, it became apparent very quickly that a serious error had been made with respect to the nature of Japanese toilet-training; Japanese children were not subjected to any severe threats or punishments in this respect, but were treated very much like European or American children. In addition, the rapidity with which the Japanese adapted to their defeat, accepted American influence, changed many of their basic patterns of behaviour and took the lead in the peace movement in the Orient, hardly confirms the wartime portrait which emphasized their frustration and their brutality.

Next we must look at 'The Case of the Swaddled Russians'. This hypothesis was put forward by Gorer and Rickman in their study of the Russian national character; it said essentially that the Russian national character could best be understood in relation to the long and severely restricting form of infant swaddling allegedly practised by the Russians. Gorer maintains that swaddling was associated with the kind of manic-depressive personality corre-sponding to the alternating constraint and freedom experienced by the Russian infant, producing a pent-up feeling of rage while swaddled, contrasting with relief at the sudden freedom when the swaddling bandages were removed. This rage is supposed to be directed towards a diffuse object because the infant is handled in a very impersonal way and has difficulty in relating the treatment to a particular tormentor. The rage then gives rise to guilt, but once again the emotion is widely distributed and not related to a particular person.

Building on this remarkable hypothesis, Gorer tried to show that such phenomena as the Bolshevik Revolution, the Stalin purge trials, the confessions of guilt at these trials, and many other events of recent Soviet history were in some sense 'related' to the generalized rage and guilt feelings associated with swaddling. One of his more amusing excursions was to suggest that the Russian concern with the expressiveness of eyes stemmed from the fact that the restriction of the other parts of a Russian child's body forced the infant to depend upon vision for its main contact with the world! Marvin Harris, in his book *The Rise of Anthropological Theory*, had a splendid comment on these theories. He points out:

Unfortunately Gorer had no firm evidence concerning the extensiveness of swaddling. Indeed, the intellectuals who confessed their guilt at Stalin's purge trials were probably not swaddled. The oppressive and fear-haunted ambience of the Stalin period can be found in association with dictatorships from Ghana to Guatemala, and the alleged compatibility between Russian national character and the despotism of the Stalin period is contradicted by the very fact of the Russian Revolution. To attribute the uprising against Tsarist despotism to rage induced by swaddling bandages is to miss the whole point of recent European history. Stalin's tyranny was founded on the corpses of his enemies. Only by filling the Siberian camps with millions of nonconformists and by relentlessly rooting out all vestiges of political opposition did Stalin manage to impose his will on his countrymen. The notion that the mass of Russians were somehow psychologically fulfilled by the terror of the Stalin period is absolutely without basis in fact.

Gorer's theory is put in terms which imply a direct causal nexus: swaddling produces the Russian character. Gorer, however, produced a disclaimer which is typical of much psychoanalytic thinking in the anthropological field. He says:

It is the argument of this study that the situation outlined in the preceding paragraphs is *one* of the major determinants in the development of the character of adult Great Russians. It is *not* the argument of this study that the Russian manner of swaddling their children produces the Russian character, and it is not intended to imply that the Russian character would be changed or modified if another technique of infant training were adopted.

As Marvin Harris points out: 'A careful reading of this disclaimer does not improve its intelligibility. Swaddling is said to be one of the *major* determinants of the Great Russian character in one sense, but in the next, it is said not to be *any kind* of determinant.' Gorer maintains that there is considerable heuristic value in the swaddling hypothesis, and likens it to a 'thread which leads through the labyrinth of the apparent contradictions of Russian adult behaviour'. It is not easy to understand the epistemological nature of this 'thread' – if there is no causal link, then there is no thread! Any hypothesis must involve a correlation of some degree of quantity or quality, i.e. some causal nexus. Take that away, and we are left with nothing.

Margaret Mead took up the defence of Gorer and interpreted him as affirming something like this: 'From an analysis of the way Russians swaddle infants, it is possible to build a model of Russian character formation which enables us to relate what we know about human behaviour and what we know about Russian culture in such a way that Russian behaviour becomes more understandable.' She does not explain how, if there is no causal relation, the hypothesis makes Russian behaviour more understandable. Mead restates Gorer's hypothesis as follows: 'It is the combination of an unusually confining version of a widespread practice, the age of the child which is thus confined, and an adult insistence on the need to protect the child from itself – the duration and the type of swaddling – which are *assumed* to have distinctive *effects* on the formation of Russian character' (italics added). As Harris comments: 'With this statement, the entire argument is returned to its initial form, and the lack of evidence for the "assumed" effects once more summons forth its full measure of amazement.'

This curious combination of claims for causality and denial of causality is typical of Freud's general attitude. As Cioffi has pointed out: 'Symptoms, errors, etc., are not simply *caused* but they "announce", "proclaim", "express", "realize", "fulfil", "gratify", "represent", "initiate", or "allude to" this or that repressed impulse, thought, memory, etc.' He goes on to say:

The cumulative effect of this is, in contexts where it would otherwise be natural to demand behavioural elucidation or inductive evidence, this demand is suspended due to our conviction that it is intentional or expressive activity which is being explained; while in contexts where we normally expect an agent's candid and considered rejection sufficient to falsify or disconfirm the attribution of expressiveness or intent, this expectation is dissipated by Freud's talk of 'processes', 'mechanisms', and 'laws of the unconscious'.

All of this, as Cioffi makes clear, is because Freud and his followers feel under the constraint to give a *causal* explanation, but they are also *afraid* of making any definite statement which could be refuted by an appeal to factual inconsistencies. This ambivalence is documented many times in this book, and it pervades all of Freud's work, and that of his followers. Cioffi's chapter should be consulted in full, as giving the best sustained account of this general tendency which makes psychoanalysis a pseudo-science, rather than a science; Gorer, Mead and others quoted here are simply following the example set by Freud himself.

In discussing the application of Freud's theories to history and anthropology, and in particular his theory of the origins of 'Totem and Taboo', it is impossible to neglect the influence of Freud's own history and personality on his theories. I have previously pointed out the impossibility of understanding Freudian theories except as a literary presentation of his own feelings and complexes; this view in fact finds support in writings by well-known psychoanalysts themselves. Thus Robin Ostow maintained that *Totem and Taboo* may be 'read as an allegory about Freud, his disciples, and the psychoanalytic movement'. This is what Ostow has to say:

The personal characteristics of the primal father represent many of Freud's own traits. Some of the basic trends of the primal drama are observable in both the evolution of the psychoanalytic movement and in Freud's fears and fantasies for his personal future and that of his theory and his organization. Adler and Stekel were two of the growing sons whom Freud exiled from the horde . . . Freud's fantasy of being dismembered and being incorporated by these creative, aggressive young men seems to contain some fear and a certain amount of masochistic pleasure. He sees his ultimate re-emergence, with unprecedented personal control over a group of now co-operative, affectionate, and remorseful but still unindividualized spiritual sons ... Freud imagined himself to be the totem of later generations of psychoanalysts; they would call themselves 'Freudians', they would revere him, and they would function in an orderly organization.

E. Wallace, who has gone into great detail regarding the dependence of Freudian theories on Freud's own personal history, adds a number of further points. He insists that among the causal factors in the writing of *Totem and Taboo* were Freud's father conflict and, more currently, his problems with Jung, who was rebelling against Freud's pre-eminence. Freud himself admitted that his intrapsychic life was characterized by considerable ambivalence towards his father, a conflict which clearly asserted itself in several symptoms. Wallace goes on as follows:

There are several ways that we can look at the relationship between Freud's own father conflict and the parricide hypothesis. On the one hand, by raising his personal dynamics (the father conflict) to the level of a phylogenetic universal, Freud could distance himself from his patricidal rage (which had been reactivated by the rebellious Jung). On the other hand, by calling it a primal fact of world history, he was expressing its importance in his own psychic life. The characterization of the primal parricide as an irrevocable inheritance may reflect Freud's partial awareness of his own dynamics – the fatalistic inevitability that he must re-enact his father conflict and suffer the guilt. Furthermore this hypothesis may have been a way of undoing previous attribution of guilt to fathers (when he relived his hysterics' fantasies) – that is, it was the sons, not the fathers, who had committed the crime. Still the element of compromise formation is plain enough, for by depicting the primal father as a brutal tyrant, Freud could in a sense justify the murderous feelings of the sons.

It is interesting to see psycho-history turned against its own creator, and the methods of psychoanalysis used to dissect the work of Freud himself. The fact that this has been done by Freud's own followers illustrates the point that Freud's work and his developmental history and personality are in many ways inseparable. The alleged scientific analysis of man which Freud believed himself to have undertaken is little more than a gigantic autobiographical essay; the miracle is that so many people have taken it seriously as a contribution to science! Can we put any faith in the application to its own originator of what we consider to be a faulty method? The reader must be left to form his own impression, preferably after reading the very extensive work of Wallace, who has specialized in this field and makes an impressive case. From the scientific point of view, of course, the whole issue must be irrelevant. Whatever may have caused Freud to put forward a particular theory, the theory must be judged on grounds of logic, consistency and factual support. This support has not been forthcoming in the fields of history and anthropology, nor in the other fields we have examined, and it is this that is the gravamen of the charge against Freud – not that he was driven to formulate his theories by his own developmental history and the events of his later life.

I shall end this chapter by quoting Marvin Harris, who has this to say about the relationship between psychoanalysis and anthropology:

The meeting of anthropology and psychoanalysis has produced a rich harvest of ingenious functional hypotheses in which psychological mechanisms can be seen as intermediating the connection between disparate parts of culture. Psychoanalysis, however, had little to offer cultural anthropology by way of scientific methodology. In this respect the meeting of the two disciplines tended to reinforce the inherent tendencies towards uncontrolled, speculative, and histrionic generalizations which each in its own sphere had cultivated as part of its professional licence. The anthropologist carrying out a psycho-cultural analysis resembled the psychoanalyst whose attempt to identify the basic personality structure of his patient remains largely interpretive and immune to normal verification procedures. In a sense, what the great figures in the formative phases of the culture and personality movement were asking us to do was to trust them as we would trust an analyst, not for the demonstrated truth of any particular item, but for the accumulating evidence of coherence in a believable pattern. Although such faith is essential to psychoanalytic therapy in which it scarcely matters whether childhood events of particular kinds did or did not take place as long as both analyst and patient are convinced that they did, the separation of myth from concrete event is the highest goal of disciplines which concern themselves with human history.

If this is true, why have so many historians and anthropologists rushed to interpret their material along Freudian lines? The answer probably lies in the ancient human desire to get something for nothing. We start out by knowing nothing whatsoever about

Leonardo da Vinci's childhood, or the factors that led Luther to behave as he did. By using Freudian interpretations of recorded dreams, fantasies, or behaviour of one kind or another, it is suggested that we can transcend the limitations of our factual material, and arrive at conclusions which are breath-taking in their generality. In biology we have learnt to build up a whole skeleton of some defunct dinosaur from just a few tiny bones and fragments of teeth; psychoanalysis holds out the hope that we can do the same in history and anthropology – just give us a few isolated fragments of dreams, behaviours or *Fehlleistungen*, and from these few indices we can reconstruct a whole culture, a person's childhood development, or the causes of a national character.

More than that: if we have no facts at all, then we can make them up, using the suggested 'scientific laws' of psychoanalysis to deduce what the facts must have been! We need know nothing about the toilet-training habits of the Japanese; if Freud tells us that rigorous toilet-training produces the kind of character exhibited by the Japanese during the war, then we can confidently assert that this is the kind of toilet-training they must have had! It is sad, of course, to be told afterwards that in actual fact the toilet-training of the Japanese was nothing like that assumed by the Freudians, but apparently it has had little effect on their interpretive ardour. As quoted earlier, T. H. Huxley said that the great tragedy of science is the slaying of a beautiful theory by an ugly fact. Freudian theories may not be beautiful, but they have proved invulnerable to any amount of factual evidence demonstrating their absurdity. Psychoanalysts, unfortunately, are unlikely to understand the insistence on factual evidence which is so characteristic of the scientist; they prefer to float on clouds of interpretation based nebulously on imaginary fantasies. Not in this way is a science constructed!

CHAPTER EIGHT

Rest in Peace: An Evaluation

Truth comes out of error more readily than out of confusion.

FRANCIS BACON

Let us now try to assess Freud's status in the world of science. Freud was very ambiguous in his pronouncements about himself. On the one hand, he classed himself with Copernicus and Darwin; as they had humbled mankind by demonstrating the insignificance of the earth in the celestial scheme, and the relationship between man and other animals, so he claimed to have shown the supreme power of the unconscious in governing our daily activities. On the other hand, his insight led him to state that he was not a scientist, but rather a *conquistador* – although he did not specify what it was that he had conquered. This contradiction is apparent in much of what he wrote; on the one hand, the desire to be a scientist in the accepted sense common to the natural sciences, and on the other, the realization that what he was doing was essentially different in kind. This conflict, of course, is not peculiar to Freud, nor is it confined to psychoanalysis; it is essentially the difference between psychology as *Naturwissenschaft* (natural science) and psychology as *Geisteswissenschaft* (hermeneutics).

Hermeneutics is the discipline concerned with interpretation and meaning. It compares the analysis of actions and experiences with the interpretive study of a text. The art of hermeneutics is to extract the meaning of a particular 'text' by knowing the implications of the symbols used, as well as their significance in relation to each other and the context in which they appear. To the practitioner, actions and experiences are regarded as encoded meanings, not as objective facts; they take their significance from the meanings they convey. Such an approach which stresses *meaning* is the exact opposite of the natural science approach which stresses the study of *behaviour*; hence the eternal struggle in psychology between behaviourists and a wide range of opponents, who include psychoanalysts, many cognitive psychologists, introspectionists, idiographic psychologists, etc. The philosophical arguments between these two groups are genuinely important in the struggle for the soul of psychology, and many writers have anguished about making the right choice, or have indeed attempted to have the best of both worlds by embracing both sides indiscriminately! Freud was one of those who hankered after the natural science of behavioural research, but whose major contribution is clearly on the hermeneutical side. Howard H. Kendler, in his book *Psychology: A Science in Conflict*, has given an excellent summary of the arguments on both sides, and the possibilities of reconciling them; but this is an issue rather too complex and perhaps recondite to enter into in this book.

Richard Stevens, in his book *Freud and Psychoanalysis*, firmly argues that Freud can be understood only in terms of hermeneutics:

> What is it about mental life which makes it so intractable a subject-matter? I would like to suggest that the problems arise because its essence is *meaning* ... By referring to the actions of mental life as meaning, I am pointing to the fact that the conduct of our lives and relationships is ordered by concepts. The way we conceptualize and feel about ourselves, other people or a situation will be fundamental to the ways we behave. In everyday life, we take this for granted.

This, of course, is true, but it does not mean that we want necessarily to abandon a natural science interpretation of behaviour, and adopt a more commonsensical one. Primitive tribes interpret many objective facts in terms of meanings and intentions; if a person falls ill, this is due to the intentions of an enemy, or a witch-doctor, or some kind of magic. This clearly is not the way to develop a sound science of medicine.

Stevens goes on to discuss the nature and potential of psychotherapy:

> We are continuously testing and modifying our interpretations either

explicitly by exchanging views with others or *implicitly* by noting their example of ways of interpreting events. One way of viewing a psychotherapy session is as a negotiation of this kind. It may not involve direct persuasion, but the patient is likely to be encouraged to revise the way he construes himself and his relationships. Thus psychotherapy is quite distinct from physical medicine. Its core is a manipulation of meaning, not of body functioning . . .

When regarded as an hermeneutic method, psychoanalysis' weakness as an experimental science becomes its very strength. Take the idea of *over-determination*. In discussing the condensation which occurs in dreams, it was pointed out that many different strands of meaning may underlie a single remembered image or event. Psychoanalytic interpretation is aimed at unravelling these. Moreover, the concepts the theory provides help us to view the meanings from different perspectives and levels . . . Although this makes it impossible to submit any interpretation to a precise test, it does offer great potential for putting together the detailed picture of all the different meanings which may be involved.

What is suggested here is something often claimed for psychoanalysis, namely that it provides us with numerous 'insights' which behaviourism and other natural sciences are incapable of doing. This inevitably presents us with a difficulty. What if these so-called 'insights' are nothing but idle speculations which are actually untrue, and do not apply to the situations in question? What if all these interpretations of dreams, slips, etc., are in fact erroneous, and lead us in the wrong direction? How are we to tell whether Freud was right or wrong? The alternatives to Freud might not, after all, be behaviourism, but the theories of other hermeneutic psychologists: how are we to decide between Freud and Jung, Freud and Adler, Freud and Stekel, and so forth? There is no doubt whatever that Freud and the other psychoanalysts mentioned would interpret a given dream in very different ways; how are we to tell which of these interpretations is 'right'? Thus, even if we accept the hermeneutic approach, we still need criteria for deciding about the truth and falsity of given interpretations, and Freud does not provide us with any of the criteria needed to fulfil this function.

P. Rieff, in his book *Freud: The Mind of the Moralist*, has an interesting passage on the way psychoanalysts use the term 'science' in a sense that is very different to its use among hard scientists. He acknowledges that psychoanalysis does not adhere to the rigorous standards of scientific theory, but expresses his concern:

Lest this label 'unscientific' be used to condemn Freud, or worse, to praise him condescendingly for just those rare qualities in him that we do not encourage among ourselves: his wide range and subtlety, his unsurpassed brilliance as an exegete of the universal language of pain and suffering, his willingness to pronounce judgements and draw out the evidence for them from his own life as well as from clinical data. His scientific motives are of a piece with the ethical implications of his thought, whose catch-phrases have seeped down from the conversations of the educated into the popular consciousness of the age. It would be an impertinence, into which no received notion of the boundary between science and ethics should lead us, to judge one of Freud's faces authentic and dismiss the other. For humanists in science, and for scientists of the human, Freud should be the model of a concern with the distinctively human that is truly scientific.

Stevens sums up the debate by saying:

If your critical criterion for science is the generation of propositions which are falsifiable, then clearly psychoanalysis is not a science. But if you mean by 'science' the systematic formulation of concepts and hypotheses based on careful and detailed observations, then I think the answer must be that it is. It is arguable, too, whether there is any other approach likely to offer better potential for the prediction of people's actions than real-life settings. For Freud, albeit reluctantly, takes on the uncomfortable but important task of confronting the Janus face of humans as they are – both biological and existential beings.

This brings us back to the problem of Freud the man, the creator of his theory, and his application of his own neurotic troubles and sufferings to the way all men behave. There is no reason to assume that Freud's 'insights' into his own suffering are in any way relevant to the behaviour of other human beings, just as there is no reason to assume that his 'insights' are in fact accurate. One would require evidence to prove this, and evidence is precisely what is missing. Indeed, as we have seen, Freud was demonstrably wrong in so many different contexts that it is difficult to see why we should, without any proof, believe all these alleged 'insights'. Many of these insights were, in any case, borrowed from others, ranging from Plato to Schopenhauer, and from Kierkegaard to Nietzsche, and to give Freud the credit for them is as wrong as to assume that they are true. A historical approach is required to assign priority, and a natural science approach is required to discover their truth-value. This is assumed by Freud's apologists, but is precisely what is at issue. In the discussion between behaviourism and psychoanalysis, behaviourism has always had a bad press for two reasons.

In the first place, it is not Freud but Pavlov who belongs with Copernicus and Darwin as the great dethroner of mankind from its pedestal; it was he who showed that many of our actions are not those of *Homo sapiens*, but are the results of primitive conditioning mediated by the limbic system and other subcortical parts of the brain. Thus he has encountered the hostility which Freud erroneously assumed, as we have seen, to have been his part. To explain neurotic conditions in terms of Pavlovian conditioning seems to many people demeaning, mechanistic and dehumanizing; they much prefer the apparently more human interpretations of subtle meanings which flavour all Freud's work.

In the second place, anyone can understand (or believe that he understands – quite a different matter!) Freud's writings and theories. After reading a few of his books, many people feel quite capable of interpreting dreams, judging other people's actions, and explaining them in terms of psychoanalytic concepts. However, to understand Pavlov, and to keep up to date with the large-scale experimental work that has been done on his theory, requires several years of study, the reading of innumerable books and articles, and a constant updating of the knowledge so acquired – all requirements which, in the nature of things, most people are incapable of undertaking. Few, if any, psychiatrists are more than remotely familiar with the essential features of conditioning and learning theory; teachers, social workers, probation officers and others who have to deal with human beings can usually repeat a few Freudian terms, and may imagine that they are able to 'psychoanalyse' their wards, but they do not normally know anything about Pavlovian conditioning, learning theory, or the wealth of factual data available to the behaviourist.

It has been my experience that abstract discussions are, in general, quite insufficient to convince the doubters. Let us look at a few simple examples to illustrate the difference between the Freudian and the behaviouristic approach. The first example I have chosen is the behaviour of head-bangers, i.e. children who for no apparent reason bang their heads against walls, tables and chairs, etc., and who may in the process blind (because the retinae become detached) or even kill themselves. How do psychoanalysts propose to treat this very serious disorder? They argue that the child acts in this way in order to attract attention, and to get his mother to show affection. The recommendation, therefore, is that whenever the child starts to bang his head, the mother should pick him up, kiss and cuddle him, and generally be affectionate. This is all very humane, and the interpretation may or may not be correct, but unfortunately it has the opposite effect to that intended. The child's abnormal behaviour is reinforced because he is rewarded for it, and consequently he indulges even more strongly in his head-banging, in order to obtain more and more attention from his mother.

The behaviourist, on the other hand, is not concerned with meanings; he simply applies a universal rule, namely that of conditioning, to the situation. He instructs the mother that whenever the child begins to bang his head, she is to lift him up bodily, place him in an empty room and lock the door. After ten minutes she is to unlock the door and bring the child back to where he was before – without any show of emotion or any scolding, and as quietly as possible. The law of effect soon penetrates the mind of the child, and the negative effects of head-banging, once realized, ensure that he will stop indulging in this abnormal behaviour. The psychoanalyst's approach may seem the more humane but his treatment in fact achieves the opposite of what is intended, while the behaviourist's method may seem quite mechanistic but his treatment actually works. If you had a son, five years old, who banged his head and was in danger of going blind or killing himself, which method of treatment would you prefer? To ask the question is to know the answer.

Let us take a somewhat more complex problem, that of enuresis (bed-wetting). It is well known that many children wet their beds at night, even at an age when the great majority have ceased to do so. Why is this so, and what can we do about it? Let us first look at psychoanalysis. Psychoanalysts regard enuresis with great suspicion; as one of them has said, 'Enuresis is always regarded in psychoanalysis as a symptom of a deeper underlying disorder.' According to this point of view, the clinician attaches fundamental causal importance to the deep-seated patterns of the child–parent relationships which are 'moulded from birth due to the complex interplay of unconscious forces from both sides'. Some of the specific theories embraced by analysts take the form of highly speculative interpretations based on psychoanalytical symbolism. For one analyst, for instance, enuresis 'represented a cooling of the penis, the fire of which was condemned by the super-ego'. For another, enuresis was an attempt to escape a masochistic situation and expel outwards the destructive tendencies: the urine is seen as a corrosive fluid and the penis as a dangerous weapon. Yet another therapist suggested that usually enuresis expressed a demand for love, and might be a form of 'weeping through the bladder'.

There are many such different interpretations, but they can be conveniently grouped under three different headings. Some psychoanalysts believe that enuresis is a substitute form of gratification of repressed genital sexuality, others regard it as a direct manifestation of deep-seated anxieties and fears, and a third group interprets it as a disguised form of hostility towards parents or parent substitutes which the victim does not dare to express openly. All these theories insist on the primacy of some psychological 'complex', and the secondary nature of the 'symptom'; concern is with the former, not the latter. Consequently, treatment is long-drawn-out, involving searching examination of the patient's unconscious through dream interpretation, word association, and other complex methods, and considering many aspects of the child's personality which are apparently irrelevant to the simple act of bed-wetting. Yet there is no evidence that this method works better than no treatment at all (most enuretic children get better anyway after a few months or years), or placebo treatment. Thus here again we have the failure of psychoanalysis to provide any evidence for its numerous suppositions.

What do behaviourists suggest as a cause, and as a treatment? They regard enuresis in the majority of cases simply as a failure to acquire a habit, and believe that this 'habit deficiency' is due to faulty habit training of some kind. Ordinary continence training teaches a child to respond to bladder stimulation by awakening. The child thus learns to substitute going to the toilet (or using his pot) for bed-wetting; when this learning fails, enuresis is the result. Thorough investigations have shown that, although there is sometimes something physically wrong with the urinary system, in nine cases out of ten bed-wetting is a habit condition. If this suggestion is right, then the method of treatment would be very simple; it would consist of instilling the habit through a simple process of Pavlovian conditioning. We use a blanket interleaved between two porous metal plates; these plates are connected in series with a battery and a bell. The dry blanket acts as an insulator; once the child begins to wet the blanket the saline urine acts as an electrolyte and a connection is made between the metal plates. This completes the circuit, and the bell rings and wakes the child, causing him by reflex to inhibit the act of urination. This method is now very widely used in child guidance clinics all over the world; it is completely safe, works well and quickly, and has been found acceptable to parents and children alike. Furthermore, many deductions can be made from general learning theory about the specific way it works, and experiments have demonstrated that these deductions are in fact verified by the experiment. The bell-and-blanket method has now superseded Freudian therapy almost universally because it is much simpler, and it works much better and more quickly. Why then should we stay with methods of interpretation which have no empirical support and do not result in cure, as opposed to a method which has good experimental support and produces cures more readily and much more frequently?

Freudians used inevitably to argue that this 'symptomatic' type of treatment does nothing to reduce anxiety which is fundamental to the condition, and that it is this that should be treated. The facts, however, appear to be exactly the opposite. It is the enuresis that produces anxiety as the child finds himself in the very unenviable position of being made fun of by his peers and blamed, and sometimes beaten, by his parents. Once the bell-and-blanket method eliminates the enuresis, the anxiety is nearly always found to subside, and the child recovers his equanimity.

Many other examples could be given, such as the treatment of obsessive-compulsive hand-washing described in an earlier chapter. We may not *like* the fact that we are descended, through evolution, from animal-like ancestors, and we may not like the fact that, like they, we are constrained in our behaviour by bodily mechanisms which appear to us primitive and unworthy. But likes and dislikes do not create facts; it is the task of the scientist to pay attention to the facts, rather than the likes and dislikes of humans. The proper way to judge theories, whether behaviouristic or hermeneutic, is to pay attention to the consequences, and these generally point to the correctness of the behavioural theories, and the errors and inaccuracies of the hermeneutic ones, particularly in their Freudian guise.

What is wrong, with hermeneutics in general, and with Freudian psychoanalysis in particular, is that it substitutes a pseudo-science for a genuine science. As Cioffi has pointed out:

It is characteristic of a pseudo-science that the hypotheses which comprise it stand in an asymmetrical relation to the expectations they generate, being permitted to guide them and be vindicated by their fulfilment but not to be discredited by their disappointment. One way in which it achieves this is by contriving to have these hypotheses understood in a narrow and determinant sense before the event but a broader and hazier one after it on those occasions on which they are not borne out. Such hypotheses thus lead a double life – a subdued and restrained one in the vicinity of counter-observations and another less inhibited and more exuberant one when remote from them. This feature won't reveal itself to simple inspection. If we want to determine whether the role played by these assertions is a genuinely empirical one it is necessary to discover what their proponents are prepared to call disconfirmatory evidence, not what *we* do.

Even from the hermeneutic point of view, then, Freud and psychoanalysis must be regarded as a failure. We are left with nothing but imaginary interpretation of pseudo-events, therapeutic failures, illogical and inconsistent theories, unacknowledged borrowings from predecessors, erroneous 'insights' of no proven value, and a dictatorial and intolerant group of followers insistent not on truth but on propaganda. This legacy has had many extremely bad consequences for psychiatry and psychology, among which we can single out the following.

The first, and probably the most lamentable, consequence has been the effect on the patients. Their hopes of cure and rescue have been dashed time and time again, and in some cases they have actually been made worse by psychoanalysis. Their sacrifice of time, energy and much money has been unavailing, and the resulting disappointment has frequently been a severe blow to their self-esteem and their happiness. When discussing psychoanalysis, we should always bear in mind the fate of the patients; the scientific pretensions of psychoanalysis are one thing, but its therapeutic effects are another, much more important from the human point of view. Psychoanalysis is a discipline meant to cure patients; its failure to do so, and its reluctance to admit the failure, should never be forgotten.

The second consequence of Freud's teaching has been the failure of psychology and psychiatry to develop into properly scientific studies of normal and abnormal behaviour. It is probably true to say that Freud has set back the study of these disciplines by something like fifty years or more. He has managed to sidetrack the scientific research of the early days onto lines which have proved unsuccessful and even regressive. He has elevated the absence of proof, devaluing its necessity, into a religion which too many psychiatrists and clinical psychologists have embraced, to the detriment of their discipline. There are great difficulties in the scientific study of behaviour; Freud has multiplied these difficulties by acting as a Pied Piper for those unwilling to undergo the rigorous training needed to be a practitioner of modern psychology, and necessary for any research worker wishing to make a genuine contribution. This, too, is hard to forgive, and future generations will have to undo the harm he and his followers have done in this field.

The third consequence that may be laid to Freud's charge is the damage to society his theories have caused. In his book on

The Freudian Ethic, Richard La Piere has shown how Freud's teachings have undermined the values on which western civilization is based, and while some at least of this undermining has been due to a misunderstanding of Freudian teaching, nevertheless his influence on the whole has been malignant. W. H. Auden, in his famous poem 'In Memory of Sigmund Freud', had this to say:

> If often he was wrong and, at times, absurd,
>   to us he is no more a person
> now but a whole climate of opinion . . .

This is a very perceptive remark, worthy of the poet, but the question must be raised whether this climate of opinion, i.e. a climate of permissiveness, sexual promiscuity, decline of old-fashioned values, etc., is one in which we would want to live. Even the egregious Dr Spock, author of the famous baby book, recanted his previous enthusiastic advocacy of Freudian teaching, and acknowledged the harm it had done; it is time we reconsidered this teaching not only in terms of its scientific worthlessness, but also in terms of its ethical nihilism.

The broad influence of Freudian notions on our life in general can hardly be doubted, and will be familiar to most people. Sexual mores, the upbringing of children, the subjectivity of ethical rules, and many other Freudian tenets have certainly filtered through to the man in the street, usually not through any reading of Freud, but through the very great influence he has had on the literary establishment and the media – on journalists, television writers and reporters, film producers and others who act as intermediaries between academic teaching, on the one hand, and the general public, on the other. Literary criticism has been as strongly pervaded by Freudian notions as have historical criticism or anthropology, and this inevitably has had its impact on society as a whole. The truth of Freudian ideas is taken for granted in these contexts, and no questions are raised about its truth-value. Thus a great inertia has built up which even the most cogent criticism finds it difficult to disturb; literary critics, historians, teachers, social workers, and others concerned in one way or another with human conduct cannot be bothered to read complex arguments and experimental studies, particularly when these threaten to undermine their faith in 'dynamic' psychology.

There are other reasons why psychoanalysis has been so successful in gaining access to and approval from the great intellectual (and even the non-intellectual) public, as compared with experimental psychology. In the first instance, experimental psychologists, like all other scientists, use jargon, based on experimental paradigms and mathematical and statistical treatments which are unintelligible to anyone without special training. Freudian jargon, on the other hand, is readily intelligible to anyone who can read English (or German!) prose. Terms like 'repression' are easily understood (or at least seem to be so); terms like 'conditioned inhibition', 'Hick's Law', or the 'triune brain', on the other hand, clearly are not intelligible without very lengthy explanation.

But beyond this, psychoanalysis clearly deals with important and 'relevant' matters, like motivation and emotion, love and hate, mental disease and cultural conflict, the meaning of life and the very reasons for our everyday behaviour; it supplies a kind of explanation (however mistaken) for our lives, our successes and failures, our triumphs and disasters, our neuroses and our recoveries. Experimental psychology, on the other hand, appears to deal with esoteric, unimportant and fundamentally irrelevant problems, of interest only to experimental psychologists themselves. This picture is sufficiently near the truth to convince many highly intelligent and knowledgeable people (including many psychologists themselves!) that our choice lies between a humanly important discipline, however unscientific its approach, and a discipline fundamentally irrelevant to our deepest concerns, even though it might be rigorous and truly scientific in its methodology.

Many experimentalists not only accept this verdict but glory in it. Like the famous English mathematician, G. H. Hardy, they enjoy experimental work precisely because it has no practical implications. Its problems are self-generated, they believe, and far away 'from the sphere of our sorrow'. This escapism is difficult to understand, and almost certainly mistaken; even Hardy's mathematics proved useful and instrumental in such practical applications as the construction of the atom bomb.

Similarly, apparently esoteric work on conditioning in dogs has proved fundamental in teaching us how neuroses originate, and how they can be treated. Pavlov certainly never doubted the practical applicability of his laws, and how right he was! But the impression of the practical irrelevance of experimental psychology still persists, and unfortunately there is much truth in that belief; many experimentalists concentrate on small problems of no real scientific significance, preferring methodological elegance to scientific importance. But while widespread, this attitude is far from universal, and there is already enough evidence of the broad relevance of experimental findings to everyday problems to convince even the most determined sceptic. This book was written in part to make precisely this point: we can combine relevance and rigour, human importance and integrity of scientific experimentalism. It remains to convince the world of this important truth. Most of our problems are psychological in nature, from war to political strife, from mental disorder to marital disharmony, from strikes to racism; it is surely time to enlist the help of science in trying to solve these problems!

The influence of Marx has been rather similar to that of Freud, not only because he too based his whole case on 'interpretations', and discounted direct evidence, but also because very few of the people who now claim to hold his views have ever bothered to read his original contributions, or look at the criticisms, however cogent, of these views. Indeed, present-day Marxists often hold views exactly opposite to those of Marx and Lenin, as in the question of the inheritance of intelligence. Both Marx and Lenin were quite explicit about their belief that 'equality', as an ideal essential to Socialism, meant *social* equality, not *biological* equality, and they emphasized their belief that the latter was absolutely impossible to attain. It is quite clear from their writings that they supported the view that intelligence and other abilities had a clear genetic foundation, but some of their followers nowadays claim exactly the opposite! Much the same is true of Freud. His followers, too, have created a 'climate of opinion' which deviates markedly from what he himself would have approved. Nevertheless, there is a traceable ancestry, and Freud cannot be completely absolved of guilt.

If psychoanalysis is of so little value, and has such dire

consequences, why has it become so influential? This is an interesting and important question, and it is hoped that future sociologists and psychologists will try to discover how it was possible that one man could inflict his own neurotic troubles on several generations and persuade the world of the importance of his theories, which not only lacked proof or evidence, but were in some cases contradicted by his own examples. It should be said, however, that Freud's message was never universally accepted by scientists and academics. It was accepted enthusiastically, and widely popularized, by two groups of people (other than avowed psychoanalysts, of course).

The first of these groups consists of people such as teachers, social workers, and probation officers, who have to deal with human problems in one way or another. Such people are faced with a very difficult job, and therefore feel they need any help they can get in terms of psychological theories. Psychoanalysis appeared to furnish them with such help, and naturally they embraced it with enthusiasm. As previously noted, it gave them the illusion of power, and a kind of expertise which they could point to as justification for their activities. It is unfortunate that this was a pseudo-expertise, but because of the prestige it offered, people in this group have been hanging on to it with grim determination ever since. It is difficult to estimate the harm that they have done in Freud's name, and it is regrettable that his teachings have virtually excluded other, more scientific aspects of psychology from their purview. Nevertheless people such as these constitute a powerful support for the Freudian system.

The second, rather different, group of Freud's supporters is made up of members of the literary establishment. For them, Freud and his teaching constituted a most welcome set of notions and ideas which could be elaborated into literary productions, whether poems, plays or novels. It took the place formerly occupied by Greek mythology, namely a set of beliefs, personalities and adventures widely known to educated people, to which reference could be made, and which could be incorporated into literary works. Instead of Zeus, Athene, Achilles and their like, we now have the censor, the super-ego, Thanatos and other mythological figures. To the second-rate writer, Freud spelt salvation; here was a rich mine which could be exploited endlessly, and consequently the literary establishment became a firm advocate of psychoanalytic ideas.

What is the position now? Freudianism had its heyday in the 1940s and 1950s, and perhaps lasted even into the 1960s, but then criticisms began to mount, and gradually psychoanalysis lost its appeal. This is certainly true of academic institutions; modern departments of psychiatry in the United States, the United Kingdom and elsewhere now concentrate on the biological side of mental disorder, particularly pharmacological methods of treatment, or else they look to behavioural methods, and incorporate these in their teaching and practice. In psychological research, too, psychoanalysis has been losing out to behaviour therapy over the last twenty years. It will inevitably take a long time before psychoanalysts, who occupy all the positions of power and prestige in American psychiatry, and some though not all of them in British psychiatry also, have retired and younger men, with new ideas, take over. The famous physicist Max Planck once pointed out that even in physics, new theories are not established because men are convinced by rational discussion and experiment, but because the older generation dies out, and the younger men are brought up in the new tradition. This no doubt will apply in psychology and psychiatry also.

What cannot be doubted, I think, is that psychoanalysis is on the way down, that it has lost any academic credibility, and that as a method of treatment it is being used less widely. All sciences have to pass through an ordeal by quackery. Astronomy had to separate itself from astrology; chemistry had to slough off the fetters of alchemy. The brain sciences had to disengage themselves from the tenets of phrenology (the belief that one could read the character of a man by feeling the bumps on his head). Psychology and psychiatry, too, will have to abandon the pseudo-science of psychoanalysis; their adherents must turn their backs on Freud and his teaching, and undertake the arduous task of transforming their discipline into a genuine science. This is clearly not an easy task, but it is a necessary one, and short cuts are not likely to prove of lasting value.

What then, in conclusion, can we say of Freud and his place

in history? He was, without doubt, a genius, not of science, but of propaganda, not of rigorous proof, but of persuasion, not of the design of experiments, but of literary art. His place is not, as he claimed, with Copernicus and Darwin, but with Hans Christian Andersen and the Brothers Grimm, tellers of fairy tales. This may be a harsh judgement, but I think the future will support it. In this I agree with Sir Peter Medawar, winner of the Nobel Prize for Medicine, who had this to say:

> There is some truth in psychoanalysis, as there was in mesmerism and in phrenology (e.g. the concept of localization of function in the brain). But, considered in its entirety, psychoanalysis won't do. It is an end-product, morever, like a dinosaur or a zeppelin; no better theory can ever be erected on its ruins, which will remain for ever one of the saddest and strangest of all landmarks in the history of twentieth-century thought.

In a more poetic simile, we may perhaps quote Francis Bacon, although he lived many years before Freud:

> That lady had the face and countenance of a maiden, but her loins were girt about with yelping hounds. So these doctrines present at first view a charming face, but the rash wooer who should essay the generative parts in hope of offspring, is blessed only with shrill disputes and arguments.

Psychoanalysis is at best a premature crystallization of spurious orthodoxies; at worst, a pseudo-scientific doctrine that has done untold harm to psychology and psychiatry alike, and that has been equally harmful to the hopes and aspirations of countless patients who trusted its siren call. The time has come to treat it as a historical curiosity, and to turn to the great task of building up a truly scientific psychology.

Acknowledgements

For permission to reproduce extracts from copyright material, grateful acknowledgement is made to the following:

W. H. Auden, *Collected Poems*: The Estate of W. H. Auden and Curtis Brown Ltd

C. P. Blacker, *Eugenics: Galton and After*: Duckworth & Co. Ltd

F. Boas, 'The Methods of Ethnology', in *Race, Language and Culture*: Macmillan and Co. Ltd

F. Cioffi, 'Freud and the Idea of Pseudo-Science', in R. Borger and F. Cioffi, *Explanations in the Behavioural Sciences*: Cambridge University Press

I. Bry and A. H. Rifkin, 'Freud and the History of Ideas: Primary Sources, 1906–1910', in Jules Masserman (ed.), *Science in Psychoanalysis*, vol. 5: Grune and Stratton, Inc.

S. Freud, *Autobiography*, *The Interpretation of Dreams*, *The Psychopathology of Everyday Life*, *The Case of the Wolf Man*, *The Case of Little Hans*, *Three Essays on Sexuality*, *Study of Leonardo da Vinci*: Sigmund Freud Copyrights Ltd

V. A. Fromkin, *Errors of Linguistic Performance*: Academic Press Ltd

H. B. Gibson, *Sleep, Dreaming and Mental Health*: Methuen and Co. Ltd

E. Jones, *The Life and Work of Sigmund Freud*: The Freud Estate and The Hogarth Press

R. M. Jones, *The New Psychology of Dreaming*: Grune and Stratton, Inc.

P. Kline, *Fact and Fantasy in Freudian Theory*, 2nd edn: Methuen & Co. Ltd

S. J. Rachman and R. J. Hodgson, *Obsessions and Compulsions*: Prentice-Hall, Inc.

S. J. Rachman and T. Wilson, *The Effects of Psychological Therapy*: Pergamon Press Ltd

G. Roheim, *Psychoanalysis and Anthropology*: International Universities Press, Inc.

M. L. Smith, G. V. Glass, T. I. Miller, *The Benefits of Psychotherapy*: Johns Hopkins University Press, 1980

R. Stevens, *Freud and Psychoanalysis: An Exposition and Appraisal*: St Martin's Press, Inc.

D. E. Stannard, *Shrinking History*: Oxford University Press

E. M. Thornton, *Freud and Cocaine*: Muller, Blond & White Ltd

S. Timpanaro, *The Freudian Slip*: Verso/NLB Ltd

C. W. Valentine, *The Psychology of Early Childhood*: Methuen & Co. Ltd

E. R. Wallace, *Freud and Anthropology: A History and Reappraisal*: International Universities Press, Inc.

L. L. Whyte, *The Unconscious Before Freud*: David Higham Associates Ltd

J. Wolpe and S. Rachman, 'Psychoanalytic Evidence: a Critique Based on Freud's Case of Little Hans', *Journal of Nervous and Mental Disease*, 1960: Williams and Wilkins Ltd

Bibliography

In the course of a long and active life I must have read several hundred books on Freud and psychoanalytic theory, as well as thousands of articles. As this book is intended for the general reader, not for the specialist, I have not documented every remark, criticism or comment, but it may be useful to list those books to which interested readers may refer for secondary sources, for broader discussion of the issues involved and, in general, for more technical details. These are listed below according to the chapter to which they are most relevant, although of course there is a good deal of overlap.

It is obvious that the reader should have some acquaintance with Freudian theory and should preferably have read some of the major works published by Freud. The major works referred to in this book are: *An Autobiographical Study* (London: Hogarth, 1946); *Case History of Schreber* (London: Hogarth, 1958); *Three Essays on the Theory of Sexuality* (London: Hogarth, 1949); *Leonardo Da Vinci* (Standard Edition of the Complete Psychological Works, Volume 11); *The Interpretation of Dreams* (London: Allen and Unwin, 1937); *Introductory Lectures in Psychoanalysis* (London: Allen and Unwin, 1933); *Psychopathology of Everyday Life* (London: Unwin, 1914); *Totem and Taboo* (London: Routledge, 1919); *The Analysis of a Phobia in a Five-year-old Boy* (Collected Papers, Volume 3. London: Hogarth Press, 1950); in Muriel Gardiner, ed., *The Wolf-Man: With the Case of the Wolf-Man by Sigmund Freud* (New York: Basic Books, 1971).

Readers not familiar with the Freudian opus will find the best and most readily comprehensible account in a book by R. Dalbiez, entitled *Psychoanalytical Method and the Doctrine of Freud* (London: Longmans, Green & Co., 1941). The writer is an adherent of Freud, but is not uncritical, and the examples of case histories, dream interpretation, etc., which he gives are particularly well chosen.

For an outstanding discussion of Freud's work from the point of view of the philosophy of science, Adolf Gruenbaum's *The Foundations of Psychoanalysis* (Berkeley: University of California Press, 1984) should be consulted. It is the definitive work on the subject, informed and informative, impressive in its logical rigour and argumentative precision, and wholly admirable in its extensive scholarship of both the psychoanalytic and the philosophical literature.

Readers who believe that only those who have been psychoanalysed have a right to criticize might with advantage consult a book by J. V. Rillaer, an eminent Belgian psychoanalyst of long standing, who has lost his illusions and written an extremely illuminating book highly critical of the theories and practices of his colleagues, *Les Illusions de la Psychoanalyse* (Brussels: Mardaga, 1980). This book is a classic, but unfortunately available only in French. For a broad criticism by an American psychiatrist, there is B. Zilbergeld's *The Shrinking of America: Myths of Psychological Change* (Boston: Little, Brown & Co., 1983), which is based on long-term psychiatric experience and written with no holds barred.

Written from the point of view of general medicine is a book by E. R. Pinckney and C. Pinckney, *The Fallacy of Freud and Psychoanalysis* (Englewood Cliffs: Prentice-Hall, 1965); this provides a salutary counterblast to those who believe that all diseases are psychosomatic. Another general criticism of psychoanalysis, based on long-term experience, is a book by R. M. Jurjevich, *The Hoax of Freudism* (Philadelphia: Dorrance, 1974), which may be read in conjunction with a book edited by S. Rachman, *Critical Essays on Psychoanalysis* (London: Pergamon Press, 1963).

A slightly different perspective is offered by two books, one written from the French point of view and one from the German: P. Debray-Ritzen, *La Scolastique Freudienne* (Paris: Fayard, 1972), and H. F. Kaplan, *Ist Die Psychoanalyse Wertfrei?* (Vienna: Hans Huber, 1982). They cover a fairly general area, and are relevant to the Introduction to this book, but in parts, of course, bear on different chapters as well.

CHAPTER I   FREUD THE MAN

We may begin by citing some biographies that have become quite well known. The most famous, of course, is that by Ernest Jones, *The Life and Work of Sigmund Freud* (London: Hogarth Press, (Vol. I) 1953, (Vol. II) 1955, (Vol. III) 1957); this is more a mythology than a history, leaving out as it does nearly all the warts and making many alterations to the portrait by suppressing data and items which might reflect unfavourably on Freud. Much the same may be said about M. Schur's *Freud: Living and Dying* (London: Hogarth Press, 1972). M. Krüll's *Freud und sein Vater* (Munich: L. H. Beck, 1979) deals with Freud's family relations.

Readers more interested in truth than in mythology are referred to E. N. Thornton's *Freud and Cocaine: The Freudian Fallacy* (London: Blond & Briggs, 1983); Thornton is a medical historian by profession, and uncommitted to the Freudian opus – the difference shows! Also critical but extremely factual is the account given by F. J. Sulloway, *Freud: Biologist of the Mind* (London: Burnett, 1979); this is an excellent book which unveils many of the myths which have accumulated round Freud. The same may be said of H. F. Ellenberger's *The Discovery of the Unconscious: The History and Evolution of Dynamic Psychiatry* (London: Allen Lane, 1970). Ellenberger has gone to great pains to demonstrate Freud's dependence on earlier writers, particularly Pierre Janet, and his account has become a classic. In smaller compass the same may be said of L. L. Whyte's *The Unconscious Before Freud* (London: Tavistock Publications, 1962), which outlines the 2,000-year history of Freud's predecessors and shows in great detail how they established the importance of the unconscious and delineated its vagaries.

The relationship between Freud and his followers has been of great interest to many people and has been used to illustrate the thesis that much of the theory is based on his own life history. Two books which may with advantage be consulted in this connection are P. Roazen's *Freud and his Followers* (London: Allen Lane, 1976) and R. S. Steel's *Freud and Jung: Conflicts of Interpretations* (London: Routledge & Kegan Paul, 1982). Both give an excellent picture of the rebellions and the conflicts, the authoritarian behaviour of Freud, and the diaspora which resulted from excommunication of so many of his followers.

CHAPTER 2   PSYCHOANALYSIS AS A METHOD OF TREATMENT

A book of great interest is K. Obholzer's *The Wolf-Man: Sixty Years Later* (London: Routledge & Kegan Paul, 1982), which recounts the fate of one of Freud's most famous patients, who had, Freud claimed, been cured, but who remained subject to the same troubles and disorders for the sixty years that elapsed between this 'cure' and his death. A good discussion of the actual cases treated by Freud, and of his erroneous claims to have achieved cures, is given by C. T. Eschenroeder in *Hier Irrte Freud* (Vienna: Urban & Schwarzenberg, 1984).

Two books mentioned in the text illustrate the fact, brought out by H. H. Strupp, S. W. Hadley and B. Gomes-Schwartz in *Psychotherapy for Better or Worse: The Problem of Negative Effects* (New York: Aronson, 1977), that psychoanalysis often has a very damaging effect on patients' mental health: S. Sutherland's *Breakdown: A Personal Crisis and a Medical Dilemma* (London: Weidenfeld & Nicolson, 1976), and Catherine York's *If Hopes Were Dupes* (London: Hutchinson, 1966). These should be read by anyone interested in what actually goes on in a Freudian analysis, seen from the point of view of the patient!

CHAPTER 3   PSYCHOANALYTIC TREATMENT AND ITS ALTERNATIVES

Two books relevant to this chapter might be read side by side. The first is by S. Rachman and G. T. Wilson, *The Effects of Psychological Therapy* (London: Pergamon, 1980); this is an outstanding summary of all the evidence regarding the effects of psychoanalysis and psychotherapy, written from a critical point of view, and giving in great detail the best available account of the facts. The second is by M. L. Smith, G. V. Glass and T. I. Miller, *The Benefits of Psychotherapy* (Baltimore: Johns Hopkins University Press, 1980); this also surveys the literature and claims to have demonstrated the efficacy of psychotherapy, but for the reasons given in this book succeeds only in demonstrating the exact opposite. Readers interested in finding out more about alternative methods of treatment, such as behaviour therapy, may turn to a popular account by H. J. Eysenck, *You and Neurosis* (London: Temple Smith, 1977).

CHAPTER 4   FREUD AND THE DEVELOPMENT OF THE CHILD

The main reference in this chapter is to a book by C. W. Valentine, *The Psychology of Early Childhood* (London: Methuen, 1942). There is also a chapter by F. Cioffi, 'Freud and the Idea of Pseudo-Science', which appears in a book edited by R. Borger and F. Cioffi, *Explanations and the Behavioural Sciences* (Cambridge: Cambridge University Press, 1970). Much relevant material also occurs in the books referred to in relation to the next chapters.

For the case of 'little Hans', I have referred to the detailed and enlightening critical review by J. Wolpe and S. Rachman, 'Psychoanalytic evidence: a critique based on Freud's case of Little Hans', in *Journal of Mental and Nervous Diseases*, 1960, 131, 135–45.

CHAPTER 5 THE INTERPRETATION OF DREAMS

There is a wealth of material to choose from for this chapter. Excellent introductions to the psychology of dreaming are available in the following works: H. B. Gibson, *Sleep, Dreaming and Mental Health* (in the press); D. B. Cohen, *Sleep, Dreaming: Origins, Nature and Functions* (London: Pergamon Press, 1979); A. M. Arkin, J. S. Antrobus and S. J. Ellman, editors of *The Mind in Sleep* (Hillsdale, N.J.: Lawrence Erlbaum, 1978). Another good account is D. Foulkes's *Children's Dreams: Longitudinal Studies* (New York: John Wiley, 1982); he starts as a convinced Freudian, but his own studies disillusion him. Then there is M. Ullman's and N. Zimmerman's book, *Working with Dreams* (London: Hutchinson, 1979), and also R. M. Jones's *The New Psychology of Dreaming* (London: Penguin Books, 1970), a psychoanalyst who has also become critical of Freud's theory. Most important of all, however, is probably C. S. Hall; in his book *The Meaning of Dreams* (New York: Harper, 1953), he produced a rival theory to Freud's, much more sensible and strongly supported by a large body of evidence.

I mention in this book the age-old tendency to symbolize male and female sexual parts by reference to pointed and round objects; a detailed study of this topic is given by J. N. Adams in *The Latin Sexual Vocabulary* (London: Duckworth, 1982), from which I have taken the various examples given in this chapter.

Regarding the so-called 'Freudian slips', I have referred to two books. The first is by S. Timpanaro, *The Freudian Slip: Psychoanalysis and Textual Criticism* (London: New Left Books, 1976); and the other is edited by V. A. Fromkin, *Errors in Linguistic Performance: Slips of the Tongue, Ear, Pen and Hand* (London: Academic Press, 1980). Both books are excellent and give an interesting introduction to the theory and experimental study of such slips from the point of view of linguistics and experimental psychology.

CHAPTER 6   THE EXPERIMENTAL STUDY OF FREUDIAN CONCEPTS

As far as this chapter is concerned, two books may with advantage be consulted. One is P. Kline's *Fact and Fantasy in Freudian Theory* (London: Methuen, 1972); this is a very detailed account of all the work done by experimental psychologists interested in the Freudian theory and attempting to test it in the laboratory. The author is not uncritical, but often fails to consider alternative hypotheses; we may accept his dismissal of a large body of evidence as failing to prove Freudian theories, but consider his more positive evaluations suspect. A book by H. J. Eysenck and G. D. Wilson, *The Experimental Study of Freudian Theories* (London: Methuen, 1973), takes the major experiments claimed by competent critics to give the strongest support to Freudian theories and tries to show that in actual fact they do no such thing. Readers must be left to decide for themselves between Kline and Eysenck–Wilson.

CHAPTER 7   PSYCHO-BABBLE AND PSEUDO-HISTORY

The discussion in this chapter has largely been based on D. E. Stannard's *Shrinking History* (Oxford: Oxford University Press, 1980), a detailed examination of the claims by Freud and his followers concerning the study of history from the psycho-analytic point of view – and a very damning account it is.

For the anthropological side of the chapter, readers may refer to M. Harris, *The Rise of Anthropological Theory* (New York: Crowell, 1968), and E. R. Wallace, *Freud and Anthropology: A History and Reappraisal* (New York: International Universities Press, 1983). Also quoted is D. Freeman's *Margaret Mead and Samoa* (Cambridge, Mass.: Harvard University Press, 1983), which demonstrates very clearly how utterly lacking in factual content anthropological theories and interpretations can be.

CHAPTER 8   REST IN PEACE: AN EVALUATION

For this chapter we may recommend a book by N. Morris, *A Man Possessed: The Case History of Sigmund Freud* (Los Angeles: Regent House, 1974). This book is also relevant to Chapter 1, analysing Freud's personality in a manner linked to our interpretation of his work as an extension of his personality, and to Chapter 2 in so far as it concerns the details of what an analysis looks like from the point of view of the victim.

The book by R. La Piere, *The Freudian Ethic* (New York: Duell, Sloan and Perce, 1961), looks at Freud's teaching from the ethical point of view and insists on the tremendous damage it has done to American, and by extension to European, society.

B. A. Farrell's *The Standing of Psychoanalysis* (Oxford: Oxford University Press, 1981) and R. Stevens's *Freud and Psychoanalysis* (Milton Keynes: Open University Press, 1983) discuss the scientific standing of psychoanalysis, and deal with many of the matters raised in this chapter. Both are written by men who are critical of psychoanalysis but accept it in ways which, as I have pointed out, ultimately reduce it to a non-scientific status.

There are, of course, many more books and large numbers of articles which might and should be read by anyone wishing to be considered competent to discuss the issues involved. However, detailed references will be found in the books mentioned above, and little purpose would be served in going beyond the list here offered.

Index of Proper Names

Index of Subjects